Mother Was A Lady

CONTRIBUTIONS IN AMERICAN STUDIES

Series Editor: Robert H. Walker

The Columbian Exchange: Biological and Cultural Consequences of 1492
Alfred W. Crosby, Jr.

The Presidency of Rutherford B. Hayes
Kenneth E. Davison

The Politics of a Literary Man: William Gilmore Simms
Jon L. Wakelyn

Visions of America: Eleven Literary Historical Essays
Kenneth S. Lynn

The Collected Works of Abraham Lincoln. Supplement 1832-1865
Roy P. Basler, Editor

Art and Politics: Cartoonists of the *Masses* and *Liberator*
Richard Fitzgerald

Progress and Pragmatism: James, Dewey, Beard, and the American Idea of Progress
David W. Marcell

The Muse and the Librarian
Roy P. Basler

Henry B. Fuller of Chicago: The Ordeal of a Genteel Realist in Ungenteel America
Bernard R. Bowron, Jr.

Mother Was A Lady

Self and Society in Selected American

Children's Periodicals ● *1865-1890*

R. Gordon Kelly

Contributions in American Studies
Number 12

Greenwood Press
Westport, Connecticut ● London, England

Library of Congress Cataloging in Publication Data

Kelly, R. Gordon.
  Mother was a lady; self and society in selected American children's periodicals, 1865-1890.

  (Contributions in American studies, no. 12)
  Bibliography: p.
  1. Children's periodicals, American—History.
  2. Children's stories, American—History and criticism.
  I. Title.
PN4878.K4   051   72-5451
ISBN 0-8371-6451-6

Library of Congress Catalog Card Number: 72-5451
ISBN: 0-8371-6451-6

First published in 1974
Greenwood Press, a division of Williamhouse-Regency Inc.
51 Riverside Avenue, Westport, Connecticut 06880

Manufactured in the United States of America

This book is for MKK

Contents

List of Illustrations

Acknowledgments

In writing this book, I have contracted a number of scholarly debts. Most of these are conventionally, if inadequately, discharged in the chapter notes, but it is a pleasant duty to acknowledge those teachers, colleagues, and friends whose influence and contributions have been more direct and substantial. The idea for this study originated in conversations with John Cawelti. Stow Persons and Alexander C. Kern gave generously of their time and knowledge throughout the months of research and writing. Whatever excellence the study may have is due primarily to their encouragement and example. A fellowship from the Graduate College of the University of Iowa facilitated the work by providing for a year free from other responsibilities. I should also like to thank Robert Corrigan, John Gerber, Sherman Paul, and my colleague Murray G. Murphey for their comments and suggestions on an earlier draft. Finally, my own lady typed what must have seemed endless drafts and corrected my stylistic lapses with unerring good sense. It is her book as well as mine, and both book and author are better for her care.

Introduction

Students of Anglo-American children's literature have not always distinguished scrupulously between children's literature in the sense of the books actually read or appropriated by children and those created and intended to edify and entertain the young. It is with children's literature in the latter sense that this study is concerned. It should be emphasized at the outset that an examination of books for children provides little direct or reliable information about behavior—what things children did or did not do at a given time in the past. For such information, we must look to sources other than narrative fiction, on which this study is based. Nor do I think we go to children's literature primarily to determine the effects that reading may have had on children, although it is interesting to know that when Theodore Roosevelt was a child, he read *Our Young Folks*, one of the periodicals discussed in this study, and that he later acknowledged its influence on his life. Rather, children's literature is significant and illuminating for the cultural historian because it constitutes one important way in which the adult community deliberately and self-consciously seeks to explain, interpret, and justify

SOURCE: Portions of this introduction were published in "American Children's Literature: An Historiographical Review," *American Literary Realism, 1870-1910* 6 (1973): 89-108. Reprinted with permission of the publisher.

that body of beliefs, values, attitudes, and practices which, taken together, define in large measure a culture—that is, a distinctive way of life.[1] "The richest settings for discovering the rules of a society," anthropologist James Spradley writes, "are those where novices of one sort or another are being instructed in appropriate behavior."[2] Although there is a long-established aversion to "didacticism" among students and custodians of children's literature, it is difficult to imagine how fiction written for children could escape being both cognitive and normative—by implication if not by design.[3]

Peter Berger and Thomas Luckmann's recent study in the sociology of knowledge, *The Social Construction of Reality*, presents an argument that has great promise as a conceptual basis on which to ground a thoroughgoing cultural approach to imaginative literature in general and to children's literature in particular.[4]

Briefly, the authors argue that reality may be said to be socially constructed. By this, they mean that the worlds inhabited by men can be conceptualized as structured systems of shared meaning, specific to a certain place and time, and consensually maintained. These worlds or "symbolic universes" are created, maintained, and transmitted by means of symbol systems, of which language is the most important, and they are arbitrary and precarious owing to what they term man's "world-openness": [man's] "relationship to the surrounding environment is everywhere very imperfectly structured by his own biological constitution." A given social world, in this view, bears minimal relationship to some underlying, stable reality defined either biologically or environmentally. Since the biological basis for culture permits extraordinary variation in customary behavior, socialization—the process by which an individual becomes a functioning member of a particular group—is productive both of individual identity and social continuity.[5] The process of socialization is a potential source of tension and concern in any society, since a measure of success in the socializing process is a necessary (though hardly sufficient) condition for maintaining a system of belief and the distinctive way of life in which it is expressed.

In the nineteenth century, conditions of rapid social change and the availability of alternative systems of belief often combined to make the process of socialization in America seem extremely difficult and precarious. The family, and particularly the mother, was expected to prepare Young America for the better future promised by the doctrine of progress, but it was not always clear, either to parents or, we may guess, to children, precisely how useful or necessary parental values would be in the altered, if better, conditions of the bright tomorrow. Standards and modes of behavior that seemed plausible, natural, and inevitable to adults had to be carefully and explicitly justified and given persuasive form if they were to be communicated with their meanings intact to the next generation. Those who were to inherit responsibility for sustaining in their day-to-day activity a distinctive world view had to become convinced of its absolute legitimacy and inevitability—and then remain convinced. Such are the implications, in part, of Berger and Luckmann's argument.

If systems of belief are not to die with those who hold them, then the constituent beliefs must be taught, and they must be learned. Cultural continuity requires not simply that a group's knowledge and beliefs be made available to the young, but that the validity and importance of that knowledge be successfully justified to and internalized by those who will eventually be responsible themselves for maintaining the belief system.

In the process of socialization, or enculturation, children's books are among the several agencies that can contribute to the internalization of a given social world, but the influence they exert is difficult to measure and varies greatly among individuals and among social classes. Nevertheless, the process of socialization within the family in our society typically generates no systematic written record, and children's literature is one of the few elements of child-rearing behavior that remains accessible for research long after its intended function as entertainment and instruction has ceased. Consequently, it is of crucial importance in our efforts to reconstruct what it was that children, growing up within a particular belief system, were expected to know and to believe—and why.

Narrative fiction, the form of children's literature chosen for this study, offers an especially illuminating source from which to reconstruct these elements. Stories for children, even those intended for very young children, typically proceed from an initial problem or conflict to a satisfactory resolution, and the terms in which these are cast provide the basis for inferences about the ways in which a group defines and symbolizes the principles of order thought to structure and sustain a given way of life. Children's stories may also specify, often quite directly, the limits of permissible behavior in certain circumstances and suggest typical and acceptable modes of reward and punishment. Stories, biographies, even fantasy, may all designate those valued attributes of character which are held to contribute most directly to a rewarding life, however that illusive ideal may be defined by a given group.

In addition, some children's literature, certainly much late nineteenth-century American children's fiction, may be regarded as an effort to make a particular way of life attractive to those considered to lie outside the boundaries of a group, whether defined in religious or secular terms —to persuade children to acknowledge, and finally to act on, particular definitions of self and society, for example. It also may be regarded as carefully formulated structures of meaning intended to confirm and reinforce the allegiance of those children already persuaded of the truths manifest in the fiction. Fiction created for children may therefore be examined for the strategies of reassurance and persuasion typically employed by a group as well as for clues to the group's assumptions about the nature of the reading experience, about the imputed characteristics of children's minds, and about the ways in which changes in personality, belief, or styles of behavior may be effected. We may properly regard a group's children's literature, then, as constituting a series of reaffirmations over time of that body of knowledge and belief regarded as essential to the continued existence of the group, for not only must children be convinced of the validity of the truths being presented to them "but so must be their teachers."[6] Repetition may be as important to the teacher as to the learner. By creating fictional order, children's authors not only direct the attention of their young readers to specific concepts, but they may also renew their own commitment to certain principles of social order—for example, shaping their fictional response, in part, to meet threats posed by alternative belief systems.

These assertions have methodological as well as substantive implications. They focus attention on certain elements of the fiction—the qualities of character that prove most effective in action, for example—and, given a particular group with known characteristics, they provide a basis for conjecture about some of the specific cognitive and normative elements that ought to emerge from a study of a chosen body of literature. Despite the logic of examining children's literature in the context of specific social groups, few attempts have been made to study the social factors shaping American books for children. The classic children's books, on which so much attention has been lavished by historians and critics of children's literature, have been identified by literary and ideological criteria hardly calculated to direct attention to the social origins of the literature. The distinction between "religious" (really, denominational) and "secular" literature for children has generally sufficed to define the social origins of juvenile literature; and most secular children's books simply have been attributed to an undifferentiated middle class. In the Durkheimian sense of relig-

ion as providing an overarching framework of meaning, a
great deal of so-called secular children's literature is, in fact,
"religious": it is concerned with representing the true
meaning of behavior and events. The fiction discussed in
this study is religious in this sense. It is also "realistic" in the
sense that it was intended to illustrate the true operation of
moral law.

A considerable body of late nineteenth-century American children's literature, exemplified by such popular
periodicals as *Our Young Folks*, *St. Nicholas*, and the *Youth's
Companion*, is more properly regarded as issuing not from a
diffuse middle class but from an American gentry class,
distinguishable on the basis of its members' commitment to
a distinctive concept of the roles and attributes of the lady
and the gentleman in a democratic society. An examination
of children's fiction produced by that group might be expected to reveal a number of tendencies, including the
following: the presence of ladies and gentlemen in the
stories as distinct social types worthy of emulation; an-
tagonism toward groups espousing different definitions of
gentility; definitions of self and personal achievement emphasizing individual discipline and public service.

The sample of children's fiction on which this study is
based reveals not only the characteristic values of the gentry
class that produced it but also the assumptions and beliefs
concerning self, society, and nature that give meaning and
significance to the values.[7] The key social roles presented in
the fiction are those of the gentleman and, more especially,
the lady. These are the definitions of selfhood that structure the social world of the fiction; these are the recogniz-
able social types that, by virtue of their attributes, are held
up as being especially worthy of youthful emulation. Taken
as a whole the stories explain the function of the gentry
(and hence define the true promise of American life, as the
gentry perceived it) in terms of a paradigm which integrates
the natural world, the social world, and the individual's own

experience of a private inner flow of feeling and thought and a public life of purposive activity. The paradigm organized, explained, and justified those central beliefs considered essential to the maintenance of gentry culture. As the embodiment of those beliefs, the social type of the gentleman or lady constituted an ideal of psychological integration, a standard of public service appropriate to a democratic republic, and a principle of social order in a society dedicated to personal freedom and individual achievement and characterized by intense social and economic competition.

Consider, for example, the first story published in the *Youth's Companion* in 1873—Louise Chandler Moulton's "My Little Gentleman." Briefly, the story recounts an episode in the life of the Shaftsburys, a prosperous, closely knit family of three who build an imposing (but tasteful) house on a hill overlooking an old New England farming community. The story emphasizes the salutary effect of the Shaftsburys' son Robert on his village schoolmates. The boy, a pale, delicate lad of thirteen, is notable for his courage, graceful manners, and sensitivity. These qualities, far from proving a liability to the boy, are respected by his rougher companions, particularly after Robert risks his life to attend a fever-stricken classmate. Although his parents attempt at first to dissuade him, Robert justifies his action as a proper expression of the golden rule, the moral imperative which compasses the code of the gentleman as he has learned it from his parents but especially from his mother. Unhappily, Robert's schoolmate dies, but Robert learns the vital lesson that Mrs. Moulton takes some pains to convey —the necessity of striving to be a gentleman by adhering to the golden rule.

Mrs. Moulton's homiletic narrative holds few charms for the modern reader. It is noticeably lacking in those qualities of imaginative freshness, liveliness, and truth required of children's books today. "My Little Gentleman" is not atypical, however, of the children's fiction appearing in the most popular and respected children's periodicals of the late nineteenth century; and Mrs. Moulton, a genteel poet and novelist, was a well-known, if comparatively minor, figure in the circle of authors, editors, publishers, and journalists who dominated American cultural life until World War I. The children's fiction produced by members of this elite may be regarded as constituting a set of responses, constrained in certain ways, to salient conditions of the Gilded Age—salient, that is, to those who accepted the gentry definitions of self and society.

In practice, society as a whole is represented sketchily in many of the stories used for this study, but the gentry author writing fiction for children could hardly avoid representing selfhood in the process of creating a fictional world. If the concept of self is the axis of a group's world view, as A. I. Hallowell has argued, children's fiction, shaped as it must be by assumptions about the nature of childhood, the effect of the reading experience, and the type of personality best suited to conditions of republican freedom, is a peculiarly suggestive kind of cultural evidence with which to explore the conceptual system, the symbolic universe, that defined America's cultural elite in the generation following the Civil War.[8]

This is a book, then, about the fiction to be found in such popular late nineteenth-century children's periodicals as *St. Nicholas*, *Our Young Folks*, and the *Youth's Companion*. It is also a study of cultural transmission and the difficulties faced—and the solutions proposed—by an American gentry class intent on perpetuating their definitions of self and society amid the turmoil and disorder—at times it seemed to them the disintegration—of American life in the Gilded Age.

Mother Was A Lady

1

Publishing: The Institutional Matrix

> Essentially, the standards of the imprint are the standards of the publisher and his editorial colleagues.
>
> Alfred Harcourt

From the end of the Civil War to the turn of the century, the market for periodical literature of all kinds expanded rapidly. Technological innovation increased the speed of printing, and improved transportation made mass distribution feasible and commercially attractive. The editorial policies of such new children's periodicals as *St. Nicholas*, however, were shaped less by the new technology than by the traditions of established publishing houses (for example, Ticknor and Fields), which had long accepted a custodial and proprietary role in providing literature for their countrymen. The editors of the periodicals included in this study, with the exception always of Frank Leslie, were members of Boston's rather closely knit and socially homogeneous literary circle and the equivalent cultural establishment in New York City.[1] Several editors wrote extensively for their magazines, and all appear to have exercised close editorial control over the moral tone of their publications. A marked degree of editorial continuity characterized the three longest-lived magazines, *St. Nicholas*, the *Youth's Companion*, and *Wide Awake*. Contributors were predominantly women, and a relatively

3

small group, perhaps no more than forty or fifty, contributed regularly and prolifically to the magazines studied.[2]

Three principal stages mark the development of American children's periodicals in the nineteenth century.[3] From the publication of the first children's periodical, the *Children's Magazine* in 1789, until the 1840s, magazines for children were dominated by religious themes and imagery; pleasure was subordinate to religious and moral instruction. Magazines begun during a transitional period from the 1840s to the outbreak of the Civil War reflected a more relaxed attitude toward the duties and characteristics of childhood and a lessened emphasis on religious conversion. After 1865, the primary intention of children's magazines, with the exception of those still produced under denominational auspices, was to provide wholesome entertainment for the children of democracy. To be sure, definitions of wholesomeness showed considerable variation and never lacked a didactic component, but the emphasis in quality children's literature shifted during the century from instruction to entertainment. If the shift seems less pronounced to us than it did to post-Civil War practitioners of children's literature, they were nonetheless responsible for producing a vigorous, imaginative literature intended for the heirs apparent of democratic progress.

Between 1802 and the outbreak of the Civil War, at least seventy-five children's periodicals were begun. Most of them were notably unsuccessful in attracting readers; fewer than one in five managed to continue publication for as many as ten years, and only about one in three was able to sustain itself for as long as three years.[4] The earliest efforts to win young readers were often cheaply printed and illustrated with simple, crudely executed woodcuts—if illustrated at all. The prospectus of the *Youth's Companion*, begun in 1827, expresses a commitment to religious instruction common to these early periodicals:

The contents of the proposed work will be miscellaneous, though articles of a religious character will be most numerous. It will not take the form of discussion, or argument, and controversy will be entirely excluded. It will aim to inculcate truth by brief narratives, familiar illustrations, short biographies, and amusing anecdotes. It will attempt to excite attention to good things by entertaining matter; and yet everything frivolous or injurious will be avoided. Its several departments will comprize religion, morals, manners, habits, filial duties, books, amusements, schools, and whatever may be thought truly useful, either in this life or the life to come.[5]

Life, even for the very young, was earnest and real in the *Companion* and similar periodicals published during the early period. Adults and children alike lived in the shadow of death, life's climactic event. The sooner children became impressed by their mortality the better; and to speed them in their understanding, the punishment meted out to sinners in the "brief narratives" was swift and inevitable. A common motif was the pious child whose virtue was symbolized by an early and moving conversion. Evidence of such religious precocity was frequently rewarded by the child's early removal to heaven. Barring this happy outcome, the child was solaced with an abundance of worldly goods during his remaining earthly days. Following the practice of the day, the authors of these narratives of exemplary piety remained anonymous; much of the material was taken from British sources.[6]

In addition to urging the necessity of pious conduct, early American children's magazines frequently advocated educational and moral reforms. Advancements in pedagogical theory were publicized, outdated instructional methods were condemned, and material designed to increase children's secular knowledge was included. Slavery, intemperance, and the use of tobacco were frequently condemned in children's literature generally. The young readers were also advised against the hidden dangers to good morals inherent in theater going, dancing, and novel reading.

Only gradually did a distinctive concept of children's literature emerge. Well into the 1840s, stories and features characteristic of children's periodicals not only reflected what adults felt children needed but made few of the concessions to the abilities and presumed interests of children that became evident in the post-Civil War magazines.[7]

During the 1840s, however, the appearance of children's magazines began to improve, complementing a somewhat lightened tone and a decreasing emphasis on such formulas as the death of the virtuous child. More than a dozen magazines were founded to publicize, in part, the cause of public education and to provide supplementary material to be used as texts for reading instruction, geography, and science. Memorization was attacked as outmoded, Pestalozzian teaching methods and subject matter were introduced, and free public education and education for women were supported. During this transitional period, stories and poems increasingly demonstrated a necessary link between education and success. They held out the promise of reward in this world to those who practiced the persistence that gradually usurped the place (or, more accurately, came to share the place) held exclusively by piety. With the increasing emphasis on education, a growing sense of the contribution that education might make to democratic citizenship became manifest. The virtues of honesty, obedience, industry, and generosity were shown as having instrumental value for those who lived in a democratic society and who took advantage of the opportunities it offered in such apparent profusion.[8]

At the same time, there was a growing recognition that writing for children was a distinctive kind of literary activity calling for capable and dedicated practitioners. Undoubtedly, an economic motive was involved as well: a writer as well known to the public as Longfellow could fatten the subscription rolls while simultaneously raising the tone of the magazine. Moreover, writers hard pressed to make a living were provided with an additional market for their work. Hawthorne, Whittier, Bayard Taylor, Longfellow, and others contributed to children's magazines or wrote, on occasion, specifically for children. In so doing, they inaugurated what was to become one of the most distinctive characteristics of children's publishing after the Civil War. Almost without exception, the most prominent literary figures wrote occasionally for children's periodicals, while a number of now nearly forgotten writers devoted themselves almost entirely to juvenile literature.[9]

In the generation following the Civil War, the institutional context in which children's magazines existed underwent substantial changes. At the same time, the children's magazine came into its own, and American children's literature entered what many were to recall as its golden day. In 1868, a writer for *Putnam's Magazine* recognized the changes and proclaimed a "new era in this country in the literature for children. It is not very long since all the juvenile books seemed conducted on the principle of the definition of duty, 'doing what you don't want to,' for the books that were interesting were not considered good, and the 'good' ones were certainly not interesting."[10]

A number of factors made possible the efflorescence of children's literature that characterized the Gilded Age. Not the least of these were technological. Even before the Civil War, railroads from eastern cities had bound the Mississippi Valley to the East Coast, making possible a larger market for publishers' wares that could be served quickly and in quantity. With the completion of the transcontinental railroad in 1869, the potential of this earlier market was extended and made truly national.

A series of advances in printing technology made inexpensive publication commercially feasible. A key invention was a machine capable of producing a continuous web of paper. Developments in rotary presses and improvements in stereotyping, engraving, and composing machinery also helped to streamline the printing process and to make mass-circulation periodicals possible at a reasonable price. Frank Luther Mott, the dean of American magazine historians, estimates that the number of periodicals of all kinds published in the United States mushroomed from 700 in 1865 to approximately 3,300 by 1885. The growing numbers of magazines were paced by swiftly rising circulation figures as well. By 1885, the *Youth's Companion*, with 385,000 subscribers, had become the most popular periodical in the country with the exception of some mail-order papers.[11]

Public school enrollments, increasing faster than the population as a whole, and a threefold increase in enrollments in academies and liberal arts colleges between 1850 and 1870, contributed to the creation of a larger reading public, but one that bore promise of being less discriminating than some commentators felt was essential. The phenomenal success of Erastus Beadle, who sold nearly four million dime novels during the Civil War, pointed to a heretofore untapped commercial potential for inexpensive fiction of a type that seemed noteworthy only for its violent and frenetic action. As early as 1877, fourteen "libraries" of inexpensive, often pirated, fiction, priced at between ten and twenty cents per volume, were competing with the more substantial children's books and periodicals that were beginning to appear.[12]

These factors are reflected in the altered character of children's periodicals begun after the Civil War. Subscription lists reveal the national character of the market, although some regions, particularly New England and the Old Northwest, tend to predominate. A significant reduction of postal rates in the early 1870s made economical distribution by mail possible. The improvements in printing and engraving practices provided the means to make children's magazines far more attractive than their antebellum counterparts.

Amid the changes that resulted from the mechanization of printing and the creation of a nationwide mass audience, certain important characteristics of the publishing world changed more slowly. The persistence of ideals formed in an earlier period appear to have had a decisive impact on several of the children's magazines included in this study. The larger and more influential publishing firms in existence after the war—almost all of them located in New York City, Boston, or Philadelphia—had been founded before midcentury, frequently to cater to a particular branch of the book trade. The founders of these firms—like G. P. Putnam, Charles Scribner, and James and John Harper —were still working after the Civil War.[13] A recent historian of publishing, Donald Sheehan, concludes that, given the character and influence of such men, the industry as a whole was "affected by a morality higher than that which is customarily associated with the [Gilded Age]."[14]

The traditions of the publishing industry reflected their origins in the antebellum period when literature was identified more with gentility, scholarship, and instruction and less with popular entertainment. In assessing the industry's leadership, Sheehan suggests that it was composed of its "most scrupulous men rather than its most grasping."[15] They were men of taste and culture, active in the intellectual life of Boston and New York City as members of various literary clubs and trustees of colleges and universities.[16] "As a rule, gilded youths don't seek publishing," Henry Holt once commented in a letter. When asked for a definition of publishing, Charles Scribner replied, "Publishing is neither a business nor a profession. It is a career."[17]

The distinctiveness of publishing was not associated with manufacture—publishers frequently contracted to have their printing done—but rather with the selection and evaluation of manuscripts and with the distribution of the completed book. Unlike other industries, general book publishing was not dominated by a handful of large corporations who monopolized the distribution of the most popular books.[18] Competition was vigorous but not generally cutthroat. Of his associates, Henry Holt recalled, "No one of them [Putnam, Appleton, Harper, Scribner] or of a few more, would go for another's author any more than for his watch."[19]

Whether ultimately to their entire credit or not, such men considered themselves custodians of morals and culture, acting in proxy for the nation, as well as gentlemen competitors in the marketplace. The responsibility for supplying books to the nation was not undertaken lightly. "The leading publishers of the 'Gilded Age,' " Sheehan concludes, "were a reasonably homogeneous group which took pride in its conservatism. As pillars of the church and guardians of the family, they were steadfastly traditional in their personal ideals as in their public convictions."[20] The publications of a particular house tend to reveal the standards and tastes of its partners.

In the face of growing competition after the Civil War, several of these established eastern publishing firms diversified their book lists and expanded their periodical publishing to include magazines for children. *Our Young Folks*, the first of the postwar magazines, was brought out by Ticknor and Fields as part of a more general and ambitious expansion into the field of periodical publishing, which included purchasing the *North American Review* in 1865 and *Every Saturday* a year later. Horace Scudder's *Riverside Magazine for Young People* was published by Boston's Hurd and Houghton, for whom Scudder was a principal editor. The idea for *St. Nicholas* came largely from Roswell Smith, who, with Josiah Gilbert Holland and Charles Scribner of the well-known publishing house, had formed Scribner and Company in 1870 to publish *Scribner's Monthly*. Daniel

Lothrop headed one of Boston's two largest publishing houses catering to the children's book trade when he began *Wide Awake* in 1875, after successfully initiating *Pansy*, another children's magazine, the year before. *Oliver Optic's Magazine*, which issued under various titles, was published by Boston's Lee and Shepard, the largest American publisher of children's books during the period. In 1879, the house of Harper added a weekly children's magazine to its list. Of the popular children's periodicals which form the basis for this study, only the *Youth's Companion* and *Frank Leslie's Boys' and Girls' Weekly* were unaffiliated with a major book publisher.

The sponsorship of these children's periodicals by leading publishers emphasizes the relatively conservative nature of the enterprise. For the men and women who edited these magazines and for the publishers whose names appeared on the title pages, children's literature was an important part of a general cultural mission they had self-consciously assumed. That this kind of legislative function was not new in American publishing is clear from William Charvat's study of antebellum critical thought.[21]

Only a handful of children's magazines survived the Civil War and, of those hardy few, only the venerable *Youth's Companion* succeeded in sustaining itself for very long in the postwar era. Begun in Boston in 1827 by Nathaniel Willis and Asa Rand, editors of the *Boston Recorder*, the *Companion* was created to provide readings that would be appropriate to the capacities and the "peculiar situation and duties of youth." The prospectus went on to declare, "Our children are born to higher destinies than their fathers; . . . Let their minds be formed, their hearts prepared, and their characters moulded for the scenes and duties of a brighter day."[22] This responsibility for progress the *Companion* zealously undertook to fulfill. At first a three-column, four-page weekly folio without illustration, it was characterized by a miscellaneous but predominantly religious content which was wholly in keeping with the conservatism of editor Willis, a deacon of the Park Street Congregational Church, who chose to send his son to Yale rather than risk his soul at the more radical campus in Cambridge. "A rather namby-pamby child's paper" was a later contributor's irreverent description of these early issues of the *Companion*.[23]

In 1857, Willis, then a crusty seventy-eight, sold the *Companion* to John W. Olmstead and Daniel Sharp Ford, who together edited and published the *Watchman and Reflector*, an influential Baptist paper in Boston. At that time the *Companion*'s circulation was a narrowly regional and rather modest 4,800. Ford's partnership with Olmstead was dissolved soon after the acquisition, with Ford keeping the *Companion* and Olmstead the *Watchman*. Although Willis remained "senior editor" until 1862, Ford controlled the *Companion* from the time of the acquisition until his death in 1899.[24]

Under Ford's editorial control, the *Youth's Companion* came to occupy an enviable position in American periodical publishing. Professor Mott calls it the greatest American juvenile published in the latter part of the century, in part because Ford assembled a talented group of assistants, many of whom later had important careers in editing. Gradually the paper became more of a family publication although the emphasis on youth remained. Ford introduced more fiction, submitting it to his own rigorous moral criteria. He insisted on stories that "stirred an admiration for healthy thinking and brave action" and contained authoritative facts.[25] He emphasized movement and dramatic effectiveness and called for stories that had "well-devised [plots] and at least one strong incident" but were untainted by sensationalism, melodrama, or improper language. Detective stories, a staple of the dime-novel industry, were proscribed, as were love stories. Crime was acceptable if it was necessary to a story, but it was to be kept in the background, and all unpleasant or unwholesome details were to be omitted; neither bloodshed nor "evil Passions" were permitted prominence. "The moral tone of the stories must be irreproachable," Ford admonished in a leaflet sent to possible contributors.[26] Final impressions of death or unrelieved calamity conflicted with the *Companion*'s desire to convey cheer; pathetic stories were required to turn toward "brightened endings."

In order to appeal to the widest audience, Ford cautioned his authors against stories containing a particular theological or political bias as well as against stories that might revive sectional feelings or tend to set rich against poor. An ethical purpose was always desirable, but the moral was to be revealed "by the story itself, not by any comment of the writer," a constraint that is difficult now to reconstruct from the stories.[27] By the time of the Civil War, a successful combination of reading had been put together, consisting of a serial and several short stories and articles by famous men and women, leavened by instructive anecdotes and puzzles of the kind that flourished during the period. This format was maintained until after Ford's death. Less and less a Sunday-school magazine after Ford's accession to the editorship (the subtitle "Sabbath School Recorder" had been added in 1834), the *Companion* remained a self-conscious force for moral improvement under Ford's long tenure as editor.

In a retrospective article published in 1907 in the eightieth anniversary issue, the editors attributed the periodical's success to its stability amid change. Some things were not altered by time, they mused, especially the sacredness of family life and the changeless love of parents for children; nor were there adequate substitutes for those elements that made a house a home.[28] Shrewd management, however, had always been an important factor in the *Companion*'s success. Soon after acquiring the paper, Ford began to solicit advertising, something Willis had refused to do; and the new editor began to benefit from the drawing power of familiar names as the tradition of literary anonymity gave way in the 1860s. About the same time, Ford began to use a premium list to attract subscriptions and to enlist what eventually became a nationwide band of children eager to acquire the tempting items to be had for enrolling three, five, or a dozen new subscribers. By the early 1880s, the annual subscription number amounted to thirty-six pages of premiums, ranging from Barlow knives to parlor organs. With articles by William Gladstone, James G. Blaine, Lord Bryce, Thomas Hardy, and many other notables from both sides of the Atlantic, the paper presumably kept the interest of the adults who might first have been attracted to it as children. And like *St. Nicholas* and *Our Young Folks*, the *Companion* was eventually able to include in its list of contributors nearly all the well-known literary figures of the period.[29] With these techniques, Ford built the *Companion*'s subscription list to 385,000 by 1885. At the time of his death in 1899, it stood at 500,000, a figure comparable to the circulation of the *Saturday Evening Post* five years later.[30] It may be, however, that the ultimate strength of the *Companion*'s appeal lay in the moral tone that Ford vigilantly protected and on his ability to make that moral commitment visible, dramatic, and reassuring.[31]

Daniel Sharp Ford was a man of modest and retiring personal habits. "He was set apart from all other men by his total lack of self-appreciation," Rebecca Harding Davis recalled. "He sincerely believed that [the *Companion*] was a lever which could uplift the minds and souls of American children."[32] After 1867, the *Companion*'s masthead never bore his name, although every story bore his personal approval. Instead, publication and editing were attributed to a Perry Mason and Company.

Ford was born in Cambridge, Massachusetts, in 1822, the son of an English immigrant father who died when the boy was six months old, leaving the widow Ford with six children to support—a situation not unlike that described in many *Companion* stories. Growing up in straitened circumstances, Ford supplemented his public school education with a disciplined regimen of reading and writing, and, like some other nineteenth-century poor boys, was able to make the printing shop his Yale College. Beginning as a compositor for the *Watchman and Reflector*, he used borrowed capital to buy into the firm in the early 1850s and subsequently into the *Youth's Companion*.

His private life was marked by strong religious commitment and generous but anonymous philanthropy. A constituent member of the Boston Baptist Social Union, he quietly supported a Baptist mission in the Roxbury district of Boston for a number of years, and during his later life gave as much as fifty thousand dollars a year to religious and charitable activities in Boston. The bulk of his estate, variously reported at between $2 million and $3 million, went to Baptist missionary and benevolent associations in New England. Three hundred and fifty thousand dollars were set aside for the Baptist Social Union with the express wish that the money be used to bring working men and Christian businessmen into closer personal relationships. According to one close friend, Ford feared that labor unrest and industrial warfare would become serious threats to the stability of democracy.[33]

Another Boston magazine, Horace Scudder's *Riverside Magazine for Young People*, was the shortest-lived of the era's major children's periodicals. Begun in 1867 by the then recently organized firm of Hurd and Houghton, the periodical was a well-illustrated monthly of forty-eight pages produced in a large octavo format. A year's subscription sold for $2.50.[34] *Riverside Magazine* ceased publication in 1871. Scudder, who edited the magazine throughout its brief career, had met Henry Houghton in 1864, soon after the latter had gone into partnership with M. M. Hurd. Despite a fifteen-year difference in age, Scudder and Houghton became close friends. Combining an interest in quality printing with considerable business ability, Houghton had made the Riverside Press into one of the finest printing shops in the country, following his establishment of the press in 1852. The addition of Hurd and Scudder was to make the firm one of the period's outstanding publishing houses.

In a memoir of his publisher, Scudder recalled the discussions that led to the decision to publish a new magazine, particularly one for children. Houghton was impressed by what Ticknor and Fields had done with *Our Young Folks*, which they had begun in 1865, and by the quality of the printing being done by the Harvard University Press, and he was anxious to continue the Riverside shop's tradition of technical excellence. But he also wanted to provide a distinctly American children's literature to offset the quantity of readily available English juvenile books whose influence he disliked, largely because their assumption of unalterable class distinctions was personally offensive to the Vermont farm boy who had learned his printing in the shop of a country newspaper before making his way to Boston. Scudder had already written successfully for the children's market, and a magazine offered a familiar mode "of exploiting juvenile literature."[35]

Scudder proved to be an editor with strong convictions about the qualities to be sought in writing for children. His series of articles, "Books for Young People," in the *Riverside Magazine* was one of the earliest efforts at applying serious literary standards to children's literature. But perhaps his best service to the young was to introduce them to Hans Christian Andersen, seventeen of whose stories appeared in the pages of the *Riverside Magazine*. Scudder also was concerned about the quality of illustration that accompanied the text and engaged such competent illustrators —John LaFarge, Thomas Nast, Winslow Homer, and F. O. C. Darley among them.[36]

Born in Boston, the son of a well-known merchant and a deacon of Union Church, Scudder was the youngest of seven children in a family that traced its antecedents to the earliest days of Massachusetts Bay. While at Williams

College, he edited the literary magazine, and after graduating in 1858, he became a tutor in New York City, where he wrote several books for children and contributed articles to the *North American Review*. Although he had determined on a literary career, he remained uncertain of the exact nature of his vocation for several years. Later in his life, in an essay on Emerson, he acknowledged the debt his generation owed to the man who had made possible "the profession of letters earlier in life without that long experimental process which took place in Emerson's case."[37]

Like so many of his generation, Scudder felt his life deeply affected by the Civil War although he did not fight in it. Impressed by what he perceived to be the consolidation of nationalism and the assertion of the personality of an organic state emerging from the war's carnage, he concluded that the sturdy individualism that had inspired and sustained the previous generation of New England literary lights, preeminently Emerson, was on the wane and was no longer capable of sustaining Scudder's generation. The shift in his thinking was symbolized religiously when he adopted the Episcopal confession. Politically, he embraced the doctrines of Christian socialism as articulated by F. D. Maurice, a founder of the Workingmen's College in London.

Scudder had joined Hurd and Houghton in 1866 as a manuscript reader, a position he was to retain throughout his life, and he began to create for himself a unique, if unostentatious, position in American letters. He was capable of prodigious and meticulous work, both as an editor and as a critic and author. His preference, he once confided to a friend, was to remain out of "the glare of publicity."[38] He helped to make books on American history an important part of the firm's list and initiated the popular and inexpensive Riverside series of well-known literary texts. He also began the Cambridge Edition series of standard English and American authors, edited the American Commonwealth and American Religious Leader series, and followed Thomas Bailey Aldrich as editor of the *Atlantic Monthly* in 1890. "America needed, as never before," he said at the time, "an insistence on the high ideals of literature and life."[39] Nevertheless, according to one friend, Scudder was a driven man. "That malady of the ideal, his own ideal, dominated him, till he almost lost vision of the practical, the commercial side of literary work."[40] Aldrich later joked wryly that Scudder was a greater man than Moses: the patriarch had dried up the Red Sea but Scudder dried up the *Atlantic Monthly*.[41]

Like Daniel Ford, who was admittedly less a critic and scholar, Scudder preferred to work anonymously through an organization to which he had dedicated his life with almost religious devotion. In the person of Horace Scudder, the New England man of letters had chosen, out of a deep conviction that consolidation was the tendency of the times, to submerge himself, to become a kind of organization man. Ostensibly praising a similar tendency in Houghton, he revealed as much about his own motivation: "He was building an institution; he was creating something which should have an organic life of its own, and the whole stream of his energy passed into its external creation. He projected himself into it, and never withdrew his hand, but he thought of it as an artist thinks of the picture he paints, the poet of the poem he writes."[42]

Two years before Scudder began editing the *Riverside Magazine* for Hurd and Houghton, Boston's Ticknor and Fields had brought out *Our Young Folks*. Mixed motives probably prompted James T. Fields to undertake a children's magazine. Childless, he may have been sentimental about children, as his biographer suggests.[43] Doubtless he was aware of the new market being created by an expanding school system, and it seems clear from his autobiography that he shared the eastern cultural elite's uneasiness over the dangers of pulp literature. *Our Young Folks*, even if it proved profitable, could be conceived of as a worthwhile contribution to good morals to set over against the pernicious influence of "sensational" fiction.

It is said that Oliver Wendell Holmes wanted to name the new magazine the *Atlantic Lighter* after the parent magazine, but the new venture in children's literature appeared in January 1865 as *Our Young Folks*, a sixty-four-page octavo monthly costing $1.50 per year.[44] Alice M. Jordon has called it the first modern children's magazine, marking the beginning of recreational reading as a desirable end in itself.[45] Like the *Youth's Companion* and later *St. Nicholas*, its list of contributors was studded with the names of familiar New England literary figures. Among the contributors to the early numbers were Harriet Beecher Stowe, Louisa May Alcott, Thomas Wentworth Higginson, Thomas Bailey Aldrich, Rose Terry, Elizabeth Stuart Phelps, Edward Everett Hale, Bayard Taylor, James Parton, Celia Thaxter, James Russell Lowell, Whittier, and Longfellow. The magazine quickly built up a substantial circulation of over 75,000.[46]

John Morton Blum, drawn to examine the files of *Our Young Folks* because of references to it in Theodore Roosevelt's personal papers, briefly examines the values apparent in the magazine in his introduction to an anthology compiled from its nine volumes. Not substantially different from such competitors as the *Youth's Companion* or *St. Nicholas*, it was more of a New England magazine than either, he argues. Pledged to furnish "healthy entertainment and attractive instruction," *Our Young Folks* reveals the anxieties of a region that sensed its values being challenged by the forces that seemed to be changing American life —immigration, industrialization, and urbanization. These changes appeared to threaten the existence of traditionally conceived virtues dependent for their nurture on the distinctive New England landscape and on strenuous outdoor activity.[47]

Our Young Folks began publication under an editorial

triumvirate composed of John Townsend Trowbridge, Lucy Larcom, and "Gail Hamilton," the pseudonym adopted by Mary Abigail Dodge. At first, Trowbridge remained in Washington, D.C., and Miss Dodge in Hamilton, Massachusetts, until a quarrel with Fields resulted in her resignation in 1867. As a result, Miss Larcom handled the periodical's major editorial responsibilities, for which she received an annual salary of $1,200.[48]

Lucy Larcom is perhaps the most famous alumna of the Lowell cotton mills. Born in 1824 in Beverly, Massachusetts, where generations of Larcoms had lived since the late seventeenth century, she moved to Lowell following the death of her father, a retired shipmaster, in 1835. Work in the mills was one way to keep the family together, and, during the 1830s, the mill offered a free grammar school, night school, lyceum, and various church activities that made it possible for the young girl to undertake a broad program of self-culture—to study German and botany and to read widely in English and American literature. She began her literary career as a contributor to the *Lowell Offering and Magazine* while working at the mills. In 1846, she moved to the Illinois frontier, where she taught school and studied at the Monticello Seminary. Graduating in 1852, she returned to Norton, Massachusetts, to teach at Wheaton Seminary. An abolitionist from early girlhood, she received a prize offered by the New England Emigrant Aid Society in 1853 for her inspirational poem, "Call to Kansas." Her later poetry was dominated by religious themes and by an evident love for the New England countryside, which seldom found distinctive enough expression to warrant the attention of literary historians.

In *A New England Girlhood*, published four years before her death in 1893, Miss Larcom examined her childhood in relationship to the New England culture, at once so distinctive and so changing, which she revered.[49] The following passage from her autobiography captures her characteristic blending of Puritan activism and self-abasement: "What a world it would be, if there were no hills to climb! Our powers were given us that we might conquer obstacles, and clear obstructions from the overgrown human path, and grow stronger by striving, led onward always by an Invisible Guide."[50] *A New England Girlhood* is the record of an education; life, in Miss Larcom's favorite metaphor, is a school: "Circumstances are only the keys that unlock for us the secret of ourselves."[51] The scenery of Cape Ann, the moral earnestness of her Puritan forebears and family, the experience of frugal living, her early work in the Lowell mills, and books, especially poetry—these shaped her own pilgrim's progress. She learned "to take life as it is sent to us, to live it faithfully, looking and striving always towards a better life."[52] From childhood she felt a "vague, fitful desire . . . to be something to the world I lived in, to give it something of the inexpressible sweetness that often seemed pouring through me." True to the best traditions of New England introspection, she sought to follow out her intuitions of the real and to become an instrument through which the "One All-Beautiful Being" might speak clearly and persuasively to others. If we are all students, we are also all teachers, Miss Larcom suggested: "What has best revealed our true selves to ourselves must be most helpful to others, and one can willingly sacrifice some natural reserves to such an end."[53] Like Scudder, she sought an appropriate mode of personal expression amid the changes in New England life which altered the traditional forms and conventions of expression but left unchanged the moral duty to express one's sense of the real and the true.

Miss Larcom's co-editor on *Our Young Folks* was John Townsend Trowbridge. Trowbridge was born on a farm in upstate New York, not far from Rochester, in 1827, the eighth in a family of nine children. The Erie Canal, opened two years earlier, was visible from the rear fence of the Trowbridge homestead. As a boy, Trowbridge went swimming in it and peddled nuts and apples to passengers on the canal boats. Later he wove these activities and the life of the canal into several popular boys' books.[54]

His father, who died when the boy was sixteen, traced the Trowbridge line to a namesake who had settled in Dorchester, Massachusetts, in 1636. When he was young, Trowbridge resisted the religious heritage such an ancestry implied, however. In his autobiography, he recalled his rejection of the doctrine of innate depravity and the efforts made by relatives and friends to sweep him into the fold on a tide of emotion. His search for a more congenial spiritual life went unfulfilled until as a young man, he encountered Emerson's essays, especially "Self-Reliance," "Spiritual Laws," and "Heroism."[55]

Although his mother was ambitious for her children's education, Trowbridge dated his own intellectual awakening from an encounter with a list of foreign words in a spelling book, which set him actively to the study of language. He began writing poetry at thirteen—behind a plow, he recalled. A growing restlessness for wider experience preceded his father's untimely death. His boyhood abruptly ended by this loss, Trowbridge lived briefly with married sisters, taught school for a term in Illinois, and in the spring of 1847, not quite twenty years old; set off for New York City, hoping to become an author. Fifteen months later, he moved on to Boston, where he gradually established a secure, if rather minor, place in that city's closely knit literary life.[56]

Trowbridge was at first a contributor to various weekly newspapers, such as the *Olive Branch* and Daniel Ford's *Watchman*, but he declined the editorship of a Boston daily, preferring fiction to journalism. His career of hack writing ended when his *Father Brighthopes* (1853) became a popular success for its appealing embodiment of practical Christianity.[57] During the next fifty years, Trowbridge wrote some forty volumes of fiction—much of it for boys —as well as several volumes of verse and an autobiography.

Like other young men from the provinces, he was able to enter the augustan circles of the Boston literati with comparative ease. When the *Atlantic Monthly* was begun in 1857 to champion Boston's literary claims, Trowbridge was the youngest contributor to the first issue.[58] No doubt the earnest young man who had given up the solace of stimulants and the comfort of tobacco to join the literati could be counted on to discharge his responsibilities in the new beacon light of New England letters. Years later, in the pages of the *The Critic*, he expressed his credo: the young should have "a literature which gives faithful representations of life, nourishes the moral fibre without sentimentality or cant, fosters a love of nature, and cultivates by example clearness and beauty of expression."[59]

In the disastrous Boston fire of 1872, James T. Fields sustained considerable losses. The panic of the following year resulted in a loss of business which, coupled with the financial drain incurred in refurbishing *Every Saturday* and in advancing money to several authors, required him to retrench. The *Atlantic Monthly* and *Every Saturday* were sold to Hurd and Houghton, and *Our Young Folks* went to Scribner and Company to be merged with their newly founded children's magazine *St. Nicholas*.[60]

St. Nicholas quickly became, and has since remained, the best-loved and best-remembered American children's magazine. As noted earlier, its publisher, Scribner and Company, had been formed in 1870 when Josiah Gilbert Holland and Roswell Smith returned from an accidental meeting in Europe, intent on founding a new monthly magazine. Holland, a sought-after lyceum lecturer, a best-selling author for Charles Scribner, and later one of the great editors of the period, had earlier turned down his publisher's request that he edit Scribner's faltering *Hours at Home*.[61] Consequently, Holland felt obliged, when he returned, to tell Scribner about the project he and Roswell-Smith were considering. Scribner offered to publish the new magazine and to lend it the prestige of his name in return for a 40 percent interest in the venture. In November 1870, *Scribner's Monthly* appeared with Holland as editor and the young Richard Watson Gilder as his assistant. The new monthly, the parent of *St. Nicholas*, was conceived as a family magazine designed to have a broad appeal and pledged to the purest of literary and moral standards. With the zeal characteristic of one of the period's most popular defenders of the moral status quo, Holland allowed himself to hope that the magazine would carry culture to a wide popular audience and be instrumental in helping to reunite science and religion. To this end, Scribner added the practical requirement that it be well-illustrated, well-printed, and well-written.[62]

The same standards of editorial responsibility were evident in the first issue of *St. Nicholas*, which appeared in November 1873, a lavishly illustrated, forty-eight-page octavo volume bound in gaily decorated red and gold covers. Yearly subscriptions were priced at two dollars. The magazine quickly established a circulation of around 70,000 copies, about the same as *Our Young Folks* and a figure that appears to have remained relatively unchanged for many years. In its early years, *St. Nicholas* benefited from the subscription lists of several magazines whose assets it purchased—*Our Young Folks* and *The Children's Hour* in 1873 and the *Little Corporal* and *Schoolday Magazine* in 1875.[63]

Mary Mapes Dodge, who was called by the directors of Scribner and Company to edit the new magazine, was in complete accord with the ideals held by the publishers. It was she who gave to the magazine the name of the patron saint of childhood. Already well known as the author of the best-selling *Hans Brinker and the Silver Skates* (1866), Mrs. Dodge had been an associate editor of *Hearth and Home* under Harriet Beecher Stowe. Born in 1831, she was one of three daughters of Professor James Jay Mapes, a scientist and inventor whose New York City home was a watering place for such literati as William Cullen Bryant and Horace Greeley. Mrs. Dodge was educated by tutors and in English literature by her father. In 1851, she married a New York lawyer, William Dodge, whose death seven years later left her with two small sons to raise. Moving to Newark, New Jersey, with her children, she began to write with more success than many women in similar straits who sought to live by their pens, and her work began to appear in the *Atlantic Monthly* and *Harpers*.[64]

As the editor of *St. Nicholas*, Mrs. Dodge succeeded over the years in gathering around her an especially able group of editorial assistants and advisors, and her literary contacts brought to the pages of the magazine a varied and distinguished list of writers and illustrators. John Townsend Trowbridge joined her staff with the passing of other assets from *Our Young Folks* to the new magazine in 1873. Frank Stockton, who had earlier worked on *Hearth and Home* with Mrs. Dodge, became an associate editor. Louisa May Alcott, her *Little Women* already a popular success; Hezekiah Butterworth, later an editor of the *Youth's Companion*; and Edward Eggleston also became associated with *St. Nicholas* in the early years. Horace Scudder was not a staff member, but Mrs. Dodge frequently called upon him for advice. William Webster Ellsworth, who joined the Scribner organization in 1878 and later presided over it from 1913 to 1915, credited Mrs. Dodge with the rare ability to persuade even the busiest and most well-known writers of the day to contribute to *St. Nicholas*.[65]

Two years after *St. Nicholas* was begun, *Wide Awake*, a Boston monthly for children, appeared (July 1875). Published by Daniel Lothrop, an established and successful publisher of juvenile books, *Wide Awake* was designed to appeal to the same age group, children from ten to eighteen, as *St. Nicholas*. Another Lothrop magazine, *Pansy*, which the publisher himself edited, had been begun a year earlier and was intended for younger children. *Babyland* subsequently appeared in 1876 and *Our Little Men and*

Women four years later. All were popular enough to survive
until Lothrop's death in 1892. The following year, *Wide
Awake* went the way of so many other children's magazines
and was absorbed by *St. Nicholas*.[66]

Wide Awake was a profusely illustrated fifty-six-page
square quarto, which sold for $2.40 per year. To edit the
new periodical, Lothrop engaged Charles S. Pratt and Ella
Farman, the latter a children's writer whose books had
appeared under the Lothrop imprint. Not unjustly, Mott
characterizes Lothrop's editorial policy as old-fashioned,
tending to emphasize what adults felt was good for
children's instruction rather than heeding children's tastes
and preferences.[67] Lothrop's firm was closely connected
with the Chautauqua movement during the 1880s. In 1882,
Wide Awake organized the Chautauqua Young Folks Reading Union, in the interests of which a supplement was
published each year until 1888. Semiannual collections
made up from the files of *Wide Awake* were issued by Lothrop as the *Wide Awake Pleasure Book*, to take advantage
of the birthday and holiday giftbook business.

Daniel Lothrop appears to have been representative of
that class of New England gentlemen who managed to
combine a shrewd commercial nature with religious
idealism and an active sense of public responsibility. He was
born in 1831 into a New England family descended from a
Puritan minister with the best of credentials: the first
Lothrop had made his way to Massachusetts Bay after two
years in prison on orders of Archbishop Laud.[68] Afforded
the usual preparation in the classics to enable him to enter
college, Daniel Lothrop chose instead to pursue a career in
business, which he began at the age of fourteen when he
took over a brother's drugstore. He soon opened two other
stores in neighboring New Hampshire towns, purchased a
bookstore in Dover, and in 1856 moved west to grow up
with St. Peter, Minnesota, then the territorial capital. With
the shifting of the capital to St. Paul and disheartened by
the panic of 1857, Lothrop returned to New Hampshire

and subsequently moved to Boston in 1868 to establish a publishing house. The firm of D. Lothrop and Company was founded to serve the growing postwar market in juvenile books and to improve the quality of books sold to Sunday school, public school, and town libraries.

At the outset of his publishing career, Lothrop successfully persuaded three ministers to act as manuscript readers and offered cash prizes for acceptable manuscripts. His considerable judgment as to what would sell, tested by long experience in New England country stores and on the Minnesota frontier, enabled him to expand the business in 1874, despite losses in the Boston fire of 1872 and the rigors of the panic of the following year. According to Edward Everett Hale, a long-time friend, Lothrop owed his success primarily to two basic principles, which Hale clearly approved—never to publish a purely sensational book, however attractive the financial prospect, and "to publish books which will make for true, steadfast growth in right living." Lothrop was convinced, Hale stated, "that literature must be of some use, and especially of use to the American community."[69] He knew that "it is the business of a publisher of large views . . . to be steadily levelling up the intelligence of those who do read, that they may, on the average, read better books in any one year than they have read in the year before."[70] This impulse, which sought to make juvenile literature a force for social uplift, also found expression in Lothrop's founding of the American Institute of Civics in 1880, an organization he hoped would contribute to increasing public knowledge about politics and to fostering a more general interest in government.[71]

Eight years before *Wide Awake* was begun, at the same time that Scudder was bringing out the *Riverside Magazine*, a children's periodical that was very different from any of these others appeared on New York newsstands as *Frank Leslie's Boys' and Girls' Weekly*. The successor to *Frank Leslie's Children's Friend*, which apparently had not been friend enough, the *Weekly* was an eight-page small folio that helped to set the style for later pulps.[72] The chief selling point of the paper was a steady succession of dime-novel serials with lurid illustrations keyed to the more sensational episodes in the stories.

"Frank Leslie," a pseudonym adopted to keep secret an interest in engraving disapproved of by his father, was born Henry Carter in Suffolk, England, in 1821. The senior Carter was a successful glove merchant, who expected his son to follow him into the business. The son insisted on working out his own economic salvation, however. At the age of twenty, he began working as an engraver for the new *Illustrated London News* and quickly became responsible for running the engraving department. In 1848, hoping to establish his own paper, he left London for the wider opportunities seemingly offered in New York City. The following year, he successfully engineered the publicity for Jenny Lind's American tour in 1850-1851, sponsored by P. T. Barnum. An unsuccessful venture in Boston and a brief stint as chief engraver for the short-lived *New York Illustrated News* followed before he brought out his first publication, *Frank Leslie's Ladies' Gazette of Fashion*, in January 1854. The following year, he bought the moribund *New York Journal of Romance*, adding his name to the title, and began *Frank Leslie's Illustrated Newspaper*, patterned on the London paper for which he had worked. Leslie illustrated the news with resounding success and was on his way to wealth and a publishing empire. Exploiting various literary markets, he branched out into children's magazines, the most successful of which was the *Weekly*. Under a fictitious name, he catered to a rather different audience with the *Jolly Joker*, which seems to have blended smoking-car jokes with police-gazette scandals.[73]

While making a good deal of money illustrating the news, Leslie adopted a flamboyant and ostentatious style of living that itself made news. He and his family occupied a fashionable Fifth Avenue boardinghouse and maintained a Saratoga cottage and a steam launch in the approved conspicuous style. Nor was he without symbolic honors. He was a United States commissioner to the 1867 Paris Exposition. In 1876, as New York's commissioner to the Philadelphia Centennial Exposition, he was elected president of the state commissioners. His splashy Fifth Avenue wedding in 1874 to Miriam Follen Squier, a divorcée, gave him a notoriety of a less desirable kind, as it climaxed his protracted, bitterly fought, and widely publicized effort to divorce his first wife. Then in 1878, his domestic affairs were news again. After a cross-country train trip, Mrs. Leslie had some uncomplimentary things to say about Virginia City, Nevada, in her account of the trip. Stung by the fashionable Eastern lady's doubtless unwarranted jibes, the *Territorial Enterprise* succeeded in discovering some interesting facts about Mrs. Leslie, including a hastily annulled marriage; a brief stage appearance as "Minnie Montez," the sister of the notorious Lola; a liaison with a Tennessee congressman; and various seamy details of the divorce she ruthlessly obtained from the patrician E. G. Squier in order to marry Leslie.[74]

It is difficult to know how much Leslie himself wrote for his children's magazine. Probably he wrote little, but his influence on the magazine was surely substantial. The popular serial writers that he frequently used, except William O. Stoddard, were not men who contributed frequently to the other children's magazines here surveyed. Bracebridge Hymyng, George L. Aiken, Matt Marling, Roger Starbuch, Captain Tom Singleton, Oswald A. Gwynne, and the versatile P. T. Barnum are not names (and pseudonyms) that routinely graced the tables of contents of *St. Nicholas* or *Wide Awake*.

The characteristic style of both the illustrations and stories printed in *Frank Leslie's Boys' and Girls' Weekly* contrasts sharply with the standards maintained by Mrs. Dodge and the editors of the other magazines. The brutality and violence evident in the *Weekly* have no counterpart in the other magazines studied, where the illustrations may be stilted or precious but never portray callous cruelty. In the *Weekly*, the careless rendering of figures, the stark tonal contrasts, and a visual preoccupation with physical injury provide the pictorial counterparts of a literary style that is frequently dominated by restless action, unconvincing motivation, meretricious diction, and a covert morality that contradicts the passages of overt moralizing casually interspersed in the narratives.

The *Weekly* is further distinguished by its relative anonymity and lack of personalization. *St. Nicholas* and *Our Young Folks* encouraged their readers to become contributors by frequently printing children's work. Through letters columns, the editors personally answered questions and gave advice. In time, a magazine like *St. Nicholas* took on the lineaments of a personality, partly because of the familiar style with which Mrs. Dodge conducted her monthly column, "Jack-in-the-Pulpit," and partly because her shrewdly chosen title invited children to imagine *St. Nicholas* as a person. Leslie, on the other hand, encouraged no such familiarity. Contributors remained largely anonymous, letters were kept to a minimum, and little effort seems to have been made to establish a consistent editorial voice in the magazine. The reading experience was kept as impersonal as possible, as if to emphasize the distance that separated the exotic fantasy of the fiction from the more ordinary events that surely made up the daily rounds of its readers' lives. The pious remarks which dot the stories accentuate the tension between latent and manifest content. The implicit logic that emerges from the play of fictional events and characters contradicts the logic of the moral framework perfunctorily professed for appearance's sake but seldom dramatically realized in the stories. Similarly, the logic of Leslie's private life contradicted the symbols of respectability with which he sought publicly to ally himself.

Leslie was one of several late nineteenth-century journalistic entrepreneurs who recognized the commercial possibilities of mass periodical publishing and who possessed the requisite talents to exploit the rapidly growing markets. His style of living links him with that group of wealthy men spawned by the Gilded Age for whom fashion and ostentatious display were sought as measures of social virtue and desirability. Fashionable society, deprecated in the better children's magazines, manifested an increasingly powerful social symbolism during the Gilded Age, a symbolism not lost on Mrs. Dodge and her allies.

The men and women who edited *St. Nicholas*, the *Youth's Companion*, and the other quality children's magazines of the period were heirs to different social and publishing traditions. In the kind of literature represented by Leslie's *Weekly*, they saw a moral incoherence expressive of the social inutility of the fashionable ideal in a democratic society. Men like Daniel Ford, John Townsend Trowbridge, and Daniel Lothrop were self-made men, even as Leslie was, but they adopted a life-style quite different from his. They and the other editors were associated with a functional elite in American society, which sought to model its ideal social expression on the type of the traditional gentleman. It is this code of the gentleman that gave a moral coherence to the events, characters, and resolutions found in the children's magazines. The evidence of personalized editorial control and the existence of a relatively small group of authors who wrote frequently for the periodicals warrant the use of these popular children's magazines as a measure of the elements central to the world view of the gentry elite.

2

Two Narrative Formulas

Carelessness is worse than stealing.
"Behaving," *Wide Awake* (1876)

A comparatively narrow, often rigid, and marked conventionality has long been regarded as one of the principal qualities differentiating mass or popular literature from serious literature. Detective fiction and westerns are familiar examples of popular forms characterized by patterns that have remained relatively stable over time. We expect that detective stories will be about crimes successfully solved by suitably shrewd or dogged individuals and that westerns will pit the forces of lawlessness and savagery against the forces of civilization. These expectations amount to prescriptive rules governing popular forms, and they have rather high predictive capabilities. To learn that a book is a detective novel is, after all, to know a good deal about what will happen in the story. Similarly, the stories published in *St. Nicholas*, the *Youth's Companion*, and *Our Young Folks* in the generation following the Civil War reveal a stable pattern of repeated elements.

It is not uncommon for the rules governing a popular genre to be formulated explicitly either by aficionados seeking to guide public taste or by editors seeking to define the qualities of desirable manuscripts.[1] In his autobiography, Ray Stannard Baker, a contributor to the *Youth's Companion* before he became famous as a muckraker for *McClure's* magazine, recalled the rules Daniel Ford and his staff laid down to contributors.[2] Early in his career, Baker had worked as a reporter on the *Chicago Record*. Learning that the *Companion* paid fifty dollars for stories and hoping to supplement his reporter's modest salary, Baker wrote to the *Companion*. In reply, he received a cordial letter and a two-page leaflet entitled "The *Youth's Companion* Story," which outlined and explained the principles authors hoping to contribute to the popular periodical should follow.

These formulas, Baker suggests, were the key to popular acceptance: they constituted "the chart for sure-fire success; which is to be sedulously followed. Don't experiment. Don't originate; repeat!" In economic terms, the rules represented what a particular audience "wanted and would pay for," although few periodicals of the time "ever set down their formula so explicitly in black and white as the *Youth's Companion*."[3]

Baker's description of the *Companion*'s rules as defining a measure of continuing public acceptance is suggestive. By implication, the rules or formula met (or were thought to meet) certain unspecified needs of a particular audience—needs that the repetition of a rather limited number of elements did not satisfy once and for all. People continued to buy and to read material characterized by simple, familiar patterns. Critics of mass culture have frequently cited this stereotypical quality as presumptive evidence that popular formula literature blunts discrimination and simplifies and falsifies experience. More perceptive students of cultural history have used the conventionality typical of popular forms as an instrument to examine widely held beliefs and values rather than as a club with which to harry cultural sinners to repentance. The works of Horatio Alger have been particularly attractive to students of late nineteenth-century American life because Alger's hundred-odd juvenile novels were enormously popular —and strikingly repetitious in terms of an overall pattern of character, incident, and reward. Those historians who have sought to explain the reasons for and the implications of Alger's appeal have done so by concentrating initially on the structure of Alger's principal motif—a boy who struggles with little success to achieve a measure of respectability and security until a fortunate encounter provides him with a powerful benefactor.[4]

The analyses of Alger's formula by Richard Wohl, John Cawelti, and others hinge on the recognition that Alger's work was ordered by a relatively stable structure of elements, varied slightly from novel to novel, and that this structure, which Cawelti terms "formula," constitutes an important kind of cultural data. In a seminal essay he defines formula as a "conventional system for structuring cultural products" and distinguishes it from such familiar critical concepts as myth, theme, medium, and genre, which, he argues, tend to be overly general.[5] More specific and limited than a myth, for example, a formula is a frequently repeated particular sequence of plot and character elements: "Westerns must have a certain kind of setting, a particular cast of characters, and follow a limited number of lines of action. A Western that does not take place in the West, near the frontiers, at a point in history when social order and anarchy are in tension, and that does not involve some form of pursuit, is simply not a Western."[6] Historically, popular formulas are created, achieve a degree of acceptance, and can persist for long periods of time. The detective story and the western, though products of the nineteenth century, remain popular today, while the seduction novel and, to a large extent, the Biblical epic have disappeared in the twentieth century.

The prevalence in popular literature of the formula, defined as a sequence of conventional elements, lends itself to several kinds of analysis. It is conceivable that some personality types may be attracted by the repetitive, highly structured nature of this kind of literary creativity.[7] Such an approach, emphasizing a personal psychological component of the writer, is complicated historically by the relatively anonymous (and pseudononymous) world of popular literature and the lack of adequate biographical data. It is also possible to approach formula fiction as a logical response to the enormous demand for quantities of material that is a conspicuous characteristic of mass publishing. Where speed and sheer volume of material become essential, as they do in periodical publishing or broadcasting, some degree of standardized form becomes a functional necessity. Such explanations of formula, however, furnish no key for understanding individual formulas nor the differences they exhibit.

A more fruitful kind of analysis assumes that a reciprocity exists in the production and consumption of popular literature. The formula can be regarded as a common ground on which a relatively small group of producers meets with a particular audience. The formula embodies the values, expectations, assumptions, hero types, and needs of a social group and perhaps resolves tensions that originate in conflicting needs.[8] The precise nature of these needs and their relation to a social group in a given historical period is a complex and difficult subject. It seems likely that the social functions of popular formulas, and especially formulas for children's literature, have their origins, in part, in the precariousness of social order and the consequent need in any society or large social group to reaffirm continually the structure of meanings, the cultural knowledge, that orders social behavior.[9]

With its biological basis in prolonged childhood and man's limited instinctual structure, cultural knowledge implies the centrality of socialization in any society. Children must learn the language of their society, its various social modes, its taboos—all that passes for knowledge among members of their particular group. The process of socialization is never complete but continues to be supported by the day-to-day activities of the members of a society. A measure of precariousness is always present because cultural patterns are never completely internalized by any member of a group—and because individuals are always acting, always choosing. Any social act ultimately has implications for the existing social order, which persists only so long as members of a group consent to, and can sustain in daily activity, the world view or conventional structure of meanings they learned as children. To focus on the transference of culture from one generation to another, then, as children's writers must, carries the increased probability of becoming sensitive to the situations that threaten social order and which must be controlled. In the context of the cultural pluralism that has increasingly characterized the American experience from the beginning of the industrial revolution, the young are a perpetual source of challenge to a particular social group's conception of reality. The world into which they are born is initially opaque to them. It must be given meaning, explicit justification, and explanation. The ways of society are not self-evident, as any parent knows. Children constantly ask "Why?" and they must be persuaded that the parental ways, the given ways, are *the* ways and warrant acceptance and allegiance.[10] By definition, children are incompletely socialized. On the one hand, they do things that would bring chaos if projected on the future as the actions of adults. On the other hand, they are weaker and less able to cope with experience than adults. Consequently, they may at any time reveal, or be used to draw attention to, the precariousness of social existence as a whole. Juxtaposed against certain institutions, they may call into question patterns of behavior that adults take for granted. As the embodiment of the future, finally, children are essential to society. They are often consciously invested with the hopes and aspirations that adults have for the maintenance of their own way of life.

A single popular formula will never mirror all the problems of a given period. The basic pattern in the novels of Horatio Alger center almost exclusively in matters of economic mobility, financial success, and the qualities considered efficacious in striving for social respectability. In contrast, the formula stories in popular children's periodicals like *St. Nicholas* and the *Youth's Companion* emphasize quite different concerns. They suggest which threats to the social order particularly exercised the social group with whom the principal writers and editors tended to be affiliated. Moreover, they demonstrate the efficacy of a particular constellation of values and assumptions about the nature of social order in a democracy. Thus, the code of the gentleman, the problem of economic security in an age of economic instability, and the destructive impact of urban environments on childhood needs were important elements in the formulas of children's domestic fiction. The child reader was asked to become self-conscious about his own behavior and to see it in relation to a moral position dramatized in the stories. This position was never called into question or shown to be a style of life to which alternatives existed. The stories defined the way things were and ought to be and illustrated the modes of behavior that are consonant and rewarding, given the principles that organize and define "reality."

Finally, these formulas probably allayed, in some degree, parental fears about the split between generations caused by widespread preoccupation with personal and social mobility, rapid social change, and shifts in the social sources of moral authority. The stories frequently dramatized a faith in the reasonableness of the child and his willingness to be guided by parental values and judgment. Children, in turn, were assured that parents know what children need for the future, however different that future may be from the experience of the parents. The apparent changes taking place with such rapidity in American society during the 1870s and 1880s did not imply the obsolescence of the parental definition of things. Their world remained subjectively plausible within the formulas of children's fiction.

In *St. Nicholas* and the four other magazines selected for study, two formulas dominate the fiction that attempted to entertain children with realistic incidents from the everyday lives of ordinary families. This editorial ideal proved elusive in practice; some very extraordinary, though usually plausible, events occur in these stories. A third group of stories suggests the possibility of another formula, but it appears so infrequently that I have discussed it as a distinctive variation of one of the others. None of these magazines published westerns, detective stories, or romances—the staple narrative formulas of the story papers and pulps such as *Frank Leslie's Boys' and Girls' Weekly* and *The Boys of New York*.

The writers who worked primarily within the restrictions imposed by the editors of the quality magazines tended to settle with impressive regularity on a single generalized situation. They most frequently dramatized an incident in which a young person (more rarely an adult) acted out an attitude, a stage of self-knowledge, or a virtue—and experienced the appropriate consequences. As I have suggested earlier, the moral framework that gives significance to the pattern of incident, resolution, and reward is the code of the gentleman modified to suit the needs and, to some extent, the interests of children. Not all of the stories that dealt with domestic life can be fitted into this schema, to be sure; formulas do not exhaust the possibilities for popular literature although they account for a large portion of it. The two or three formulas in the children's fiction sampled may be considered ideal types, created abstractions with which few stories coincide perfectly but toward which many tend in the arrangement of plot and character elements.

For want of more incisive labels, I have chosen to call the two major formulas the "ordeal" and the "change of heart." A third formula, a variation of the change of heart, I call the "gentry mission." Aspects of the first two, and occasionally all three, may be found in some serial stories. About 90 percent of the stories I read, however, are quite short (the *Youth's Companion* story, for example, was limited to 3,000 words) and the formulas, while not totally exclusive, are useful in describing the primary impulse of a given story.

In the ordeal, a child or young person is temporarily isolated from the moral influence of adults (generally parents or other family representatives, though occasionally teachers, ministers, or other professionals who might symbolize the demands of society at large). Beyond the aid or influence of adult experience, the child undergoes an experience that requires him to respond decisively. Often, very little time is permitted for reflection; his reaction frequently suggests the force of instinct. Having proved himself in action, the child returns to the safety of the family or the supervision of adults and is rewarded. The circumstances of the trial and the kinds of temptations confronting the isolated child are suggestive of the social stresses to which the adults writing for these children's magazines were sensitive. The narrative rhythm of the ordeal resembles the characteristic movement of ritual rites of passage, the three phases of which, according to Arnold Van Gennup, are separation from society, a period of isolation and transition, and finally incorporation into a new social world or reintegration with the old.[11]

A conventional realization of the ordeal is "Nellie in the Lighthouse" (1877) by Susan Archer Weiss, a story which takes place on the Carolina coast.[12] At first, Nellie, a little girl of seven, is surrounded by the adults—her father and an elderly black couple—who have reared her and her brother since their mother's death several years before. Soon after the story opens, the family begins to disperse, leaving the children isolated: Nellie's father leaves for the mainland to pick up needed supplies, and shortly after his departure, the family's black housekeeper is called away to nurse a distant neighbor. When a sudden squall blows up, their elderly black companion collapses with a stroke, leaving Nellie and her panic-stricken brother to operate the

Susan Archer Weiss, "Nellie in the Light-house," *SN* 4
(1877): 577 (facing).

lighthouse alone. A broken window in the tower and Nellie's general unfamiliarity with the equipment make it impossible for her to light the beacon her father will need to guide himself home. Consciously resisting the temptation to panic, Nellie suddenly remembers a hymn her mother used to sing. In the moment of calm that follows, through some process of association the author chose not to de-lineate, the girl recalls that pine knots will burn even in a high wind. Hastily gathering as many as she can, Nellie again climbs the long stairs to the tower and successfully rekindles the light. Her father, caught in the squall, is guided safely home by his daughter's improvised beacon.

A similar drama of fortitude, tested and sustained in crisis, is evident in Louisa May Alcott's "Bonfires" (1873). Phebe, the twelve-year-old daughter and only child of a charcoal burner, braves a stormy evening and the subtle terrors of a treacherous, desolate landscape to warn an approaching train of a washed-out bridge.[13] For her pres-ence of mind and self-reliance, qualities nurtured by her lonely life in nature where her only playmates are the woods creatures, Phebe is generously rewarded by the train's passengers, whose dress, manners, and speech iden-tify them as ladies and gentlemen. Like Nellie, Phebe is completely isolated from adults who might have aided her. Her father is away, her mother is ill, and the nearest neigh-bor lives too far away to be of any help.

Sudden, potentially bewildering isolation overtakes chil-dren in story after story based on the formula of the ordeal. Without warning, the family, a central symbol of stability, may be dissolved, leaving a young person to manage as best he can amid hardship and the loss of a taken-for-granted framework of expectations and relationships. A story enti-tled "Charlie's First Doughnut" (1882) makes explicit that this pervasive symbolism of isolation is rooted in the very conditions of American life.[14] The freedom that Americans enjoy demands of them great individual restraint and re-sponsibility, the author emphasizes. Charlie has been reared in Italy by his mother, a sculptress who has often described to him the delights of American doughnuts. For unexplained reasons, he has never had one, however. Clumsily contrived, to be sure, these improbable circumstances are designed to make clear and certain his temptation when a friend of his mother's gives him a box of doughnuts and tells the boy to take them home to his mother.

Going up into a garden overlooking Rome, young Charlie struggles to resist the temptation to eat one of the doughnuts on the spot and say nothing to his mother. She, after all, will never know how many doughnuts the box originally contained, so it will not be a lie exactly to eat one without admitting it. Uneasy perhaps over the apparent triviality of the situation she has created, the author breaks in to interpret, lest her readers fail to recognize what is going on: "It was a fateful time for our little American—a time in which his young nature was the battle-ground of good and evil; the scene of one of those terrible conflicts that we all of us have known, and perhaps yet know, and the issues of which are mighty, no matter how trifling their causes."[15] Charlie, poised on the brink of knowing himself forever hence a liar and a thief, hesitates, as well he should. He goes so far as to take a bite, but seeing a group of Italian schoolboys go by, he recalls his mother's saying that they never faced temptations like the one facing Charlie because of the formal restraints placed on their lives. Never trusted as children, they were never free—nor could they be. Americans, by contrast, were free—free to face temptation and, if sufficiently strong, free to conquer it. Temptation, Charlie learns, is the price of freedom. Fortified by his insight, he chooses to go home and to confess the stolen bite to his mother, who thereafter cherishes the box as a symbol of a "great victory." To make the moral uncomfortably explicit, the woman who gave Charlie the doughnuts happens to be present when he gets home, so he would have been caught in the lie he contemplated. We are left with the uncharitable suspicion that our hero has been badly used.

Charlie's honesty, like Phebe's courage, is tested in isolation, in situations that suddenly arise and leave no opportunity for consultation with others. Such unforeseen trials, these stories suggest, are to be expected, but they are not to be taken lightly or assumed to have purely individual relevance. The wrong decision may imperil a trainload of passengers or threaten the affection and trust on which the family—and beyond it, society—depends. Children who read these stories were invited to regard every moment of life as precarious, unpredictable, and inevitably serious. Americans, including children, were free, but they were frequently alone, uninsulated from sudden temptations and dangers. In variations of the ordeal formula, courage and self-reliance emerge as the virtues most often tested.

The second formula, the change of heart, often proceeds according to the same rhythm of separation, isolation, and incorporation that characterizes the ordeal. In the ordeal, however, the child is assumed morally capable, and the events of the story satisfy us that he is indeed. On the other hand, the change of heart almost invariably proceeds from a moral stance that varies from the merely inappropriate and embarrassing to one that is personally dangerous and socially vicious. As in instances of the ordeal, a wide variety of possibilities exists. The key element in the formula, with certain exceptions to be noted later, is a species of moral conversion, a dramatic shift in perception, which combines a conscious recognition of the erroneous nature of the individual's former behavior with a conscious resolution to do better. The change of heart is made manifest in useful and appropriate activity following the individual's conversion.

The great majority of stories in the five magazines (excluding Leslie's) follow this pattern, perhaps in conscious recognition that, given the nature of childhood, young readers might better identify with fictional children who still displayed thoughtlessness, pride, or impatience, the three failings which recur most frequently.

"Charlie Balch's Metamorphosis" (1867) is a model of the change of heart except in its setting—a private boarding school.[16] Charlie Balch enters the story a sullen, lazy, and withdrawn boy. His mother is dead, and his father, a politician, has little time for the boy. Without a mother's love or a father's guidance, Charlie is ill equipped for boyhood, which is at best a time of trial. Character, if left to form itself, becomes selfish and idle, the author warns, and we are given abundant evidence that this is true. Charlie quickly falls in with the school's less principled boys, yet an inextinguishable spark of reverence remains, hidden beneath Charlie's "unpromising exterior" and capable of being fanned into flame under appropriate circumstances—in this case a sermon. Charlie suddenly recognizes that "probably there is no such thing as an indifferent moment,—a moment in which our characters are not being secretly shaped by the bias of the will, either for good or evil."[17] In this recognition, the author announces, "the change had commenced." Charlie emerges from the chrysalis of apathy and idleness slowly, however. Success and reward are not immediate, for his resolution must be tested. Gradually his character and manners improve, his disposition grows more cheerful, and even his appearance changes. Charlie was a "hard case," but his successful redemption provided a lesson in the responsibility, which those of "gentle feeling" have, for aiding others.

European visitors to America during the nineteenth century commented frequently on the degree of freedom enjoyed by American children in contrast to their European counterparts.[18] Charlie Norton successfully resisted the temptation that was the price of that greater freedom, we recall, but it is the province of change-of-heart stories to explore the problems raised by children who chose to use their freedom irresponsibly. "When Book Meets Book" (1886) tells of a socially prominent mother who could no longer cope with society life or with her two sons, spoiled by an indulgent father and by inappropriate reading.[19] Off to Europe to rest her shattered nerves, she intrusts her sons to her brother, a Boston gentleman. He refuses to allow their misbehavior to go unpunished as had their father, for whom "boys will be boys" furnished an easy absolution to any mischief.

When the boys' carelessness in his house results in damage to the furnishings, their uncle questions their sense of honor: "I thought that my sister's children, boys twelve and ten years of age were old enough to have the simplest instincts of gentlemen," and, as rarely happens in these stories, invites them upstairs for a whipping.[20] Besides being destructive, their pranks, they are told, would be detrimental to their mother's need for peace and quiet when she returned. The fiction that they have fed on and the storybook boys whom they have emulated do not provide fit models for behavior, not in Boston at least. It requires more to be a gentleman, they discover, than merely to appear well mannered and to speak truthfully. Their every act must speak what they know, but may not like to admit, is right. Absolute congruence between moral knowledge and even the most seemingly insignificant act defines the standard of the gentleman, which they are expected to meet.

Unwarranted pride and a treacherous romanticism frequently combine to bring about the isolation and suffering that characterize the change-of-heart formula. In "Jenny, the 'Flying Fairy' " (1888), a young girl is forced to quit school after her father dies and leaves his widow with Jenny and four other children to support.[21] Jenny has had the education of a lady, but unfortunately it has borne little fruit in her behavior: she remains blindly self-centered and concerned exclusively with "her own success and amusement." She will have nothing to do with her mother's suggestion that she take a position as a governess or a maid for a family in the country. Although her mother had held such a position before her marriage without feeling degraded by it, Jenny is sure no lady could submit to such an arrangement.

Refusing also to go back to school, Jenny fears that she will never be a lady as a consequence of her misfortune. Her self-pity is transformed, however, when she sees a poster advertising a circus wintering nearby. She imagines herself supporting her family while living a glamorous and stylish life as a bareback rider, although she is appalled and frightened by the squalid quarters and the coarse, rough men she encounters at the circus. Nevertheless, she applies for a riding job and, self-conscious in a skimpy costume provided by the circus owner, a predictably lecherous foreigner, is ridden around in a practice harness. Knocked unconscious in a fall, she comes to her senses to find that her mother has rescued her. Humbled by her experience, she agrees to become a governess. Ten years later, the reader learns in the last paragraph of the story, Jenny has successfully finished her education and become a teacher, wife, and mother—and, most importantly, a true lady. The willingness to serve is the beginning of wisdom—and redemption.

Suffering is proportionately greater in change-of-heart stories in which an adult is the central character; those few who, refusing all help, defy the moral assumptions on which the stories are grounded experience disaster. Such is the case in "The Fatal Fire-hunt" (1876).[22] Pierre Estrin, a morose and impatient, if famous, hunter gives in to his only son's pleas to go on a hunt one evening in spite of his wife's intuitive uneasiness about the venture. The boy tires quickly on the trail, and Pierre pushes on into a swamp where he becomes confused in the darkness. Impatient at finding no game, he finally fires unhesitatingly at the first hint of a target, mortally wounding his son. The event shatters his reason, and Estrin, involved later in several murders, is eventually assassinated himself. He "did not profit by the teachings of his misfortunes," the author informs her readers.

The significance of the story would appear to be in three related attitudes that define Estrin's flawed character. He is antisocial and impatient, and the latter finds concrete expression in the fatal shot. Second, he ignores his wife's intuitions, the unreasoned promptings of a more reliable moral nature than his own. Finally, he fails to benefit from his misfortunes with an appropriate change of heart. He remains oblivious to the moral organization underlying reality, and his subsequent murders are evidence of the degree to which his initial antisocial bias becomes overtly destructive in a social context. In this way, his own destruction, which takes place, presumably, at the hands of similar moral outcasts, is justified. Estrin's impatience results in the destruction of the family just as his violence outside the family, if not stopped, would result in the destruction of society.

There is often little drama or suspense connected with the change-of-heart process. The child is always viewed not by another child but by the adult author from the outside. The suspense or dramatic interest that might arise as the child struggles to decide what is right remains hidden. The child's recognition of his responsibilities can be made visible only in activities that embody the new knowledge. Because a happy ending is expected, indeed required, the sense that there was ever a possibility of moral failure is almost always lost. Only in rare situations, and usually when an adult is the central character, can the possibility for moral failure exist. The principal interest is not primarily in how the change of heart occurs but in the fact of its occurrence.

In the third pattern common in the gentry fiction, the civilizing possibilities of the code of the gentleman are acted out, sometimes with explicit reference to its efficacy for the rawest kind of economic competition. The basis of the gentry mission is a figure who embodies the moral values of gentility and whose moral force brings about a change in the values of others. Several stories show how the loneliness and frustrations of elderly persons are dissolved by a younger figure. Others present a young college graduate taking over and bringing order to a rural school. Perhaps the best example of the motif, however, is "Naylor o' the Bowl" (1873), a story by Rebecca Harding Davis.[23] Miss Davis's characters are a motley group of young men, most of them mill hands, who are drawn to western Virginia about 1859 in hopes of making a rich strike on the petroleum lands being developed there. They soon discover, however, that their capacity for cooperation deteriorates steadily amid the frustration borne of their unsuccessful drilling. As mill hands, according to the author, these rough, irreligious young men lack the shared fun, friendships, and courtesies that would have provided a more stable basis for a group of college students in similar circumstances. Moreover, because none of the men are married or even related to each other, the only grounds for their uneasy and brittle alliance are dependence and greed. Given these circumstances, violence is almost inevitable.

Conditions begin to improve, however, when Naylor, the grandfather of one of the men, arrives unexpectedly to live with his grandson. Although the old man has lost both his legs and is confined to a makeshift wheelchair, he has accepted his impairment with grace and dignity. He is carefully identified as a gentleman, and as his quiet strength of character gradually invigorates and purifies the camp's atmosphere, a true community begins to emerge where none had existed previously. We are to understand, it seems clear, that Naylor's moral strength and courage are sufficient to compel, in his rough companions, a particular response—a recognition that character is the only basis for an orderly society of freely competing individuals. It is no accident that soon after Naylor arrives, his grandson begins to think about the existence of God for the first time in years; the basis for character, in turn, is seen to be an understanding of the universal principles of order. When Naylor dies peacefully after a short illness, the men's memories of the old man's moral force cement the group in friendship and cooperation, for their mutual recognition of Naylor's character establishes an essential basis for social order—the shared recognition and acceptance of a compelling ideal.

Thus, the terms of Mrs. Davis's justification of the gentry ideal are readily apparent: because his moral authority derives from universal law, the gentleman is capable of bringing order into the rawest kind of economic competition, that which characterizes the scramble to exploit the nation's natural resources. The code of the gentleman softens the rigors of such competition (but does not destroy it) and fosters a sense of community without impairing either initiative or self-reliance. After Naylor's death, the drilling goes on, but it goes on efficiently and harmoniously, or so Mrs. Davis would have her readers believe.

The three formulas contrast with the fiction that appeared in the cheaply printed, flamboyantly illustrated weeklies—*Frank Leslie's Boys' and Girls' Weekly*, for example—as well as with the work of the period's most popular juvenile author, Horatio Alger. In the *Weekly*, the adventure of the isolated child remains prominent, but the values, settings, experiences, and moral framework assumed in the stories are radically different. The hallmark of the *Weekly* and its numerous competitors was the serialized dime novel, which emphasized continuous and rapid action, violent encounters, and hairbreadth escapes, all of which occurred amid exotic settings. The stories are populated by a cast of conventional stereotypes blended from the nineteenth-century western and sea story, the gothic romance, and the sentimental novel.

"The Magician" (1867), for example, delineates a series of incidents that would never have occurred in a gentry magazine like *St. Nicholas*.[24] Carl, a young boy, later revealed to be an Eastern prince, is the sole survivor of a shipwreck. Taken into a family living in an isolated coastal town, he is taught English and matures pondering the classics. But his real interest is in the supernatural and the occult. No snob, he is friendly with a poor boy, but he can move in other circles as well, and he falls in love with a girl who lives in a beautiful castle. There Isabel entertains him in the lush splendor of her "boudoir"—where, we are told, "the days passed, glorious with dawn and dusk. Weeks, held together by God's golden links of the Sabbath, came and went."[25] With the coming of spring, however, a rival intrudes to break this splendid chain. The girl's cousin, Reginald Booth, quickly forces Isabel to forget Carl. Vowing revenge, Carl tears up his apartment in a rage and disappears. A body which seems to be his washes ashore soon after. Twenty years go by. A magician comes to the castle to perform before Isabel and Reginald, long since her husband. During the performance it becomes clear that Reginald tried to kill Carl years before but killed instead a fisherman disguised in the young man's clothes. The day after this revelation, Reginald lies murdered and Carl, revealed as the magician, is gone again, accompanied and comforted by Isabel's only daughter whom Carl, it is revealed, had stolen from her parents at the age of four.

The theme of unrestrained passion and revenge, combined with the undercurrent of sexual dalliance and indulgence suggested by Isabel's incense-laden bedroom, conveys markedly different attitudes toward experience, character traits, and children's reading needs from the attitudes implicit in the formulas to be found in periodicals like *St. Nicholas*.

The works of Horatio Alger also differ significantly in attitude from the quality children's periodicals. No one knows how many Alger books were produced, but the number has seemed sufficiently large to require explanation of his popularity: "Frozen into a host of clumsily written novels," Alger's formula, R. Richard Wohl writes, "has many times been picked out . . . as characterizing a fundamental and crucial aspect of American culture."[26] Alger's "gospel of thrift, hard work, and endurance" and his preoccupation with attaining comfort, security, and respectability appear to echo the nation's absorbing interest in material achievement, in getting and spending, in self-aggrandizement rather than self-culture. Recent commentary on Alger has questioned whether he should continue to be regarded as an unambiguous spokesman for the self-made man and for the virtues of rugged individualism. Shifting historiographical perspectives on the Gilded Age impose limitations on Alger's usefulness as a cultural symbol also. In an important recent synthesis, Robert Wiebe argues that during the Gilded Age massive changes in population distribution, new patterns of industrial organization, and new ideas worked together to undermine the structure of values and meanings that had ordered the lives of most Americans prior to the Civil War.[27] The period from 1877 until after World War I is conceptualized best, according to Wiebe, as a "search for order." The values that had effectively organized life in small, relatively isolated communties began to seem inadequate for promoting social order in large urban centers characterized by ethnic heterogeneity, corporate organization, and industrial working conditions.

Alger's stories evidence little concern with the problem of sustaining social order in an aggressive, competitive democratic society. Instead, the emphasis is on success, economic opportunity, and the values judged most instrumental and useful in achieving the kinds of secure clerkships to which Alger's heroes aspire. But the fiction characteristic of *St. Nicholas* and similar children's periodicals often speaks directly to the problem of maintaining social order under democratic conditions of competitive individualism and of nurturing those qualities of character which would stimulate a sturdy self-reliance without threatening the stability of the community. The ordeal and the change of heart were designed, as we have seen, to display those qualities of character in bold relief.

These formulas were intended to facilitate socialization—and doubtless they did, but the effect of the stories concerns us less than the striking similarity between the structure of the fictional experience and the process of socialization as explained from the perspective of social role theory.[28] This approach to socialization, or enculturation, owes much to the work of George Herbert Mead and recognizes "that a child is born into an ongoing society with common symbols, established patterns, and recognized positions, and that it is through others that a child learns these elements of the social world."[29]

A key concept in this approach is that of *role*, a pattern of expected behavior associated with a given social status or position in a social structure. Roles are symbolic forms in the sense that they are vehicles for communication and the means by which a person expresses himself in society. To function in society, the child must develop the ability to judge his own behavior against the role expectations he has learned to associate with his several statuses—as child, brother, student, Little League shortstop, or whatever. Acquiring the ability "to designate to himself that he is or is not acting appropriately" is the essence of the socialization process.[30] Only gradually does he relinquish the egocentrism that characterizes the very young child and come to possess a sense of self, to be able to regard himself from the outside, and to shape his behavior on the basis of that recognition.

Both formulas, the ordeal and the change of heart, dramatize the origins of self. The stories provide opportunities for the child as reader in the experiences of the fictional child to see the consequences of values and attitudes which initially are taken for granted in the context of the fiction. In the change of heart, the child character frequently learns that intense self-centeredness, issuing variously in selfish, careless, or thoughtless behavior, leads to isolation and suffering. Psychologically, the heart of the formula is the conscious recognition that the old habits and attitudes are unacceptable combined with an equally conscious resolution to adopt more appropriate patterns of attitude and behavior. To the extent that a child reading such a story is led to participate imaginatively in its resolution, he may gain vicariously the same salutary perspective on self.

Often the new perspective is dramatized in a dream or metamorphosis. A boy who longs to escape the irksome restraints of home by going to sea is dissuaded when he dreams of hard work and harsh discipline. Another lad, prone to being distracted from his duty, falls to dreaming about a land of short memories. He experiences a world whose only order is the logic of forgetfulness. He cannot discover who he is or where he is and awakens with relief to the recognition of his folly.[31]

In the ordeal, however, the morally capable child seldom expresses a dramatically altered perception, although his experience of isolation and even suffering may be similar to that encountered in the change-of-heart formula. He seldom comes to a conscious recognition of the connection between the values he has absorbed and his triumph over temptation. Instead, the child reader seems expected to supply the necessary recognition and to realize that, like the child in the story, the hymns he learns at his mother's knee have implications for his experience beyond the cozy warmth of hearth and home. The family is a magic circle of safety surrounded by subtle and hidden dangers. The proper attitude toward that fact is certainly not morbid fear. A decent respect and a proper prudence, combined with self-control and self-knowledge, are essential if one is to remain free.

The ordeal carries a measure of reassurance to both the children who read the periodicals and to the adults for whom socialization was a constant, and no doubt often problematic, concern amid the turmoil of the Gilded Age. Children are reassured about the social utility of the values that are justified in the home but must find their ultimate legitimation outside the family. Similarly, the stories, written by adults, continue to sustain the plausibility of adult values in the midst of social and intellectual uncertainty.

The change of heart implies reassurance of a different kind, for the formula confronts, though not always directly, the problem of social control. Here, I shall consider briefly what might be called the problem of consent—the assumptions concerning the means by which individuals, in this case children, who are free to pursue "wrong" activities, come to recognize their error and to change their behavior. This is a central and recurrent, but still largely unexamined, problem in democratic thought. The traditional model for the transformation of character frequently affected in the change of heart is religious conversion. Purged of doctrinal and institutional trappings, conversion appears in these stories in situations which dramatically juxtapose deviant values against accepted ways. Forced to perceive and to evaluate his behavior in the new context, the individual chooses, and is able to will, behavior more consonant with his altered perception. Thus, the formula, from the child's point of view, encourages a cluster of values by dramatizing the penalties—fear, pain, isolation—that attend adopting (or maintaining) the deviant ways. On the other hand, the writers may be said to be acting out *their* faith in the accepted norms and values of their group by demonstrating the inevitable punishment and suffering that attend the transgression of those accepted ways. Further, the formula may be said to act out the writers' faith, or will to believe, in the ability of the young to perceive things as the writers did as well as their belief in the willingness of the young to act on that perception and to persist in the ways of righteousness in spite of temptation.

Writers who used the change-of-heart formula tried to avoid overt preaching as a means to stimulate the shift in perception that signals conversion. A speech made by one of Rose Terry's characters puts the matter clearly: "I don't approve of talking to or at children, myself; it always exasperates me and why not them. Help 'em to use their eyes, and see for themselves, if they're not fools; if they are—why let 'em alone."[32]

Both formulas encourage children to use their eyes, to become self-conscious of the impact which even their most trivial behavior could have on the lives of others—first in the family and then, by extension, in society at large. What if everybody behaved that way? is the mirror held up to the child reader. He is asked to recognize and to judge, in the fictional lives of children supposedly just like him, the necessary consequences of the daily deeds that, he was prodded to acknowledge, formed the iron links of character and thus shaped the future.

3

Gentility: A Basis for Order

> . . . we must keep alive in the vernacular the
> distinction between *fashion*, a word of narrow
> and often sinister meaning, and the heroic
> character which *the gentleman* imports.
>
> Ralph Waldo Emerson, "Manners"

Only a handful of children's magazines survived the Civil
War. With the exception of the *Little American*, which issued
briefly, and perhaps appropriately, from West Point, New
York, the only significant new venture in children's periodical publishing undertaken while the nation occupied itself
with exorcising the sin of slavery was Ticknor and Field's
Our Young Folks, begun in January 1865. But with the coming of peace, there was time once more to think about other
problems, time to consider the training of a generation of
democracy's children for what Samuel Osgood called, in
the December following Appomattox, "that marvellous
American life that is now opening to us its new and eventful
chapter in the history of man."[1] The slaveholder's rebellion
was successfully quashed, Osgood continued, but the question posed by the "never-ceasing revolt" of the young, who
were destined to inherit the brighter tomorrow, remained:
"How keep our Young America under the thumb of his
father and mother without breaking his spirit or blighting
his destiny?" One answer was to create a genuinely American children's literature, "true to all our just American

56

ideas" and capable of helping to bring out what was latent in each child. "Children not only want the true thing said to them, but want to have it said in a true and fitting way," Osgood asserted.[2] On that note, an era of unprecedented publishing for children began.

Such staple fare of the antebellum periodicals as stories portraying the fortunate consequences of youthful conversion gave way, as we have seen, to the formulas of the ordeal and the change of heart. In the pages of *St. Nicholas* and the other magazines, religious conversion was transmuted to social conversion. The child was still saved—but for this world, not the next—and the agency of his social conversion was no longer a denominational creed but the code of the Christian gentleman. Protestant Christianity justified and explained the role and power of the gentleman. A democracy perfected would manifest the same principles as Christianity: "Christianity and democracy alike crown men with equal rights and privileges, make them individually responsible, and pass through accidents of birth, circumstances, and position, to lay their claims and their awards upon every soul," wrote one of the founders of *St. Nicholas*.[3] The true gentleman was the type and expression both of Christianity and democracy.

The lady and, to a lesser extent, her male counterpart dominate the domestic fiction that was intended to give children a sense of the social world in which they lived but of which they were largely unaware because of their limited perspective and experience. The fiction pervaded by the gentry definition of things presented a world of apparent coherence, stability, and meaning to the Gilded Age child, a world in which the social tensions of the age found temporary, if uneasy, resolution. The familiar gentry figures expressed traditional values, which served to structure the moral order informing the stories in the quality children's periodicals. The social types of the lady and the gentleman provided models for behavior and a concept of self that complemented the conditions of political and social egalitarianism. Although the values may be analyzed and treated as abstractions, they are always manifest in the stories in carefully structured relationships between character, incident, and reward. The spirit of Christian gentility, often simplified to and symbolized in the golden rule, is at once an attitude toward experience and an interpretation of it.[4] The ideal of the gentleman controlled the moral implications of the ordeal and change-of-heart formulas and provided a way to shape the relationships of their constituent elements. But before we examine the role of gentry values and discipline in organizing this fictional world, we must consider the tradition of gentility in nineteenth-century America.

European visitors to the United States in the 1830s and 1840s remarked the existence of a group of Americans whose cultivated manners, refined speech, and allegiance to the code of the gentleman effectively set them off from most of their countrymen.[5] These antebellum ladies and gentlemen no longer formed a virtual ruling class as had the eighteenth-century gentry in Virginia and Massachusetts, and they were increasingly less prominent in American politics as the century wore on. They were not necessarily a wealthy group as a whole. What held them together was neither money nor political position but a commitment to culture and discipline. Longfellow's remark that "all literature, as well as all art is the result of culture and intellectual refinement" serves equally well to describe the discipline of character that was at the heart of the gentlemanly ideal.[6] The gentleman was both a social and an aesthetic ideal. Unostentatious in dress and democratic in outlook, the gentry were engaged throughout the century (and with considerable success) in efforts to influence the level of American manners and the tone of American cultural life. In effect, they functioned as a culture-bearing elite until late in the nineteenth century.

The ideal of the gentleman had been outlined by classical writers long before it found concrete historical expression in a particular social type. Truth and honor, as well as fortitude, temperance, prudence, and justice, were virtues traditionally associated with the ideal. To these, Renaissance writers had added liberality and courtesy. Preeminently a man of moral force and independence, the gentleman was, in Emerson's words, "a man of truth, lord of his own actions, and expressing that lordship in his behavior; not in any manner dependent and servile, either on persons, or opinions, or possessions."[7] He was also a man of gracious manners, whose natural instincts for courtesy had been disciplined by training and use. Ideally, such discipline issued in a dignified, graceful bearing, polite speech, and an instinctive courtesy that put others at perfect ease but contained no hint of ostentation or affectation. In a letter to his grandson, Thomas Jefferson summarized this aspect of the gentleman: "Honesty, disinterestedness, and good nature are indispensable to procure the esteem and confidence of those with whom we live, and on whose esteem our happiness depends. . . . Above all things . . . practice yourself in good humor [courteous disposition]; this of all human qualities, is the most amiable and endearing to society."[8]

Wealth was not a necessary mark of the gentleman, but the seventeenth- and eighteenth-century gentleman was very likely to be a man of means, and by the eighteenth century gentility was not simply a model for social excellence, but a way of life, powerfully expressed by a social class.[9] In the absence of an hereditary nobility, the colonial gentry class monopolized social, political, and economic power until the turn of the nineteenth century. Louis B. Wright has suggested that in colonial Virginia the gentry class probably numbered fewer than one hundred families. These held and worked vast tracts of land, assumed the obligations of public office and military leadership, decisively influenced church affairs from their positions as vestrymen and wardens, and maintained a cultivated manner of living and an interest in books and learning.[10]

In New England, the success with which that region's gentry preserved the ideals of gentility and perpetuated themselves as a class has been characterized by Edwin Cady as "one of the fateful cultural achievements in American history. . . . What civilized persons value as civilization exists in America now in significant measure because of the traditions of the gentleman."[11] New England culture was organized around an aristocracy of scholars who accepted responsibility for the public good. As in the South, the gentleman enjoyed economic and political advantage, social prestige, and religious distinctions since his abilities and position were bestowed by providence.

Although the conditions of frontier life, North and South, conspired against the code of the gentleman, the Virginia planters and the New England gentry managed to preserve their traditions and power until the Revolution and the democratization of American politics in the first generation of nationhood began to undermine and divide the gentry's political position.[12] The political, economic, and social power which had been concentrated in the hands of the colonial gentry in the eighteenth century was increasingly distributed among specific, functionally distinguished elites in the nineteenth century.[13] Political power, although clearly allied to influential economic, social, and professional interests, was increasingly wielded by elected officials or party functionaries who were neither identifiable as gentlemen nor as members of another increasingly visible group, a social-economic elite out of which fashionable society organized itself.

In attempting to explain the diminishing influence of gentlemen on American politics in the two decades before the Civil War, E. L. Godkin, long the editor of the *Nation*, suggested that around 1835 the timidity of the northern, especially New England, gentry toward the issue of slavery resulted in an erosion of public confidence that was never successfully retrieved after the Civil War.[14] Politics increasingly became the domain of self-made men. The white gloves, which symbolized in dress the gentry's sense of refinement, lost their value as political assests. The last gentlemen to occupy the presidency conducted themselves, according to Godkin, "with such a shocking want of manliness, courage, and truthfulness that good clothes and polished manners got to be associated in the popular mind with moral turpitude and mental imbecility."[15]

Allegiance to the code of the gentleman continued, however, to unite a loosely defined group of professional men, educators, publishers, and intellectuals who held and wielded the cultural power formerly concentrated in the hands of the colonial gentry. To some extent, the growing urban class of wealthy manufacturers and merchants also thought of themselves as ladies and gentlemen, but in outlook and manners the two groups became increasingly separated as the century wore on.[16] The social-economic elite, organized into fashionable society and enjoying the insulation provided by great wealth, increasingly practiced an exclusiveness and defensiveness symbolized and hallowed eventually by the identification of a New York "Four Hundred" and the establishment of the *Social Register*.[17] Dedicated to fashion, ostentatious display, conspicuous consumption, and a jealous perpetuation of hereditary symbols, the fashionable elite increasingly affected Continental manners and sought to ally themselves with the European aristocracy they admired by marrying their daughters to the minor princes of Europe and building Renaissance-style townhouses on Fifth Avenue.[18]

The gentry elite, however, was not an elite of wealth but one of culture and refinement. It sought to exercise broad educational and cultural influence by undertaking responsibility for formal education, for a standard of democratic manners, and for the general well-being of the cultural life of the republic as they defined it. The nineteenth-century gentry encouraged and supported artistic creativity consonant with the discipline and refinement inherent in the traditionally accepted accomplishments of the gentleman. Unlike the fashionable elite, they committed themselves to the democratic ideology and readily accepted into their ranks those of undistinguished social background who showed the capacity and willingness to adopt the appropriate values and interests of gentlemen.[19] The capacity for refinement varied, as did any innate talent, from individual to individual, but all men were conceded some ability to benefit from gentry discipline. Everyone should be an "accomplished gentleman," maintained an anonymous contributor to the *Overland Monthly* in 1885, with the implication, of course, that everyone could be.[20]

The gentry commitment to democratic social theory is evident in George Henry Calvert's essay *The Gentleman* (1863), which went through three editions after its initial publication by Ticknor and Fields.[21] Calvert, a man of independent wealth and distinguished Maryland antecedents, could have readily joined the fashionable elite had he so desired. Indeed, he made his home in that prominent bastion of Gilded Age fashionable society, Newport, Rhode Island. Calvert chose instead to pursue a less flamboyant life as a gentleman-scholar. While he emphasized in his essay the discipline and dedication to self-culture which alone refine an individual's requisite natural aptitude for gentry status, he rejected the notion that the gentleman is primarily, or in any important way, a product of heredity—or even necessarily of family influence. In this view he differed markedly from Oliver Wendell Holmes who, in Edwin Cady's words, "ignored the special insistence of American theorists [Jefferson, especially] that the success of democracy must come from its discovery and use of its natural gentlemen."[22] From all classes spring individuals capable of becoming gentlemen, Calvert maintained, for gentility is only partially inheritable at best, and nature does not countenance monopolies—at least not in a republican society.[23] Discipline, refined sensibilities, graceful and dignified manners, and a readiness to serve society are recurrent themes in Calvert's essay, as they are in a great deal of the courtesy literature that issued throughout the nineteenth century.

Formal education, especially as it was embodied in the traditional liberal arts college curriculum, with its emphasis on the Greek and Roman classics, was the principal means by which those with aptitude and desire gained the discipline and developed the interests to be proper gentlemen. In his autobiography, Massachusetts Senator George Frisbie Hoar commented on the rough country boys, who, if they had it in them, emerged from study at Harvard as gentlemen in behavior and character.[24] But gentry spokesmen like Godkin conceded, on occasion, that the appropriate home influence, even individual study, if sufficiently enlightened and rigorous, could serve equally well to nurture the gentleman. The essentials of the process —the hard work and self-denial which purified and tempered a person's ideals—could be found elsewhere than Cambridge and New Haven.[25] Pernicious influences on character, such as the rapid acquisition of wealth, encouraged people to believe that they had easily reached the summit of social and moral culture and this delusion might eventually precipitate mental and moral chaos, Godkin feared, unless the process of mobility was mediated by the kind of discipline inherent in the concept of the gentleman.[26] Edward Everett Hale, one of the age's leading moralists and an occasional contributor to children's magazines, made the same point in his tribute to Daniel Lothrop, the publisher of *Wide Awake*, following Lothrop's death. Quick and showy success engaged neither heart nor mind. The process of struggle and application produced "a thorough-going, sound, reliable man," according to Hale, but a meteoric rise to social prominence could not be counted on to produce character.[27]

Historically, the ideal of the gentleman had implications for social control, and the colonial gentry had accepted as their due broad responsibilities for public service and leadership. Moreover, the ideal provided a familiar set of expectations having wide social utility in a democracy. In ordinary transactions, Godkin remarked in an essay on social classes, people rely more on an estimation of character than on legal sanctions for protection; and character, in the sense of integrity and dependability, was central to the gentry's concept of the gentleman. Noting the greater individual freedom enjoyed by Americans, another writer urged the necessity of a commensurately greater emphasis on honor in American education. The ideal accomplished gentleman furnished a concept of honor capable of offsetting the disintegrative tendencies inherent in individual competition, which was otherwise largely unchecked by explicit social sanctions.[28]

As an integrative ideal, then, the social type of the gentleman stressed a necessary reciprocity between freedom and responsibility. Courage and self-reliance were tempered by the gentleman's obligation of service and by an insistence on courtesy and disciplined self-control. The threat to social order inherent in the development of the former qualities was balanced by the latter imperatives. The code of the gentleman provided that freedom and initiative were preserved, the process of competition was restrained, and its rewards were a function of character rather than luck, ruthlessness, or chicanery.

The social power residual in the gentry ideal at the end of the nineteenth century was examined by Chicago sociologist E. A. Ross in his *Social Control*, the first systematic analysis of that subject. Ross began his investigations into social controls by trying to account for the stability of American society in the face of what appeared to be powerful forces for social disintegration—for example, the conditions of urban living and factory labor and the influx of (allegedly) racially inferior immigrants. Formal controls, embodied in legal and governmental institutions and supported by appropriate sanctions, were familiar, visible forms of social control, but taken together they still did not fully account for the maintenance of social order in the increasingly competitive and secular industrial society of the late nineteenth century. Ross argued that informal controls, located in tradition, class consciousness, educational and religious organizations, and public opinion, all operated powerfully through persuasion and through the process of socialization to maintain social continuity. Crucial among such informal controls was the power of personal ideals, conceived as social types, manifest in particular styles of life and available for wide popular emulation. With the decline historically of supernatural sanctions, the influence of such personal ideals, and especially the ideal of the gentleman, had been extended. "With us the type has become so popular and supreme that one must descend quite low in the social scale," Ross thought, "to find common the man who does not wince at being told he is 'no gentleman.' "[29] Thus, it is no surprise that John Townsend Trowbridge, in recommending Walt Whitman to Secretary Chase for an appointment to the Department of the Treasury, should choose to counter the poet's self-proclaimed image by emphasizing that Whitman was "as quiet a gentleman in his manners and conversation as any guest who enters your door."[30]

In order to account for the existence and power of personal ideals, Ross made a distinction between the "social ethos" and the "folk ethos." Such ideals as that of the gentleman were elements of the former. They were products of superior men or classes, and they were readily distinguishable from elements of the folk ethos, which were rooted largely in racial, hence hereditary and unconscious, instincts and as such were resistant to conscious control and deliberate change. Specific groups belonging to what Ross designated "the party of order" accounted for the conservation of personal ideals against the downward pull of instinct. Rulers, priests, and magistrates, as well as publicists, editors, educators, property owners, and an ethical elite concerned with the general welfare of society contributed to the maintenance of progressive social ideals. To account for the consolidation of influence by ethical elites, Ross noted the part played by what he called "dramatization." The prophet dressed his sociology as ethics and his ethics as religion.[31] Ross might well have added that ideals are perpetuated in the same way.

The ties between Christianity and gentility were historically close from the seventeenth century, and they remain close in the children's literature produced by the gentry after the Civil War. "Only God can make a gentleman," a character remarks in one of Roswell Smith's stories for *St. Nicholas*, and this statement sums up much that is implicit in essays on the gentleman in etiquette books and in children's periodical fiction of the nineteenth century.[32] As an ethical ideal, the social type of the gentleman held out the promise of harmonious social relationships in addition to the possibility of personal success. In an industrial society dominated by aggressive economic and social competition, the type of the true Christian gentleman at his best offered an attractive alternative to less-principled versions of the self-made man that glorified getting and spending, placed a high premium on competitive individualism, and made character subservient to business routine, profit making, and expediency.

The principles and values of the businessman as a social type, however scrupulous his practice, are almost never the focus of stories in the gentry children's magazines published during the Gilded Age. The values that are present are indisputably middle class, but they are given organization and expression in the personal qualities and activities of ladies and gentlemen and are validated in the adventures of children who successfully act out these values under the aegis of gentry figures or in the isolation and suffering of those who choose to ignore gentry values. There is a steady emphasis on self-discipline, conscience, and character. Psychological sanctions are far more common than physical punishment, a pattern consistent with the reduced use of corporal punishment urged in most of the child-rearing literature of the period. The familiar motif of getting ahead is softened, or more often replaced, by the gentry emphasis on service and duty. Despite the gentry's status as a functional elite, the stories reflect a commitment to democracy. Every American child, the fiction promises, can be a gentleman or lady in the essentials of character and service, if not in the desirable virtue of refined taste. Recruitment into the ranks of gentility is shown to be possible regardless of class or regional origin. Education and self-discipline are considered capable of nurturing the simple but sound virtues borne of regional life. In other words, the values and preoccupations found in these stories are just those that one would expect to find in children's periodicals edited and written by men and women who considered themselves to be ladies and gentlemen and who sought to sustain and to communicate their vision of American possibilities in the literature they made available to children.

The essence of the cultivated gentleman or lady was the congruence in their behavior between impulse and act, a "graceful consonance" between mind and manners, according to Calvert, which was wrought only by "a patient cultivation of the finer and better sensibilities and a severe unremitting self-culture."[33] The best society exists, Lucy Larcom wrote, "when people meet sincerely, on the ground of their deepest sympathies and highest aspirations, without conventionality or cliques or affectation."[34] This ideal was threatened by the spirit of fashion which fed on all that was showy, superficial, and external. "The idea that [the word] 'lady' means something external in dress and circumstances has been too generally adopted by rich and poor," she remarks in her autobiography.[35] Fashion perverted true gentility because it was ever compelled to seek out new stimulants. In a version of the drunkard's progress, the search for novel stimulation led to satiety—and finally to callousness and cynicism. Like alcohol, the spirit of fashion led to "intolerable aberrations and illegalities."[36] In one *Youth's Companion* story, fashionability is partly to blame for a young couple's unfortunate decision to marry too early, a decision that brings hardship and unhappiness to both.[37] In a similar story, the same false standard, expressed in a girl's irresponsible flirting, leads to the moral destruction of a young man who takes her coquetry too seriously.[38]

The fashionable elite of the large seaboard cities, since they too claimed to be ladies and gentlemen, were at once a threat to the gentry ideal and a useful foil to children's writers whose own interpretation of gentility was significantly different. In the gentry children's magazines, the standards of fashionable society are held up as effete, devitalized, and superficial. In a few stories, the gentry ideal is threatened by the confidence man who assumes the guise of respectable gentility to cover criminal intent.[39] But this species of sham gentility, a clear threat to social order, represents a less insidious threat than the fashionable manners and ostentatious style of the nouveau riche who offered an attractive but, for the gentry, pernicious model for popular emulation.[40]

False standards of gentility, whatever their social origin or intent, provided the contributors to the periodicals with a means of leading children to crucial distinctions between appearance and reality. Rightly understood, the code of the gentleman made it possible to size up and place others in a fluid, competitive society that had largely abandoned traditional symbols of social rank. In the literature, the ideal of the gentleman was considered capable of structuring the social world; but in actuality, of course, the sham gentleman was a constant possibility and threat.

John Townsend Trowbridge's serial "His Own Master," which appeared in *St. Nicholas* during 1876, exemplifies some of the ways in which the values of gentility shaped fictional patterns in the periodicals. With the death of his aunt at the outset of the story, Jacob loses what little family he had. The young orphaned hero is suddenly his own master in fact, though he reveals little self-mastery at first. His ability to discriminate between the real and apparent in character and motivation is shown to be dangerously inadequate; throughout much of the story, he is deceived by a variety of men who either attempt to victimize him or who present irrelevant models for behavior.

Jacob first encounters a neighbor—a deacon—who, seeing the boy's grief and uncertainty about his future, attempts to comfort him but only succeeds in being irritatingly self-righteous and sententious. Meeting a farmer soon afterward, Jacob sees through the man's efforts to beat him out of the value of his aunt's cow. Later, he sturdily refuses to be drawn into the "unmanly" sports proposed by a group of schoolmates intent on mischief. But when Alphonse Pinkey, a foppish young dancing master, happens along, Jacob yields to his buoyant, treacherous enthusiasm and air of self-confidence. Pinkey is fashion personified, and Jacob is enthralled with his new-found companion. He agrees to auction his aunt's belongings, to trust Pinkey with the proceeds, and to leave her debts unpaid while he and the dancing master embark on a search for a vaguely remembered, long-lost uncle of Jacob's. For the moment, Jacob is completely taken in by Pinkey's spurious gentility.

Pinkey's character is gradually revealed as the young men travel together aboard a riverboat. Pinkey gambles at cards and attempts to ingratiate himself with two sisters whose light and affected manners reveal their membership in fashionable society. Jacob, on the other hand, finds himself drawn to a woman whose dignity and quiet manners show her to be a true lady. Under the prodding of her gently pointed questions about Pinkey, Jacob is gradually won to the gentry definition of things and begins to recognize the dancing master for what he really is. Before the trip is over, however, Pinkey disappears in a boating accident and Jacob leaves the boat to search for him.

During the picaresque journey that follows, Jacob encounters an eccentric New England river peddler and is aided by a Quaker farm family but fails to find any trace of his missing companion. Taking up again the search for his uncle, he is unwittingly lured into the theft of a wagon by a skylarking group of rough-looking boys and is later jailed briefly as a witness against a professional gambler with whom he had innocently traveled for some distance. When he finally locates his uncle, Jacob is unprepared for the lonely old man's misanthropy and initial distrust. In the meantime, however, Jacob had met again the lady whose questions on the boat had stirred him to consider the relationship between character, motives, and actions. She and her husband, a schoolteacher, advise Jacob to make a home with his uncle and to pay the debts left by his aunt. Jacob agrees and, in time, the influence of the younger man softens the older. Preferring to make things rather than to engage in the trading of goods manufactured by others, Jacob prepares to learn the foundry business by mastering the menial, dirty work of the shop, after a brief period of formal schoolwork. His self-mastery accomplished, he is ready to coordinate and direct the productive labor of others.

"Boys that have good homes never know how well off they are!" Trowbridge admonishes his readers, through Jacob, at one point in the boy's adventures along the road to self-mastery.[41] Stripped of the family's protection, Jacob finds as he travels that it is only in families, and especially from mothers, that reliable advice may be obtained. His conscience, reawakened on his journey of self-discovery by the lady on the boat and tested and strengthened in various subsequent encounters, is the internalized voice of the family, symbolized by the mother who is also a lady. The men that he meets lack understanding or are treacherous and hostile or, like the Yankee river peddler, too eccentric to provide Jacob with the key to self-mastery: the conviction that patience, perseverance, and self-control form the basis for character. Jacob's gradual recognition of Pinkey's true character is the index by which Trowbridge charts his hero's moral progress. The achievement of character bestows moral vision. When Jacob encounters Pinkey a last time as the story ends—the treacherous friend had survived the boating accident and run off with Jacob's money—he sees Pinkey clearly for the sham he was all along and wonders at his own earlier failure to perceive the patent incongruity between the dancing master's actions and the clothes and manners he affected.

Although Jacob is at one point the recipient of a new suit and eventually gains social and financial prominence, Trowbridge hints, his rewards differ from those frequently received by the Alger hero. Early in the story, Jacob rescues the daughter of the lady who befriends him on the boat—a favorite motif of Alger's—but Jacob gets from the mother neither the money nor the clerkship so often bestowed on Alger's heroes and from which largesse their success stems. Instead, he receives advice. Similarly, from his uncle he gets advice and a chance, glossed with a rather pointed speech about boys who feel superior to getting their hands dirty and who seek genteel positions in commerical firms. Finally, Jacob changes; he develops a perception of the world that subordinates economic security to self-respect and the desire to serve society. "It is sometimes worth the while," Jacob learns, "to obey conscience . . . at whatever seeming sacrifice. . . . That precious satisfaction is, to every noble nature, more than all worldly ends unrighteously attained. Many a man, and many a youth, would to-day give up all he has ever gained by unworthy means, to be able to say to his own soul, 'I resisted the temptation—I did right.' "[42]

If young men in these stories are far more likely to get their values from ladies, they do learn from gentlemen on occasion—sometimes with results that are unconsciously but bitterly ironic. In a *Youth's Companion* story entitled "Jim" (1879), a gentleman working as a mine engineer becomes interested in the welfare of an Irish boy whose father has been killed in an accident and whose mother is an alcoholic.[43] Characteristically, the boy refuses to accept "charity"; what he wants is knowledge. His favorite reading is Benjamin Franklin and George Washington. But as if to mock the dream encouraged by that reading, the story ends in disaster. Warned by the boy that his life is in danger from Molly Maguires, the narrator discovers the boy several hours later, dying from a blow to the head. Unsupported by the family, the isolated gentleman, amid the savagery of industrial warfare, is unable to save Jim.

In "Jim" and in the majority of stories, it appears to have been increasingly difficult to create effective male characters who were not only gentlemen but also responsible professional men. Men who were gentlemen were most often teachers, frequently bachelors, or else they were, like Trowbridge's first popular figure, Father Brighthopes, elderly and frail.[44] Fathers with moral strength were almost invariably natural gentlemen; that is, unlettered men living close to the rhythms of nature, whose character and vocation seem inextricably related.[45]

In these narratives, the appearance of the traditional gentry virtues—fortitude, temperance, prudence, justice, liberality, and courtesy—is shaped by several considerations. Daniel Ford, as noted earlier, knew the commercial value of, and sought to include in the *Youth's Companion*, stories involving lively, rapid action and in which courage would be a conspicuous and appropriate virtue. This recognition helps to explain the relative absence of stories concerned primarily with problems of courtesy, manners, and etiquette, virtues less readily dramatized in ways that could compete with the enticing but treacherous tales available in the dime novels. Moreover, courage and self-reliance are the qualities most appropriate, given the frequent, sudden isolation that occurs in these stories and epitomizes the essential condition of American life. Although it is difficult, and not too informative, to categorize stories as exemplifying this or that single virtue, stories which demand of their characters physical or moral courage, presence of mind under difficult circumstances, or self-reliance outnumber the stories tending to dramatize problems of duty, faith (sometimes itself a species of moral courage), honor and integrity, or generosity. I am referring now only to stories previously categorized as ordeals—that is, stories in which a particular moral stance, already internalized by the child, proves sound in the face of conflict or threat. Of the stories so classified, about half seem to emphasize courage, self-reliance, and presence of mind, singly or in combination.[46]

Stories that conform to the change-of-heart formula, however, do not reveal a parallel distribution of inappropriate attitudes or values. Cowardice, for example, is rarely a problem in these stories despite the emphasis on courage and self-reliance in the ordeal. Instead, the failure to discipline oneself and various modes of egocentrism are dominant motifs in change-of-heart stories. A number of these portray the problems of children who are characterized by some form of thoughtless behavior, manifested variously as carelessness, recklessness, or irresponsibility. Stories portraying the wages of pride, conceit, and pretentiousness—all the varied forms of ungentlemanly self-assertiveness—are almost as frequent. Narratives dealing with impatient, self-indulgent, or quick-tempered individuals are somewhat less frequent. Stories in these three categories comprise a little more than half of the total number of change-of-heart stories in the five magazines.

By way of contrast, the values found by Irvin Wyllie in his examination of self-help literature include industry, frugality, sobriety, perseverance, punctuality, loyalty, obedience, and initiative.[47] None of these are dominant themes in the five popular children's periodicals here surveyed. Successful socialization to the code of the gentleman made self-control of supreme importance. In a representative *Youth's Companion* story, for example, a thief is outwardly indistinguishable in manner and appearance from a gentleman except in one respect: he cannot control his temper. This failure is as revealing as his record of thefts.[48] Sensitivity to the needs and rights of others complements self-control. Financial success and the so-called employee virtues evident in Alger, especially, are subordinated in the gentry's view to the development of character and self-control and the fostering of a willingness to serve society well.[49] A representative gentry story like Louise Chandler Moulton's "Coals of Fire" (1868) does not demonstrate that luck and pluck finally triumph in the commercial world of New York.[50] Rather, the story traces the circumstances in which a boy learns to govern his previously uncontrollable temper and to express his passionate nature in acceptable ways. It deals not with the theme of upward mobility and the myth of the self-made man but with the problem of locating and sanctioning social controls appropriate to the conditions of social and political equality, a matter which exercised de Tocqueville, Cooper, and others throughout the nineteenth century. The story also raises the problem of controlling individual aggression, which sociologist W. Lloyd Warner, for example, has argued is historically one of the two most problematic areas for the middle-class American child.[51]

In the first scene of "Coals of Fire," fifteen-year-old Guy Morgan returns home from school angry and frustrated. Because of a promise to his mother, he had not been able to stop a bully by the name of Osgood from tormenting some younger boys. When Osgood had turned on him, Guy refused to fight back, and he fears that he will be considered a coward by his schoolmates. He asks his mother to release him from the promise he made to her to control his "naturally fierce temper." His mother, however, is relieved that her son has finally demonstrated the self-control which she, without a husband's help, has tried, unsuccessfully until now, to instill in him. She reassures him that his will can control his impulsive nature and insists that he remain obedient to his promise for the rest of the year.

In the second and final scene of the story, it is the last day of school. Guy reluctantly attends a picnic with the rest of his schoolmates, from whom he still feels ostracized. The happy mixture of exuberant youth and natural scenery is suddenly interrupted when Osgood's sister Hetty falls into a river. Not surprisingly, Osgood is powerless in the situation; he cannot swim. Guy, of course, can, and he vindicates himself in an act of public courage. He saves Hetty, testing in the crisis the limits of his strength now fully exerted in an acceptable kind of conflict. The following day, a delegation of boys, led by the chastened Osgood, seeks Guy out at home, acknowledges his courage, and returns him to his former place of prestige in the group. But the author makes pointedly clear that the greatest reward for his exploit is not the tribute of his peers but the "few fond words" spoken by his mother and the "pride in her joyful eyes" at the evidence of Guy's triumph over himself.

Readers familiar with Alger's work would recognize several marked similarities between it and Mrs. Moulton's story. Like many an Alger hero, Guy Morgan has lost his father. He and his mother are poor, but in a lucky moment the boy is able to render a distinguished service for which he is then rewarded. Whereas the Alger hero frequently finds his reward in a modest white-collar position bestowed by a benovolent employer, Guy Morgan's reward is far less tangible. Moreover, the rural setting, the moral strength of Morgan's mother, the emphasis on personal character development in the traditional context of the Christian gentleman, and the stress on self-control suggest a significant variation from the cluster of values, rewards, and preoccupations that have been read out of the Alger books. Nourished in the family and sufficient to temper the rigors of a competitive individualistic society, the code of the gentleman is presented as sustaining social order by making self-discipline and self-control the basis for personal development.

The fact that these stories take place most often in the context of family life is important. It helps to correct the unfortunate extent to which much of the children's literature of the period has been shadowed by the Alger formula and dominated by the Alger symbol. The point of the periodical stories here discussed is rarely economic success. The concern is more fundamental than that, for it is the problem of a basic social stance, of basic social knowledge. The family is a social microcosm; behavior is assessed in relation to a world, not simply in terms of the institutions of commerce. Put another way, the real world is a collection of families, not, as Alger implies, a collection of paternalistic businesses. The values learned in the family in these periodical stories are sufficient for the operation of business, but the values of the marketplace are not sufficient for family life and consequently are not sufficient to structure society in any satisfactory way.

The virtues of the gentleman were conceived, then, as having very broad social utility. They were not narrowly vocational, instrumental, or professional: "When we think," Calvert reminded his readers, "how intimate, diversified, unavoidable, indispensable, how daily and hourly are our relations with our fellow-men, we cannot but become aware, how much it concerns us . . . to be affable and gentlemanly, and arm ourselves with a bearing that shall be the expression of self-respect, purified by respect for others."[52]

Consistent with the value placed on acquiring self-discipline, children in the stories are rarely subjected to corporal punishment, even in school. Instead, punishment is psychological—the temporary withdrawal of parental affection, trust, or esteem, for example—or else discipline is meted out by the seemingly impersonal but natural logic of events set in motion by the child's folly. The assumption underlying the latter possibility is perfectly captured in a statement by one of Louisa May Alcott's characters, Mrs. Minot, the "true gentlewoman" who acts as the moral center in Miss Alcott's *St. Nicholas* serial "Jack and Jill": "Our actions are in our own hands, but the consequences of them are not. Remember that . . . and think twice before you do anything."[53] Both of these modes of discipline appear in a variety of change-of-heart stories, but rarely is the process of psychological control presented quite as directly as in a story by one of the steady contributors to children's periodicals of the period, Abby Morton Diaz. "Little Dilly, or The Uses of Tears" describes several episodes over a two-year period during which Dilly, a rather spoiled child of six at the outset, learns to control her emotions as she discovers the uses and abuses of tears.[54] Dilly is shamed into appropriate behavior first by her mother's gentle reproach, then by the hint that she is also failing to meet her heavenly father's expectations, in addition to those of her earthly family, and finally by having her behavior interpreted to her by the community, represented by two friends of her mother's whom Dilly overhears discussing her behavior.

In the second half of the story, Dilly acts out her newly won self-control. She remains dry-eyed at the discovery of her smashed rocking horse; she has learned that one doesn't cry over one's own troubles. But she weeps, with her mother's approval, out of pity for a neighbor's tragedy; and when her brother is caught in a lie, she joins the entire family in weeping—for one can't help crying when a friend has transgressed. Her self-control firmly established, Dilly demonstrates the final use of a lady's tears: a sanction against the erring male.

Impatience, carelessness, and pride, manifested in all their variety, may also be punished more impersonally. A child's thoughtless act in a moment of mischief leads directly, in one instance, to the death of his pet horse, impaled on a fence.[55] In another story, a boy feels guilt when, as he hesitates briefly in a moment of temptation, he recalls his dead mother.[56] A vain and disobedient child who resists her mother's discipline recognizes her error only after her stubborn willfulness leads to her being kidnapped in a rough section of New York City and suffering the indignity—one is tempted to say the symbolic ravishment—of having her hair cut off to be sold, after which she is released.[57] In another story, a family's four unruly children are forced to become quietly self-controlled in the wake of an accident in which the fifth child injures her spine while playing. Because of her need for quiet "every one of us began to see, even then, that we must try to overcome our faults, try to be quiet instead of noisy, gentle instead of rough, *for another's sake*."[58] Gradually, the injured girl's room becomes a family shrine, "a little bit of heaven with the dust and the wrong all shut out." Just before the girl's death, her mother confides to her, "I truly don't know how your father and I could have brought up these children without your help."[59]

Accidents, fatal injuries, memories of dead faces looking reproachfully out of the past—such sanctions covertly speak what could not be faced directly. Mother was a lady, to be sure, and that should have been enough; but it wasn't. Father was a gentleman, but increasingly the women who wrote for these children's periodicals found him a difficult figure to draw convincingly. He hovers on the periphery of many of these domestic narratives but exerts little or no moral force, or else, no gentleman at all, he is dulled by alcohol, casually maimed, or killed off. Sometimes he simply is never referred to.

The notion of freedom that lay at the heart of the democratic social theory espoused by the gentry ironically cut two ways. Free to become what he could, his individuality compelling respect, the child was still expected to take on the manners and modes of gentility, to recognize, as Calvert stated, that "a community or people that cannot produce and maintain gentlemen, is doomed to sapless mediocrity."[60] The child in real life, however, was free to reject the ideal. Physical compulsion violated both the spirit of democratic theory and the tradition of the gentleman as, above all, a free man. In the battle for social converts, psychological compulsion occasionally verged on the hysterical, as some of these stories suggest.

The idea of the gentleman encompassed more than a theory of manners and a discipline for self-culture, however; it was also an ideal of public service, which continued to be strongly expressed in the children's fiction issued under the aegis of the gentry throughout the latter part of the century. Whether through the agency of providential good fortune or not, getting ahead for the sake of getting ahead is rarely dramatized in these stories. The emphasis, as we have seen, is primarily on self-culture; but in situations where ambition and economic insecurity combine, the ideal of service is seldom absent as a measure of success and a constraint on self-assertiveness. Characters in these stories are likely to discover their economic salvation in producing the requisite goods or services to fill a particular social need, generally one they have identified themselves. Jacob, the hero of Trowbridge's "His Own Master," deliberately chose to become a maker, an iron master, we remember; he had no taste, and said so specifically, for merely distributing the products created by others. Necessity breeds invention and productive capabilities in these stories. Making superior pickles and selling them to Boston hotels, repairing broken dolls, raising strawberries or prize roses for market, or manufacturing covered buttons at home result in both economic security and personal fulfillment.[61]

The pattern emerges with particular clarity in "The

Assistant," published in *Wide Awake* (1882).[62] The story presents the struggle of two brothers and their sister to establish a newspaper in a raw western town. It is the girl's heroic combination of courage, energy, tenacity, tact, and moral vision—her gentility, in short—that holds the family together when discouragement threatens to undermine her brothers' will. "But wherever one stands," she remarks in good Emersonian rhetoric, "the centre of the earth is always exactly beneath him, and the centre of the heavens exactly over his head."[63] If they succeed in their endeavor, she continues, the rewards are "honor, influence, home," perhaps political position and a chance to travel, but always the opportunity to exchange ideas, to punish the mean and support the good. One could hardly ask for a set of rewards more consistent with, or expressive of, the gentry's conception of service. The price of such a future may be a precarious present—"one must always be prepared for accidents"—as well as constant diligence. As another *St. Nicholas* sketch makes clear, America owes no man a living. The nation's history reveals a progressive triumphing over the wilderness, a victory won at the cost of great effort. Those free spirits who built the canals, railroads, public schools, and libraries, who built ships and invented fire-fighting equipment worked "manfully" and well. In turn each individual who follows is expected to live up to the example set by such men, to "do something, go to work and show that you are a man."[64]

Accession to gentry status, even during the eighteenth century when the colonial gentry was a virtual ruling class, was always possible for talented individuals whose energy, abilities, and force of character were their only paternity. In the nineteenth century, education continued to provide the primary avenue by which individuals assumed the interests and manners of refined gentlemen. Regional religious and cultural traditions produced a kind of vigorous natural gentility, a sturdy self-reliance, integrity, and character. Nurtured in small towns and villages, the natural gentleman might then be polished by the discipline of the traditional curriculum of the small liberal arts college. But formal education was not essential to the making of gentlemen; it simply worked a little faster, as Frank Stockton, the assistant editor of *St. Nicholas*, suggested in his story "What Might Have Been Expected" (1873).[65] A conversation on fashionable society in another story summarizes the concept of natural gentility. Rural life produced an instinctive courtesy; urban life, characterized by extremes of poverty and wealth, did not: "I've seen city girls do things that a country girl would be ashamed of. *I* believe politeness comes from the heart, and that a person can be brought up in the backwoods and yet never do an impolite thing, because he'll follow his good feelings."[66]

The problem of gentry recruitment is a recurrent theme in the periodicals. Phebe, the heroine of Louisa May Alcott's "Bonfires," who successfully flags a train to a stop in front of a ruined bridge, is an only child largely dependent on the natural world not only for her amusement but more importantly for her moral nurture. Her act not only defines her courage and reveals her presence of mind but suggests that she possesses a developed sense of social responsibility. However isolated from society she may seem to be, she displays the poise and conscience, if not the polish, characteristic of a true lady.[67]

The beneficent influences of nature, however, were not proof against erring human will or unforeseen events which sometimes combined to maim the spirit, even in pastoral settings. For Jack Ramsdale in Louise Chandler Moulton's "Against the Wind and Tide," education, personfied by a young gentleman, is not the finishing touch to character but the saving touch itself, accomplishing what nature and family had failed to achieve.[68] As the boy is first described in the story, he is bitter, antisocial, and potentially destructive. His mother is dead; only a dim memory of a woman who prayed for him remains. His father, too weak to sustain himself without her, drinks himself to death. Jack

THE BOY WHO WORKED.

By Roswell-Smith.

"DON'T YOU WANT A RIDE?"

Roswell-Smith, "The Boy Who Worked," *SN* 1 (1874): 147.

hires out to a neighbor, Deacon Small, whose hard-driving demands and hypocritical self-righteousness combine to destroy the boy's slender store of self-respect and self-confidence. When a new teacher, a recent Harvard graduate, arrives in the district, Jack joins a group of rowdies intent on making Mr. Garrison's tenure a brief and unhappy one. When Jack is caught in the mischief-making, however, he yields to the persuasion of the young schoolmaster's strong right arm; more importantly, he is persuaded of the truth of Garrison's assertion that "the forces of law and order are what rule the world."[69] Embodied in the character of the vigorous young schoolmaster, the gentry influence kindles a sympathetic response in the recalcitrant, lonely, much-exploited boy, and Jack learns from his encounter with a gentleman that neither fate nor poverty can limit him if he wishes to improve himself. The key to renewal is Jack's conscious resolution to become a better person—a resolution which, expresssed in appropriate behavior, validates his prior intuitive response to the character of the gentleman.

If an individual proved blind to the opportunities of rural life or was too poverty-stricken to attend school, a chance encounter with a gentleman or lady might still be enough to kindle and focus a poor boy's initiative. In Roswell Smith's *St. Nicholas* story, "The Boy Who Worked" (1874), a gentleman, defined in this case as "one who always does all he can to help others and to make them happy," meets a fatherless boy on a midwestern country road.[70] The boy is impressed by the manners, speech, and moral force of the man and seeks his advice periodically afterward. He does not ask, and would have been refused, Smith implies, the more tangible aid bestowed by the benefactors characteristic of Alger's fiction. The boy's education comes only with struggle, but Smith bestows a familiar symbol on his persevering young hero in the end: the boy achieves gentry' status, successfully establishing himself as an editor and marrying a lady. The familiar success story—shaped by concepts of the educational role of the gentry, the inspirational potential of gentry values, and the theory of natural gentility—reaffirms central elements of the gentry world view.

Waxing euphoric over the advent of the year 1871 ("a great strange book in heaven's own blue and gold"), the editors of *Our Young Folks* announced an essay contest in the January issue, the subject of which would best test the moral perception of their young readers. That subject, perhaps inevitably, was the nature of the true gentleman "in the best sense of the term." Boys were encouraged to "describe such a character as they would wish to become" while girls were asked to "give their idea of what a gentleman should be."[71] In return for these expressions of character, the editors offered, apparently without recognizing the irony, a series of cash prizes!

They received more than four hundred replies, mostly from young ladies. The winning essays, published later in the year, were doubtless selected by Lucy Larcom, perhaps aided by John Townsend Trowbridge, and thus provide unique evidence from which to infer their concept of gentry selfhood. Integrity, modesty, pleasing manners, purity of heart, and dedication to service were the qualities emphasized in the two first-prize essays, worth twenty dollars. The familiar lineaments of the gentleman were filled out in the remaining prize essays with the addition of bravery, justice, generosity, temperance, self-control, and cultivated taste. The editors gave the last word on the subject to a Muscatine, Iowa, girl. Her essay was not among the winners but her letter accompanying her entry apparently summarized perfectly the impulse for the contest. The editors, with a fervent amen, joined her in hoping that their readers might "all better *illustrate* than any can *define* the characteristics of a true gentleman."[72] Performance, not understanding, after all, was the crucial test of gentility.

The contest makes explicit what is evident in the formula

domestic fiction published in *Our Young Folks* and the other gentry children's periodicals throughout the Gilded Age. It consistently demonstrated and reasserted the efficacy of gentry values. It offered the social types of the lady and the gentleman as models for behavior to be emulated by young Americans destined to inherit the nation's brighter tomorrow. "Can any one fancy what our society might be, if all its members were perfect gentlemen and true ladies?" asked the compiler of one of the period's numerous etiquette books.[73] Those who wrote for and edited the popular children's periodicals cited here made every effort to delineate that society in their domestic fiction, to dramatize in an entertaining but truthful fashion the necessary and sufficient basis in individual character of personal achievement, social order, and progress in a democratic society.

4

Fiction and the Republican Child

A good home story can express as much of the law and economy of the household as a chapter of Paley or Wayland.

Samuel Osgood
"Books for Our Children" (1865)

Throughout the nineteenth century, a running skirmish over the nature of the child flickered across the intellectual landscape. As alternative, more benign definitions of the child challenged older notions of innate depravity and childhood became invested with a diverse but powerful symbolism, concepts of children's literature shifted to accommodate, and in some cases to define and champion, the newer attitudes. Agencies that might influence young Americans were anxiously weighed by various groups having a proprietary interest in the nation's future. After the Civil War, the gentry grew increasingly dismayed by the potentially harmful influence implicit in the rising popularity of inexpensive literature aimed at children—much of it poorly printed and luridly illustrated. Critics of this new threat to democracy called for the creation of a body of literature that was appropriate to the conditions of American life and to republican institutions and that met certain standards of critical excellence and moral integrity. Dime novels, which might lead impressionable boys to seek adventure in the West behind the muzzle of a revolver, could not be directly suppressed, but their influence could be vigorously disputed and hopefully minimized if morally sound stories, attractively produced and shrewdly marketed, could be created as an alternative.

Philippe Ariès, the French social historian, has argued that an awareness of the "particular nature of childhood" was not characteristic of medieval society; only in the sixteenth and seventeenth centuries did competing notions of child nature emerge. Children became a source of both amusement and relaxation, at first among the members of the upper class, and objects of psychological interest and moral solicitude for moralists and educational reformers intent on transforming children into reasonable adults and good Christians.[1] Childhood, conceived of as an intermediate stage between infancy and adulthood, lengthened with the recognition that the child was not ready for adult life until disciplined by the school.[2]

In Puritan New England, this discipline was permeated and shaped by the religious convictions of the colonists. Students of children's literature unsympathetic to that theology or imbued with an uncritical romanticism have frequently condemned as harsh and grim the children's literature produced in the shadow of the doctrine of infant depravity. Monica Kiefer concludes from her study of early children's books that fear and repression were the lot of colonial boys and girls until the Revolution.[3] This view of Puritan nurture is convincingly refuted by Edmund Morgan, who argues that although Puritans were not disposed "to allow the unimpeded development of personality . . . at least children were not subjected to a preconceived discipline without reference to their individual needs and capacities. A parent in order to educate his children properly had to know them well, to understand their particular characters, and to treat them accordingly. Granted its purposes and assumptions, Puritan education was intelligently planned, and the relationship between parent and child which it envisaged was not one of harshness and severity but of tenderness and sympathy."[4]

The child was born evil and ignorant, to be sure. Original sin was a fact, however unpleasant, and each child needed to become acquainted with it and its implications as soon as possible. The child was not incorrigible, however, and the Puritans, perhaps paradoxically, assigned enormous importance to education. Firmness was necessary in handling children, but it was always better to persuade the reluctant to holiness than to attempt to whip them into the Kingdom of Heaven. The notion that each child was a good seed to be nurtured into individual flower may have been alien to seventeenth-century Puritans, but it is clear, Morgan concludes, that children were cherished in colonial Massachusetts.[5]

As the inherent instability of orthodox Puritanism was progressively revealed by the events of the late seventeenth century, the traditional view of the child was attacked in the course of the wider debate over Arminianism. By the middle of the eighteenth century, the doctrine of infant damnation, isolated from its complex theological context and used as a rhetorical strategy in the debate, seemed distasteful, even to some defenders of the old orthodoxy.[6] Rejection of the concept in popular child nurture literature, however, was not complete until the outbreak of the Civil War.[7]

Whether expressed in the liberal theology of Charles Chauncey and Jonathan Mayhew or in the secular rationality of the Revolutionary political leaders, faith in the child's ability to learn and rejection of theological determinism characterized many leading eighteenth-century thinkers. Their position raised two particularly important issues that were to echo through the next century: the problem of vindicating the emancipated child against the stultifying tendencies of tradition and authority and the problem of locating appropriate rational sanctions for limiting his freedom as theological sanctions progressively weakened. Their guarded optimism added a second important cluster of ideas about childhood to the child nurture debate that emerged in the 1830s as part of the more generally expressed uneasiness of that period that the Revolutionary ideals were being subverted.[8]

The disturbing appearance of social change, uncertainty over the child-rearing practices most appropriate to republican institutions, and the beckoning promise of the unshaped but better future complicated and blurred that debate. The stakes were high. Individual salvation and the nation's promise—"the last, best hope of earth," Lincoln would later call it—were both implicated; (the concern suggests the accuracy of the observation that few societies have expressed so pervasive an anxiety about child-rearing as has ours throughout the nineteenth century).[9] Still, European visitors persisted in characterizing as unruly and disobedient the children being raised in republican freedom.

The debate over child nurture focused on the earliest years of childhood and on the mother's role, too often inexpertly performed it was charged, in creating an appropriate atmosphere for that small part of the democratic future entrusted to her care. Her responsibilities were further enlarged as she assumed responsibility for those functions once performed but, as the nineteenth century wore on, largely abandoned by the father, particularly disciplining the children and conducting the family's daily religious exercise.[10] The mother came to be recognized as the moral center of the family. If she had done her work well, her memory was a lamp by which her children's feet might be guided long after they had left home. "Happy, thrice happy, is he whose early years have been watched over by a pious, intelligent mother," wrote one successful "empire builder" in the conventionalized appreciation of maternal influence common to nineteenth-century autobiography.[11] "Nellie in the Lighthouse" (discussed in another context) is only one of a number of stories in which memories of a mother's words preserve a child in danger or inspire him to the right.[12]

Parents were encouraged by all parties to the debate over appropriate child nurture to consider child-rearing as a rational, self-conscious process and to train their offspring as soon as possible in the universally approved standards of orderliness, cleanliness, and neatness. But there was no agreement over the use of corporal punishment amid the irreconcilable debate over the true nature of the child or the best means of encouraging moral development. The hardy strain of religious orthodoxy that had resisted the ideas of the enlightenment continued to urge that infant depravity necessitated curbing the child's will with the unsparing use of the rod if all else failed.[13] Infant conversion was considered a desirable testimony to the child's victory over self-will, and stories of such conversions, often climaxed by the child's death, as indicated in chapter 1, constituted a popular form of children's literature until the middle of the nineteenth century.

Obedience was also the aim of nurturists of whatever theological persuasion. Those who condemned corporal punishment were no advocates of an indulgent permissiveness. In fact, they may have been better psychologists, for they frequently argued that the guilt felt by a child who abused the love and trust of his parents constituted a more effective potential control than the memory of a beating or the fear of another.[14] (The impulse to relax corporal punishment and to make discipline fit the offense was part of a more general recognition of children's dietary, recreational, and clothing needs. Healthy bodies could contribute, it was rediscovered, to healthy characters.[15])

Even though parties to the debate differed on the nature

of the child and the methods to use in rearing him, there was a surprising uniformity in what they wanted the child to become, according to Bernard Wishy. Children were expected to evidence well-defined moral ideals of character and to manifest the will to live those ideals; they were also to be trained in service to the creator.[16] But there was no easy answer to the problems of freedom and responsibility, of social control in a democracy, that were part of the Enlightenment legacy. Each competing notion of the child was vulnerable in the vortex at the heart of the shaping American experience; here a new faith in progress jostled with an old persistent fear of man's unaided effort, with the felt need for social stability amid apparent change, and with the ambiguous celebration of individual will, energy, and worth. Whatever the position, each party to the debate had to maintain the plausibility of the world as he knew and lived it and had to attempt to transmit successfully the values sustaining that world to his children, who would nonetheless, by the law of progress, live in an altered world.

Conditions of widespread social equality would profoundly affect the form and uses of literature in a democracy. De Tocqueville, attempting to assess the impact of equality on various institutions in America, concluded that, "accustomed to the struggle, the crosses, and the monotony of practical life," the restless mass of men would "require strong and rapid emotions, startling passages, truths or errors brilliant enough to rouse them up and to plunge them at once, as if by violence, into the midst of the subject."[17] Literature then would no longer be an aspect of order as it was in societies dominated by an aristocracy: "Its form, on the contrary, will ordinarily be slighted, sometimes despised. Style will frequently be fantastic, incorrect, overburdened, and loose, almost always vehement and bold. Authors will aim at rapidity of execution more than at perfection of detail."[18]

After 1865, the enormous popularity of so-called

sensational literature, much of it aimed at children, seemed to bear out de Tocqueville's predictions. Before the war, children's fiction had been characterized by a uniformity of purpose and a unanimity of moral structure. Such pre-Civil War fiction as Jacob Abbott's popular Rollo series had been written primarily to instruct children rather than to amuse them. Moral lessons were embodied in pointed didactic statements as well as in the dramatic texture of events and resolution.[19] Less didactic writers like "Oliver Optic" began to write during the 1850s, but no body of popular children's literature before the war challenged the moral consensus in the work of Abbott, "Peter Parley," and others or threatened to provide a commercially competitive alternative form of literary experience.

Reading was considered a serious matter, and children's books were expected to be above reproach. In New England, Lucy Larcom recalled, "There was much questioning . . . as to whether fictitious reading was good for children. To 'tell a story' was one equivalent expression for lying."[20] Although she admitted reading "a great many romances," she considered the effects of skimming such books, wondering only how they ended, to be detrimental.[21] Both the promise and the threat of literature are clear in Margaret Sangster's summary of her early reading: "In the beginning of my life books were to me as real as people, and the characters on the printed page as much a part of my being as those whom I met on the street or talked with at the table."[22]

After the war, the child's right to read exclusively for pleasure became the cornerstone of literary policy for the new popular children's magazines sponsored by the gentry. They resolutely turned their faces away from what they now were pleased to recognize as the cheerless didacticism and the overt religiosity of their predecessors. With the improvements in printing technology available to them, they sought to raise standards of design and illustration in children's books and periodicals. Unlike their predecessors, they found they had to compete with a growing body of inexpensive literature which exploited that combination of rapid action, heightened emotion, debased style, and lack of moral consistency which de Tocqueville had feared would become popular with the uprooted, competitive, unreflective personality type bred of social and political equality.

Those concerned with the morality implicit in fiction addressed to children feared and hated the weekly story papers for boys and the popular dime and half-dime novels of adventure and romance. They thought sensational literature appealed primarily to the passions and to an unhealthy craving for excitement. Because it failed to touch the sentiments, such literature threatened to upset the balance and self-discipline that formed the psychological core of the gentlemanly ideal. Literature, it was assumed, was ever a stimulus to expression—hence the great concern over its social implications. Reading that merely excited individuals almost certainly would find expression in activity threatening to the gentry definition of social order.

Examples of the evils wrought by sensational fiction were not difficult to find. In April 1875, James T. Fields, the founder a decade earlier of *Our Young Folks*, visited young Jesse Pomeroy in a Boston jail to learn whether it was true that reading dime novels had led him to a murderer's cell. It had, the boy admitted.[23] Prior to his crime, he had read dime novels in prodigious quantities. Dismayed at the widespread popularity of the sensational literature intended for the juvenile market, William Graham Sumner attacked such reading in a vigorously written essay for *Scribner's Monthly*. The characters, incidents, language, rewards, the views of life inculcated, the code of manners and morals taught—all were "indescribably vulgar,"[24] Sumner charged. Manliness, in these stories, was compounded of a brawler's strength, a blackmailer's morals, and the courage that carried and used a revolver. Cheap fiction teemed with hypocritical parents and blundering policemen, with pirates, highwaymen, gamblers, vagabond boys, and dissipated city youths; the effect was to poison minds "with views of life which are so base and false as to destroy all manliness and all chances of true success."[25]

Anthony Comstock, in his exposé *Traps for the Young*, condemned the dime novel habit in an orgy of vituperative self-righteousness, claiming that such reading led to "vulgarity, profanity, loose ideas of life, impurity of thought and deed. They render the imagination unclean, destroy domestic peace, desolate homes, cheapen women's virtue, and make foul-mouthed bullies, cheats, vagabonds, thieves, desperadoes, and libertines." If that were not enough, these stories struck at the very heart of the accepted relationship between hard work and reward: "What young man will serve an apprenticeship, working early and late, if his mind is filled with the idea that sudden wealth may be acquired by following the hero of the story?"[26] One erring boy's confession summarized the danger: "I never thought of stealing until I began to read these stories."[27]

The novels of Horatio Alger and Oliver Optic were not beyond the taint of sensationalism, according to some gentry critics. Of the latter's heroes, a reviewer for the *Nation* wrote, "They encourage youthful impudence and 'smartness,' and do nothing at all to take the average New England boy away from the Boston *Herald*, from a Young American belief in his foolish self, and from general insufferableness."[28] Optic also attracted the attention of Henry Ward Beecher, who called him coarse, and Louisa May Alcott, who sniped at him in the pages of "Eight Cousins," a serial she wrote for *St. Nicholas*.[29] Such attacks as these continued during the 1870s and 1880s, and the books of both men were banned from some public libraries. Alger's preoccupation with financial success, his excessive fondness for the lucky break, and his tendency to embody social virtue in the businessman, however characteristic of

American culture these motifs may have seemed to later generations, were unacceptable to those committed to the social ideal of the gentleman.

Even books intended for Sunday-school libraries did not escape indictment on grounds of moral inadequacy. Memoirs of saintly children, those staples of the prewar child's literary diet, were disparaged; they might encourage impossibly priggish behavior or lead to the logical conclusion that religion was unhealthy since so many of the pious youngsters died young. According to George Bacon, religious novels often taught bad morals and worse religion or else exemplified a "thin and drivelling goodishness."[30] The inevitable triumph of virtue was true to doctrine but not to life: "The youth who, guided by such pious fictions—not to call them pious frauds—should proceed to the conversion, right and left, of the ... personages among whom his lot was cast, would scarcely find such uniform and facile success."[31] As for books of thrilling adventure which might be present on Sunday-school shelves, "Healthy children do not want to be thrilled; and morbid children do not need to be."[32]

Good literature refined and elevated the sensibilities; sensational literature evidently brutalized and coarsened them. The problem facing those concerned about the state of American culture, particularly the literature accessible to children, was clear: how to attract and influence the social classes who most needed culture without sacrificing the principles of democracy on the one hand or gentry standards of culture on the other.

In his autobiography, Trowbridge tells of an incident that illustrates the problem. Offered a high price to write a serial for a New York weekly noted for its sensationalism, he hesitated, worried about the propriety of being associated with the publication. He sought the advice of various friends and decided, finally, to follow the advice Longfellow gave to him:

"Accept it, by all means!" [Longfellow said.] "Of course you will not write down to the level of such a paper, but try to bring it up to your level. You will have an audience that you would probably reach in no other way." And he added something more as to the good work I would do by showing that literature could be entertaining without being melodramatic.[33]

Sensational literature was a threat to the future of democracy to the extent that it glorified false values, but one question could neither be faced directly nor ignored completely: What if those who most needed culture refused and disdained it? One strategy to improve the quality of literature for children, which avoided confronting that dilemma, was to draw up and distribute lists of approved books. Throughout the rest of the century, a great many lists were devised by denominational and professional groups. A well-organized and ambitious effort was begun as early as 1865 when a group of Unitarian ladies, many of them ministers' wives, was called, under the auspices of the American Unitarian Association, to select a library of books that could be confidently recommended to the association's churches.[34] During the next four years, members of the commission examined 5,674 titles but found only 1,526 of them suitable. Their work was widely publicized and their advice sought on selecting books for specialized audiences, such as "factory operatives," which they had not originally intended to consider.

The commission excluded books on the basis of four general criteria: incompetent style, ignorance of human life and character, "general injudiciousness," and sensationalism. An evident lack of culture or the frequent hint of ignorance was as culpable as the actual vulgarity of faulty grammar. Inconsistent motivation, lack of character development, and absence of sequence in action (lack of moral coherence, perhaps) accounted for other failures. Books about children were considered injudicious when they tended to create a harmful self-consciousness in children. Even more dangerous were stories in which adults seemed stupid or silly until redeemed by the child hero. Sensationalism, defined as the exploitation of the "startling and often horrible character of events," was potentially most harmful; as the depiction of scenes of viciousness and violence, sensationalism threatened to force on children an awareness of evil that cut childhood prematurely short.

An even more influential list was Caroline Hewins' *Book for the Young* (1882) which grew out of her own pioneer library work with children. Like the Unitarian ladies before her, Miss Hewins rejected books that made "smartness" a virtue, as well as books which "encourage children in cruelty, rudeness, or disrespect to their elders, contain much bad English, or make their little everyday heroes and heroines leap suddenly from abject poverty to boundless wealth."[35]

A second strategy formulated to improve the quality of children's literature was to enlist the natural interests of the child himself in the gentry-sponsored effort to protect him from unsatisfactory literature. Such an approach reflected the greater respect being accorded children's "natural" needs and the rhythm of their development. Boys desire adventure, conceded Martha Brooks, a member of the Unitarian Ladies Commission, at the second annual meeting of the American Library Association convened in 1879; but they lack the discrimination borne of experience to separate caricature from realism in their reading. The natural desire for adventure did not have to lead to reading "poor and vicious" books. If a boy is given "bright, crisp narratives of real life and adventure" before his taste is spoiled and told "what men and boys have done already in Arctic Sea or Great Desert . . . he will not need to seek for fictitious adventure."[36]

A third strategy, the influence that could be wielded collectively by librarians as custodians of traditional culture, was aired and debated during the 1879 Boston meeting of the American Library Association, which featured papers on "Fiction and the Reading of School Children" by such leading gentry figures as Charles Francis Adams, Jr., James Freeman Clarke, Thomas Wentworth Higginson, and Mellen Chamberlain, then superintendent of the Boston Public Library.[37]

This meeting testified to a growing uneasiness over the power of public libraries, one participant observed. More people were reading, but they were reading more fiction, and a large part of that reading was sensational—"false to life, tawdry in sentiment, full of impossible incidents."[38] Few of those present were willing to act on Charles Francis Adams' pessimistic view of the lower classes and deny such fiction any place at all in public libraries. Only two alternatives seemed available: one, free access for all patrons, even to sensational novels, was considered an abdication of the gentry's moral and cultural responsibility; the other alternative, restriction—de facto censorship—was undemocratic but a necessary bulwark against the harmful social effects of bad reading, particularly on the lower classes, who were, by definition, less disciplined than the cultured elite. Restriction might seem necessary in principle, but in practice there was no agreement about authors like Alger who fell into a gray area of marginal acceptability.

Mellen Chamberlain's address to the conference bluntly glossed the major issues discussed. The lie at the heart of sensationalism had infected statesmanship, theology, and art, as well as literature. The issue was not a matter of squeamishness or of a well-bred revulsion at unpleasant but realistic literary description: "It is a question of literature or no literature; and as the same vice manifests itself in all departments of life, it becomes part of a larger question —that of civilization itself."[39] Those who expected a return to normality after the upheaval of war or who expected a growing cultural maturity to reduce the demand for sensational literature were fooling themselves. Appetite grew with what it fed on, Chamberlain argued, and since "librarians have to do with a mass of minds not healthy, nor so surrounded by healthful influences," their responsibility was plain: "For such [minds] we have to legislate."[40]

Given his premises, Chamberlain's conclusion was inevitable, but those who pay the piper call the tune, and libraries were supported increasingly by taxes. S. S. Green, director of the Worcester Library, stated uncompromisingly what they all knew: "Men and women who pay taxes have a certain right to insist that books which please them should be bought for their use and for that of their children. Many persons, too, who read poor books believe that they are good, and this, notwithstanding they know that cultivated readers differ from them in opinion."[41] This admission is as close as anyone at the conference came to the unspeakable—the possibility that the less cultured would persist in reading Ouida's novels, fully mindful that the arbiters of culture condemned such reading. The wages of sensational reading were spiritual death, but the cultural sinners, like all other sinners, remained unconvinced.

Still, the idea of some principle of restriction tantalized those who attended the conference. The worst of the dime novels could be unanimously dismissed; but discussion of the works of Alger and Optic, especially, exposed the impossibility of any general agreement on where to draw the line against sensationalism. Those who condemned the stories of these worthies were countered by others who argued that their novels might encourage mill boys, who otherwise would not read at all, to adopt the reading habit. If nothing else, Green urged, "It is certainly better for certain classes of persons to read exciting stories than to be doing what they would be doing if not reading" (i.e., threatening the peace and stability of the community).[42] The debate ended where it had begun. They agreed that sensational literature was a danger to social order, but if the uncultivated read it, perhaps it could be an instrument in the economy of cultural salvation since they were unlikely to read anything else, at least initially. It was better than street brawling, after all. Moreover, since "legislative inter- ference with personal reading is not republican . . . be- nevolence can only clothe itself with moral suasion and library associations."[43]

Thomas Wentworth Higginson may have been whistling in the dark when he reminded the conference that "chil- dren are children" and not as depraved as other speakers seemed to assume, but there was surely no comfort in any less generous faith. Perhaps the desire that led boys to read Oliver Optic's novels was, as Higginson suggested, the same love of adventure that had made the "Anglo-American race spread itself across a continent, taking possession of it in spite of forests, rivers, deserts, wild Indians and grizzly bears."[44] Children have a right, he continued, to demand what they had always demanded—"that if we wish them to read good books we shall make such books interesting."[45] Good books, stirring books, needed to be written; reversing Gresham's law, good books would drive the bad from liter- ary circulation. Mary Mapes Dodge had used the same argument six years earlier when she launched *St. Nicholas*.[46] The child's natural desire for enlarged experience is the basis for his interest in fiction, Higginson concluded: "We cannot suppress it; we can only out-bid it by making the truth more interesting."[47] The nature of the child was the rock on which to found a saving literature.

Lists of approved books and shrewd appeals to the innate adventuresomeness of boys depended finally, for their suc- cess, on the ability of individual authors to create a demo- cratic children's literature out of the memories of their own childhood, out of their faith in the essential beneficence of the child nature, and out of their faith in the nation's future. Children could no longer, even theoretically, be forced to read what was merely good for them, except perhaps in school and church. Granted a measure of autonomy by changing definitions of their nature, children became a public whose opinion was courted, even if the nation and civilization itself hung in the balance, dependent on their choice.

Dedication to the new image of the innocent child was the hallmark of *Our Young Folks, Wide Awake*, and especially *St. Nicholas*. Mrs. Dodge sought above all to please her young readers, to offer in *St. Nicholas* a refuge—from the pressures of school particularly—where the child spirit might freely indulge itself in a healthy and regenerating fantasy. Here, she said, was no place for sermonizing or the "wearisome spinning out of facts."[48] Instruction and moral teaching were not to be eliminated, of course, but they ought to emerge indirectly "by hints dropped incidentally here and there; by a few brisk, hearty statements of the difference between right and wrong; a sharp, clean thrust at falsehood, a sunny recognition of truth, a gracious application of politeness, an unwilling glimpse of the odious doings of the uncharitable and base."[49] In practice, however, those clean thrusts at falsehood, even in *St. Nicholas*, must often have seemed like the blow of a sledge; certainly they seem so now.

Two examples will suggest that the new antididacticism was at least partly a rhetorical strategy. In her *St. Nicholas* serial "Jack and Jill" (1879), Louisa May Alcott stated directly and uncompromisingly the moral implications of an incident: it provided "one of the three lessons all are the better for knowing,—that cheerfulness can change misfortune into love and friends; that in ordering one's self aright one helps others to do the same; and that the power of finding beauty in the humblest things makes home happy and life lovely."[50] Similarly, at the end of a series of short stories about two young ladies, Harriet Beecher Stowe urged her readers: "Now remember to be a good girl, and live to help other people. Begin by being, as Pussy was, a kind, helpful daughter to your dear mother, who has done more for you than you have any idea of; and remember that your happiness consists in what you give and what you do, and not in what you receive and have done for you."[51] Such moral tags as these suggest the difficulty that gentry authors had in striking a proper balance between entertainment and instruction, despite their avowed intentions to let the moral implications of their stories emerge indirectly.

A remarkable body of children's literature was, in fact, created; but, as in the debate over restricting sensational novels in the public libraries, much of it reveals unresolvable conflicts and unsatisfactory compromises. Even in theory, these were evident from the first. (George Orwell's efforts a half-century later to argue the possibility of a socialist-oriented popular boys literature confirms the difficulty inherent in any attempt to strain the chaos of experience through the coarse mesh of ideology.)[52]

The effort to fit conceptions of American literature to conceptions of the American republic has a long history in this nation's thought, as Howard Mumford Jones has made clear.[53] Nathaniel Willis' prospectus for the *Youth's Companion* sounded a note that was seldom absent again from discussions of American children's literature: since the republican child is the heir apparent of a brighter tomorrow, the influences that are allowed to shape his growth must be consistent with republican principles. In 1865, when Samuel Osgood called for an American children's literature, he made no predictions about the form it would take, but he was confident about its spirit. It would have none of the class consciousness characteristic of imported British juvenile literature, it would avoid the tone of moral priggishness so evident in earlier American writing for children, and, by implication, it would be an attractive and morally sound alternative to the increasingly popular sensational formulas of the dime novels.

The new literature for American youth, exemplified by the popular magazine fiction studied here, may be seen from one perspective as strategies of order, as modes of communicating and legitimating certain values to the next generation. In short, the literature may be seen broadly as an agency in the process of socialization. From another perspective, these formula stories may be examined and analyzed as strategies for competing with the sensational literature, which seemed at once so dangerous and so distressingly popular. Moreover, the formulas reveal tensions generated by the efforts to preserve the essential instructional element in the literature without jeopardizing the new principle of pleasure and entertainment, largely the offspring of the more generous view regarding children's rights and needs and the nature of childhood. The notion of childhood as play proved difficult to incorporate into fiction, and the stories reveal an unresolved conflict between the desire to preserve childhood as a period of pleasure and the necessity to prepare children for adult responsibility, which, for a variety of reasons, might suddenly confront even very young children. The new concept of childhood as play interfered with assumptions about the necessity of character in a precarious world.

In confronting the popularity of sensational novels, the gentry recognized that a major source of their attraction was the fantasy of the child who moved casually, surely, and without restriction through a series of desperate situations. The gentry heartily despised the child paragon who knew no limits and experienced none, but they could not abandon the figure of the child alone who struggles, suffers, and triumphs. Both formulas, the ordeal and the change of heart, depend largely on the motif of the isolated child. By altering certain aspects of character and incident, the gentry authors were able, up to a point, to exploit that popular figure, while they maintained an appropriate moral structure by carefully manipulating the patterns of reward and resolution.

A Civil War story appearing in the first issue of *Our Young Folks* (1865) suggests one way in which the capable child

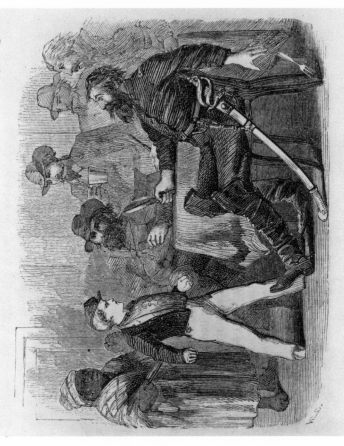

a pore, lone mudder, dat doant know but he'm dead, and he'm jess gwine

ter har. Can'n. — jess a gwine ter har. I'se been a nussin' him all o' dis

Edmund Kirke, "The Little Prisoner," *OYF* 1 (1865): 329

might experience adventure but avoid the freedom from limitation and responsibility that, in the gentry view, jeopardized character and the social order as well. James, the hero of "The Little Prisoner," like many a fictional boy of the time, is the only son of a widowed mother.[54] He has read of the fighting and longs to make himself famous in a righteous cause. When his mother finally consents to his enlistment, he goes to war as a drummer boy and is wounded—bayoneted—trying to save his dying captain during the Wilderness, his first battle. Injured and alone, he thinks of home and of his mother's God. In answer to his prayers, he is rescued by a slave and taken to a nearby farmhouse, where he is nursed back to health.

A month later, he is captured by Mosby's raiders and taken to their camp. Mosby threatens to hang the boy, but James refuses to be frightened. Mosby, never having seen this kind of courage, backs down. "It was not physical, it was moral courage," the author explains. James had learned from his mother that even the sparrow's fall was ordered by the principle of infinite right. "On her bended knees she gave it to him, and so he took it, took it into his heart until it became a part of his being," until he, "a young boy, with that in his heart, could singly meet a hostile universe."[55] Later, James is released and returns to his mother.

Although the boy has triumphed, his reward is not the fame for which he longed but rather life in the face of death and a return to the safety of the family. He learns through experience the truth of his mother's definition of the world as fundamentally ordered by benign law. The South's defeat is implicit in the irreligious nature of the slaveholder in whose house James is nursed, in the southern wife's desire for diamonds, and in the appearance of plantation house itself. Although built on the lines of a New England farmhouse, it seemed curiously comic to the boy—as if a country clown were aping a gentleman's attire.

Almost everywhere they appeared in the gentry magazines, children, isolated from adult guidance and protection, suffered, even though they were almost never defeated. Taken as a whole, the stories suggest that character can be achieved only with difficulty. Occasionally a story appeared that seemed especially aimed at deflating any romantic notions readers might hold about the freedom and romance of the child adventuring beyond the warm confines of the family. "Boys that have good homes never know how well off they are!" Trowbridge reminds us, at the end of "His Own Master."[56]

Several stories demonstrate the folly of running away to sea, none more emphatically perhaps than "Ran Away" (1873), which appeared in the *Youth's Companion*.[57] Deluded by the pulp adventures of "Jack Mainstay" into believing that sailing before the mast would be a more fitting career than working as a machinist, a boy rejects the vocation for which he is fitted, his own family, and the family he might have headed. Coarsened by his associations at sea, he disregards the wishes of his beautiful fiancée and signs for another voyage but never lives to complete it. His death off the coast of Africa is the price exacted for his persistently rejecting home and family, the honest and useful calling for which he was fitted, and the redeeming love of a beautiful woman. In trying to realize in his own life the fantasy world of sensational fiction, the boy is striking at the basis of social order. To live the values of sensationalism is to put oneself beyond the law and to live for the senses, seeing only deceptive surfaces. Fittingly the young man is lost at sea off the "dark continent," a victim of his perversity and willful self-reliance.

Self-reliance, then, was a two-edged sword that needed to be tempered by conscience and knowledge and handled with some care. Allied with courage, it is the quality of character that appears most frequently in stories conforming to the formula of the ordeal. The opposite quality, an overweening and unreliable self-assertiveness, often appears in change-of-heart stories, a good example being "Dandy Lyon's Visit to New York" (1873). Fresh in from the New Jersey countryside where his father owns a large, prosperous farm, Dandy ignores his cousin's instructions to come directly to his house. Having acquired a certain reputation for prowess at home, Dandy perceives no limits on his ability to cope with urban life. Before he is finally rescued by his cousin, Dandy has been humiliated in an encounter with street arabs, threatened with arrest, manhandled by a waiter, and caught by a policeman as he tries to flee Delmonico's, unable to pay his bill. The moral is given to Dandy's cousin to make explicit: "It's a great deal wiser and safer when [someone] . . . finds himself in a strange position . . . not to assume too much, but to be willing to be led by the knowledge and experience of others."[58]

Dandy's self-reliance is a little too cocksure, a little too presumptuous to be acceptable. To be capable of shifting to an adult role and averting a train wreck is one thing, but Dandy's self-confidence is treacherous; he mistakes bravado for the force of character. He has not earned the confidence he pretends nor is it an expression of genuine character. His cocky self-reliance is merely the product of his success in various competitive activities at home—a rather crude competition, uncomfortably close, perhaps, to the cash nexus.

Criticism of sensational literature was aimed most frequently at the violence and the aggressiveness constantly erupting in the dime novels and story papers of the period and with the inferences for behavior which impressionable children might make from such materials. Less frequently, critics of children's literature attacked the implications of reward patterns that might raise unrealistic expectations in young readers. In his survey of Sunday-school library books in 1870, George Bacon was disturbed by the "false and unnatural system of rewards and penalties" in many stories. Too often little girls who successfully converted aged unbelievers emerged as the old men's heiresses; too many boys who faithfully observed the Sabbath became wealthy. The discrepancy between fiction and real life might lead some children to doubt the fact of retribution, Bacon concluded. The rewards of piety were not well illustrated or adequately symbolized by gaining property or making a socially advantageous marriage.[59] And we recall that Caroline Hewins on similar grounds excluded from her list those books which made "their little every-day heroes and heroines leap suddenly from abject poverty to boundless wealth."[60]

It is the rare story in the gentry children's magazines where money plays an important part in the scheme of rewards. As I noted earlier, the characteristic reward, broadly speaking, for the change-of-heart formula was an altered perception, a recognition of past error coupled with the resolve to do better. This latter frequently takes the form of a promise to parents and is rewarded by some token of affection or by the symbolic reconstitution of the family, if, as often is the case, the family has been disrupted.

The ordeal formula, if one chooses to emphasize the fact, enacts virtue rewarded. Here the temptation toward providing more tangible tokens must have been greater. Still it must be said that gentry heroes did not experience sudden wealth or elevated social status in tribute to their virtue, although in one story an employee's honesty results in a better-paying job. An act of remarkable courage may simply confirm a boy's faith in the code of the gentleman or barely save a family of children isolated by a blizzard.[61]

If a boy does rise, as in the story "Jack's Treadle" (1873), the process takes years of hard work and diligence, even though Jack possesses enormous reserves of ambition, energy, and intelligence.[62] Moreover, we are not permitted to see the extent of Jack's success. We know only that he is skilled at his work and has embarked on the study of law. His prospects are good, but his accomplishments are not expressed or evaluated in concrete social or monetary terms. Unearned wealth or unmerited position, according to gentry standards, was not a reward but a plague to the soul. Character, not wealth, was the valued achievement. Wealth without character led to social chaos, to "intolerable aberrations and illegalities" as both Calvert and Godkin took great care to point out.

The adventures of the children portrayed in the gentry magazines were nearly always undertaken in the name of some higher principle rather than out of a desire for thrilling experience. Those who seek only adventure, like the boy in "Ran Away," find disaster. Most often, it is in the name of the family, especially the mother, that the autonomous child faces and overcomes danger or temptation. A mother's illness may necessitate a lonely walk through dangerous woods to get a doctor. Danger, and the child's reaction to it, can hardly be experienced in the family; to be proved, the child must venture beyond its confines, but only temporarily. Inevitably the child's movements in the story describe a looping curve back to a family relationship of some kind. The extravagant individualism, typified by fictional children seeking their own fortunes, which Horace Scudder, Caroline Hewins, and others found so objectionable in many popular children's books, was avoided in a variety of ways by the gentry authors and their editors.[63] The story paper hero, completely and aggressively self-sufficient, was a dangerous and subversive figure, especially since his popularity underscored the unhealthy attractiveness of the type. Removed from his exotic settings, deprived of his revolver and slang phrases, and subjected to the discipline of the family, he could be made to appear more nearly the perfected child of democracy—deferential to authority but boldly self-reliant when unusual circumstances required him to act independently. The gentry authors recognized that American life demanded a certain self-reliance from everyone, and children were expected to exhibit the quality within limits. The code of the gentleman offered an ideal of self-reliance moderated by concern for the welfare of others; the model for this concern was almost invariably discovered in family relationships, in the reciprocal obligations of parent and child.

The editors and authors were less able to moderate successfully a problem growing out of the greater sensitivity to children's needs and stages of development. We have seen that the attitude toward children's literature shifted during the middle of the century to an emphasis on pleasure. "The ideal child's magazine," Mrs. Dodge stressed, "is its pleasure ground," where butterflies, flowers, wind, and sunshine delight the carefree visitor but "where toads hop quickly out of sight and snakes dare not show themselves at all."[64]

The acceptance of pleasure as a legitimate motive for children's reading undoubtedly made *St. Nicholas* and its competitors far more varied in content and illustration than their prewar counterparts. As a motive, pleasure alone was perilously close to sensationalism, however. Reading was still the royal road to knowledge and to culture. In some sense, literature, especially literature for children, had to be true. "It is to the best story-tellers that we owe the greatest portion of what knowledge we have of the life led in other lands," S. S. Green reminded those attending the second annual convention of the American Library Association.[65]

If literature merely conveyed information of that kind, however, there would have been little problem reconciling it with pleasure. More significantly, books were decisive forces shaping character because they gave dramatic and memorable form to moral truths. "Many a man traces all his failures in morality to some living sentence, dazzling because of the genius in which it originated, yet a veritable Sodom apple, brilliant to the sight, but ashes to the taste," wrote Mary A. Denison, one of the more prolific contributors to the *Youth's Companion*.[66] Books directed behavior and molded character by providing goals and incentives. Kate Gannett Wells warned librarians that "many a girl's sentimentality or foolish marriage, and many a boy's rash venture in cattle ranches or uneasiness in the harness of slight but regular salary, is owing to books that fed early feeble indications of a tendency to future evil."[67] Even a single sentence "sometimes determines the influence of a book, and sometimes—of a life."[68] Forced to weigh the potential for character development against the disadvantages of the older tradition of overt moralizing, Caroline Hewins chose to include the works of Jacob Abbott, the author of the unremittingly didactic Rollo stories, in her *Books for the Young* (1882), explaining that "although old-fashioned, [they] contain so much practical wisdom concerning the everyday life of children, and so many lessons in honor, truthfulness, and courtesy, that they should not be left out of the libraries of boys and girls."[69] Pleasure was clearly not an exclusive principle.

Added to the gentry reverence for culture, the environmentalism evident in the newer ideas about the nature of the child could only increase the overwhelming sense of responsibility that went with writing for the gentry magazines. "A book is such a fact to a child, its people are so alive and so heartily loved and hated, its scenes so absolutely real!" Kate Douglas Wiggin wrote, recalling the books that influenced her as a child.[70] Caroline Hewins' celebration of her own childhood reading in *A Mid-Century Child and Her Books* summarizes perfectly the life-enhancing power of books that constituted an article of faith for the gentry children's authors.[71]

Finally, concern over the destiny of the American child as the heir of progress exacerbated further the problem of providing a children's literature that was attractive enough to be commercially profitable and faithful to the child's need for spiritual nourishment as well as transient pleasure.

There did not appear to be an easy solution to the problem. Samuel Osgood, in an essay for the *Atlantic Monthly*, urged that books for children should spring from a concept of self-culture: "True culture brings out the common human mind in all, and the rare gifts that are in the few."[72] He also argued, as would Mrs. Dodge a few years later, that the new literature must appear as a playmate. This did not mean it would lack serious purpose, for "there is no form in which exalted characters or sacred truth are brought home more effectually to the hearts both of young and old than in the stories and dramas that make life speak for itself, and play themselves into the affections and fancy."[73] The playmate was expected to be a truthful one, true especially "to all our just American ideas," and it was precisely at this point that "truth" became problematical. Osgood hoped that "our children should be brought up to regard American principles as matters of course; and their books should take these principles for granted, and illustrate them with all possible interest and power."[74] These same books should rebuke the most evident American failings—"the haste to be rich, the passion for ostentation, the rage for extravagance, the habit of exaggeration, the impatience under moderate means, the fever for excitement, and the great disposition to subordinate the true quality of life to the quantity of appliances of living."[75] Books must "stir the muscles, and quicken the will, and set the hand and foot to work and play under the promptings of a cheerful heart."[76] Osgood's truth, not surprisingly, was a very special truth compounded of the gentry's vision of a perfected American society and of their distaste for exaggeration, fashion, and impatience, all filtered by a notion of culture, which tended to make books social weapons.

The earnestness of the gentry mission effectively made every story a potential turning point in a child's life. A critic for the *North American Review* might note the monotonous triumph of good in books for children generally and long for some catastrophe to "remind us that heroes too are mortal," but few contributors to the *Youth's Companion* or the other magazines provided so strong a truth as that.[77] If a single story might decisively alter a life, every story stood alone, charged with drawing the line clearly between good and evil and with delineating the relationship between action and consequence. The knowledge communicated to children could hold few ambiguities and no moral alternatives. Any story that touched on a question of conduct "may, and must, suggest the right answer, not by 'moralizing,' but through its incident, action, and development of character," the *Companion*'s editors advised prospective contributors.[78] The only general rule was that "all stories shall be pure in tone and true to life."[79] The gentry's world view narrowed the range of experience capable of satisfying both of these requirements.

Only rarely was a hint of doubt expressed over the essential justice of events. At the end of the *Companion* story "Jim" (1879), in which a boy is killed by Molly Maguires after warning the gentleman mining engineer who has befriended him, the engineer finds it impossible to pray over the boy's body; the death was completely undeserved and unjustified. It shakes the narrator's world and leaves him no easy answer to the problem of evil.[80] It also defines the enormity of the threat of industrial violence that Daniel Sharp Ford so greatly feared. Certainly other catastrophes occur in these stories, but they are the merited punishment earned by wrongdoing or, more rarely, the consequence of inexplicable accidents, and are generously compensated. The principle of inevitable reward for merit was almost never challenged although, as I have suggested, the rewards themselves were commensurate with other gentry values.

The concept of childhood as play introduced tensions similar to the ones generated by the concept of literature as pleasure. It proved impossible to assess character in play or to create conflict out of anything less than serious personal or economic problems. Trowbridge's Father Brighthopes once made explicit an assumption that is seldom absent from the stories—children should enjoy their childhood but recognize at the same time that no one, even a child, can afford to live only for the present. Childhood was the foundation for later life. Every act, thought, or wish contributed to the individual's destiny during the time when human nature was most easily influenced and molded.[81] "People who do great things and good things at such times [of crisis as the Civil War] do them because they have been laying up strength beforehand, and training themselves in body and in mind," Harriet Beecher Stowe reminded her readers.[82] It is this kind of early discipline that makes it possible for the young heroine of "Fayette's Ride" (1875) to conquer her fear and summon help for her aunt who lies dangerously ill: "Nerves and imagination were running wild; but Fayette, from her earliest years, had been trained to self-control and duty."[83] In these stories, childhood is dominated by the future, which must be prepared for, and by the sudden intrusion of unexpected responsibilities requiring self-control and a developed sense of self-reliance and integrity if they are to be satisfactorily discharged. Training in these essential qualities of character could not be started too early: "Girls are the future mothers, nurses, teachers of the race, and should feel how much depends on them," Miss Alcott wrote in her *St. Nicholas* serial "Jack and Jill."[84]

Children, moreover, were not exempt from suffering the consequences of their actions. Neither carelessness nor thoughtlessness could be condoned under the name of play. The responsibilities of childhood occasionally made even innocent amusements suspect: reading novels and writing verses were "quite innocent in themselves, but not the stuff to live on," a mother thinks to herself in Miss Alcott's "Jack and Jill," justifying the "housewifely lessons" she gives her overly romantic daughter.[85]

The preoccupation with struggle, the frequent fact of pain and suffering in the stories, however muted, objectifies the deeply felt perception of the world as one of ceaseless struggle. "The game of the world is a perpetual trial of strength between man and events," Emerson wrote in his essay "Aristocracy." Character was achievement; it was not unhindered, gradual flowering. It emerged through discipline and was tested in adversity, and the achievement of character was simultaneously the loss of childhood. To move beyond thoughtlessness and the other attitudes so frequently altered in the course of change-of-heart stories was to become less childlike, more aware of the demands made by family and community. Childhood might be play but life was earnest—hence the gulf that widened between childhood and adulthood; hence, too, the poignancy of the adult who looked back nostalgically to a personal golden age forever after barred to him. In the first volume of *Wide Awake*, a short poem, "Vale of Childhood," suggests the chasm between childhood and adulthood over which the unstable bridges of the gentry formulas were thrown:

> Is it warm in that green valley,
>   Vale of childhood, where you dwell?
> Is it calm in that green valley,
>   Round whose bourns such great hills swell?
> Are there giants in the valley—
>   Giants leaving footprints yet?
> Are there angels in the valley?
>   Tell me—I forget.[86]

The writing of children's literature is, in part, a way of reaffirming and maintaining continuity with the child spirit—with the naiveté, the innocence, the capacity to find joy in simple things and wonder in a world still new, fresh, and unjaded. But children, especially American children, were never destined to remain very long in that warm green valley. In the very act of affirming their faith in childhood innocence, the gentry were driven by their anguished sense of moral purpose and by their sense of the intrusive future to expose the child who read their stories to the fever of the adult world. They helped accomplish, perhaps unconsciously, what Samuel Osgood and others had inveighed against—that premature awareness (and, too, often,

the competitiveness) that robbed American children of
their naturalness and contributed to a precocity of manner
which European visitors often found so notable. Children
demanded truth, the critics said—but the only truth was,
finally, that childhood ceased as one realized the true nature of the world.

5

At Home in the Country

> A town that still has a great deal of the country
> in it, one that is rich in beautiful scenery and
> ancestral associations, is almost like a living
> being, with a body and a soul. We speak of
> such a town, if our birthplace, as of a mother,
> and think of ourselves as her sons and daugh-
> ters.
>
> Lucy Larcom, *A New England*
> *Girlhood*

As we have seen, the domestic fiction characteristic of *St. Nicholas* and its competitors reveals a structure of values dependent upon, and emphasizing, interrelationships between the family and the social ideals of the gentleman and lady. Each reinforced and complemented the other. The conditions of city life, however, seemed to threaten or negate each of these essential factors in the nurture of democracy's children, and in the gentry children's magazines there proved to be no easy way to incorporate the family and the lady and the gentleman into the city in the context of the fiction. Perhaps this is why, in 1893, twenty years after Miss Alcott's heroic Phebe ("Bonfires") had saved a train in the pages of the *Youth's Companion*, the editors of the paper, in an article for *The Writer* describing the kind of stories suitable for the *Companion*, declared such exploits to be passé. They had also grown impatient with another popular motif: "The mortgage-raising hero must, if he would impress himself upon the editorial mind, be very dextrously manoeuvred," they warned.[1] In place of these time-honored narrative patterns, Daniel Ford and the *Companion*'s assistant editors suggested alternative sources for fictional inspiration. The "questions of business ethics that hourly confront every tradesman might be resolved in fiction, to the lasting pleasure and benefit of a nation of practical people."[2] They also considered the theme of the counterplay of diverse races huddled in the nation's growing urban centers to be "alive with dramatic possibilities."[3] Contributors were challenged to "get close to the hearts and lives of the people."[4]

This call for stories that would reflect the economic and social conditions of urban life acknowledged indirectly what emerges clearly from a sampling of the files of the *Youth's Companion* and the other children's magazines: the domestic fiction they contain is decisively shaped by the spaciousness, the rhythms, and the manners of rural and village life. Only one story in three (it seems to make no difference which formula) is set in a recognizably urban location. If we consider the stories in which the urban location materially affects the terms of the problem presented or clearly conditions the lives of the characters, the percentage is lower still; no more than half of the stories having urban settings are really stories about the experience of city life. In the other half, the conflicts and problems do not arise out of the pressures generated by the size, density, and heterogeneity of settlement, which Louis Wirth suggests are the sociological parameters of urbanism.[5]

In these stories of urban life, the attitude toward the city is ambivalent at best.[6] New York City may provide a salutary, though temporary, discipline for a country bumpkin like Dandy Lyon, discussed in the previous chapter, since his encounters there teach him a needed lesson.

Nevertheless, his movement from the country to the city and back to his rural home symbolizes an important truth manifest in the urban stories: the city is no place for children growing up.[7] Country life is family life. The relatively isolated village community is defined in these periodicals as a group of families. Older unmarried people, especially if they live alone, tend to appear as eccentric and neurotic types. The city, however, is not conceived of as a group of families; rather it is an environment deeply inimical to family relationships and dominated by rootless, exploitative men. In contrast to the rural landscape, which is frequently perilous but, on balance, supportive of gentry discipline, the city is simply perilous.

　The qualities of the urban environment, the characteristics attributed to children and parents living under urban conditions, and the general failure, in the stories, to resolve the problems produced by those conditions suggest that gentry authors found it very difficult to imagine children maturing normally under conditions of city life. The reasons for this are undoubtedly complex, but three seem especially important. On the basis of their own experience, the authors tended to associate childhood and country life. Secondly, the concept of natural gentility was traditionally linked to rural rather than to urban nurture. Finally, the conditions of city life in the 1870s and 1880s appeared increasingly to threaten the stability and quality of family life. The generation of children's authors writing after the Civil War, most of whom were born in the 1820s and 1830s, was the first that had to deal with what children's authors are still uncomfortable about—the constricted space available for traditional childhood activity in crowded urban centers. In spite of the fact that economic opportunities became increasingly centered in the cities—as to a great extent did the cultural opportunities prized by the gentry—the noise, crowding, and tempo of city life appeared to distort the lives and personalities of adults and seemed

potentially destructive of the gentry concept of childhood.

The sentimentality of a poem like "Vale of Childhood"
reveals a very real sense of personal discontinuity, an ab-
rupt shift from the status and roles of childhood to those of
adulthood. The poem also hints at the cultural discontinuity experienced by many children's authors who, like
John Townsend Trowbridge and Rebecca Harding Davis,
were raised in the rural culture of the 1830s and 1840s but
who later found their livelihood as adults in postwar Boston
and New York City. Only sojourners in an urban culture,
they made their living but not their homes there; in spirit,
they remained at home in the country.

According to many anthropologists, persons raised in
different cultures live in different perceptual worlds. Their
sense of spatial relationships and of time, their attitudes
toward work and play, are often quite different. Loren
Eiseley, for example, suggests that "there is a difference in
our human outlook, depending on whether we have been
born upon level plains, where one step reasonably leads to
another, or whether, by contrast, we have spent our lives
amidst glacial crevasses and precipitous descents. In the
case of the mountaineer, one step does not always lead
rationally to another save by a desperate leap over a
chasm."[8] Speaking as generally, if less impressionistically,
of the very complex problem of early conditioning influences, microbiologist René Dubos writes, "Early experiences . . . do much more than condition behavioral patterns.
They also affect profoundly and lastingly all physical and
physiological characteristics of the organism at all stages of
life. . . . Many, if not all, effects of early influences are
indeed so lasting that they appear to be irreversible."[9] The
cultural and physical environment "conditions the manner
in which the genetic endowment of each person becomes
converted into his individual reality."[10] The power of the

"personal past" is so great, Dubos concludes "that it can distort the meaning of any event and magnify trivial happenings into momentous experiences."[11] Stimuli become invested with symbolic qualities that can outweigh their objective characteristics. The "effective environment does not consist only of the external forces and substances that impinge on the organism at a given time, but includes also the genetic, social, and individual memories of related past experiences."[12] Home, then, is more than a place: it "is that environment to which a particular person becomes adapted through biological and socio-cultural mechanisms, and to which he becomes emotionally attached through the traditions of his group and his own personal experiences. Home is less a physical place than a locus with which past experiences are identified."[13] Most of the men and women who edited and wrote for the gentry children's magazines during the two decades following the Civil War had grown up in small, rural communities. Their childhood was thus inextricably linked with the tranquil spaciousness of the cultivated rural landscape.

That the differences between a rural culture (antebellum New England, for example,) and the urban life of New York City in the 1880s and 1890s were great enough to significantly affect people moving from one to the other has been argued by Paul Johnstone and Carl Degler.[14] Farming, the activity which unified rural life, was the one occupation that could not be sustained in the city. The common dependence on weather and the seasons, the sense of common earth and fortune that characterized rural life, vanished in the city, where men held diverse jobs, had diverse interests, and came from diverse backgrounds. Urban life is competitive, indoor, sedentary, and anxious; but density of population, given the diversity noted above, does not often bring intimacy or community.[15]

Johnstone finds the rural culture during the 1830s, with

the exception of the slave states, to have been marked by relatively little social stratification or by the extremes of wealth and poverty that were so visible later in cities like New York, Boston, and Chicago. Before the Civil War, the small town was more integrated with agriculture than it would be later when the farmer became dependent on national and international markets for his products. Nearly all its people were farmers at heart. Language habits, patterns of amusement, and social usages, according to Johnstone, bore the impress of agricultural life. The family tended to be an economic unit capable of facing and surviving economic depression. Life may have been hard and crude, but it was relatively secure.[16] In a recent tribute to the discipline of such a life, long since passed for most Americans, John Hay writes: "There is a fitness in natural experience, an intimacy, that may not be superseded. How many . . . now live through a lifetime of tides, nights of clean wind and clear stars above the roofline, know genuine exposure to cold rain, cold water and stiff fingers, know how to be steady there? Are you not also made of what you receive?"[17] Today, this doubtless will be dismissed by many as naive romanticism, but it strikes the authentic note of an attitude that finds persuasive expression in the autobiographies and reminiscences of many whose childhoods were spent under that discipline in the 1830s and 1840s and who later wrote for children in the pages of *St. Nicholas* and *Our Young Folks*.

The autobiography was a convenient form by which to celebrate the distinctive regional cultures that were largely disappearing at the end of the nineteenth century. At the same time, autobiography provided a means of asserting continuity in the face of wrenching discontinuity. In the recollections of Celia Thaxter, Rebecca Harding Davis, and Margaret Sangster, all of whom wrote at least occasionally for children's magazines, as in other autobiographies of the period, several themes emerge. The open hearth with its blazing fire is a central, recurrent symbol of familial warmth and intimacy.[18] The relaxed tempo of life, which took its rhythms from the turning of the seasons, provided "space . . . for the full growth of personality," as Mrs. Davis expressed it.[19] Many recalled the comparative social equality of the towns or villages in which they grew up. "The people in the community were mostly of the comfortable middle class who possess neither poverty nor riches, but live quiet, self-respecting lives, taking the days as they come, performing duties simply and exchanging friendly courtesies as a matter of course," wrote Margaret Sangster in terms that differ little from George Frisbie Hoar's description of Concord before the Civil War or Rebecca Harding Davis's memories of the West Virginia village of her childhood.[20] With the directness that often characterizes the less-gifted writer, another memoir catches a sense of muted alienation that is frequently evident in these autobiographies: "I have been swept on with my race and my time and while sharing all their tendencies, at heart what I value most, that which is most native and dearest to me is the simple undisturbed life, full of friendliness, piety and humble amusements into which I was born."[21]

The remembered culture, the vale of childhood, differed radically from the city encountered by the adult. Small-town life was more favorable for habits of reading than was life in the large cities, Edward Everett Hale reflected in his essay "Social Forces in the United States."[22] The city's jarring rhythms and frantic tempo, its cluttered visual organization, its tradition of the new, of growth and change, and its disturbing evidence of unequal wealth, of inescapable dirt and congestion, which translated as moral qualities—all of these characteristics defined the shift from rural childhood to urban adulthood.[23] In creating literature for children, the gentry authors looked backward and inward to their own childhood. They tended to see the world through their own memories. In writing their formula dramas of

order and virtue triumphant, they created a sacred place
—the unpretentious home in the small, classless village.
From it, their young heroes and heroines journeyed forth
and either proved their worthiness of that home or learned
their need for it through suffering and humiliation.

The author's memories of the discipline of modest circumstances, of the simple democracy of the village, and of
the open fireplace that drew the family together in front of
its warmth found support in the relationship presumed to
exist between the personality borne of such conditions and
the qualities of the refined gentleman. As I suggested in an
earlier chapter, a heritage of hard work close to nature did
not, in itself, unfit a person for gentility. Indeed, it fostered
an integrity and independence of spirit that might form the
basis of character, which formal education could refine and
perfect: "It is interesting to observe how little the character
of the gentleman and gentlewoman in our New England
people is affected by the pursuit, for generations, of humble occupations, which in other countries are deemed
degrading."[24] George Frisbie Hoar noted in his autobiography. In a similar vein, Rebecca Harding Davis recalled
that, during her childhood, "You were only truly patriotic if
you had a laborer for a grandfather and were glad of it."[25]
Thus, the link between the cultured elite and the conditions
of rural and village life was intimate. Because they were not
a hereditary class, the gentry depended for their perpetuation on the continued existence of the rural culture to which
they traced their own roots and from which they expected
to draw recruits, like Lucy Larcom and John Townsend
Trowbridge, to their ranks. We have already seen that a
minor motif in the formula stories is the importance of
rural nurture in producing the indispensable qualities of
courage and integrity.

In contrast, no strong intellectual tradition linked the
conditions of the city with the character foundation appropriate for gentility. Instead, to most observers in the

late nineteenth century, the city appeared to be a debilitating environment for children, one that stunted moral growth when it did not actually promote viciousness. Alarmed at discovering that more than half the Boston children entering school in 1882 had never seen a plow, a spade, a robin, a squirrel, or a sheep, the pioneer psychologist G. Stanley Hall pessimistically concluded that "city life is unnatural, and that those who grow up without knowing the country are defrauded of that without which childhood can never be complete or normal."[26] In light of such pronouncements, it is appropriate in an early *St. Nicholas* story, "Mrs. Pomeroy's Page" (1874), that a street boy who has earned a scant living by begging is sent to the country to be civilized. After he has proved his good character there, he is allowed to return to the city as a youthful servant in the home of the well-to-do lady who had plucked him out of the gutter.[27]

The threat to children's needs posed by the city was widely discussed during the Gilded Age. In "Child Life in City and Country," Charles Kellogg weighed the economic and psychological cost imposed by the physical conditions of urban life. Congestion and pollution affected all children but particularly the children of the poor. The latter were frequently denied parental supervision since economic necessity often dictated that both parents work long hours outside the home. Without books or pictures, seldom washed, habitually ill-clad, and frequently hungry, the children of the urban poor, Kellogg warned, could take only the moral direction of their surroundings.[28] Noted reformer Charles Loring Brace graphically illustrated the potential threat to society posed by these young victims of the city when he compared them to the feral children of India:

Did the children who read *St. Nicholas* in comfortable

homes ever think that there are wolf-reared children in
such a city as New York?—boys and girls who were
born to hunger, and cruel treatment, and who live in
miserable dens and holes; who are as ignorant of love
and hope, and of the missions, and churches, and
schools of this city as are the infants found in wolves'
dens of the mountains of Oude; who have been taught
only in the schools of poverty, vice, and crime; whose
ways are not our ways, and who have wolfish habits;
whose brain makes them more cunning, more dangerous, than the animal, and who if they grow up thus, will
be more dangerous to this city than wolf or tiger to the
villages of India.[29]

The conditions of urban industrialization and of tenement and boardinghouse living focused attention on the
conditions of family life and convinced some observers that
deteriorating family life in the city was the primary social
problem of the period.[30] Only as long as the family was
generally sound could it present a barrier to the disintegrative forces that were eliminating all intermediate social
structures between the individual and the largest conceivable forms of organization.[31] But in the view of many observers, the urban family was increasingly unstable; the legal
expression of this instability was a divorce rate increasing
faster than the population.[32]

Industrialization disrupted the home, it was argued, by
drawing mothers into the laboring force and by forcing
individual family members into economic competition with
each other. If a primary function of the family was the
conservation of social order and the transmission of the
"spiritual possessions of the race," such conditions reduced
parental influence and threatened the stability and progress of American society. The climax of industrial en-
croachment on the family was the utilization of child labor,
which effectively destroyed childhood, set children

to competing economically with their parents, and made socialization subservient to standards of industrial efficiency.[33]

Housing conditions in the city also threatened the family. Tenements, wrote Willystine Goodsell, an early historian of the family, are not homes "in any true sense of the word. . . . It is idle to expect that a squalid tenement in the slums, sending forth in the morning all but its youngest members to labor and receiving them at night to eat and sleep without privacy or comfort, can nourish the sentiments of family loyalty, love and responsibility . . ."[34]

The apparent instability of the American family was discussed throughout the Gilded Age. The problem was not peculiar to the city, but it was in the cities that a combination of conditions seemed most destructive of family life and most portentous for the future in view of the evident migration from rural areas into the cities. During the latter part of the nineteenth century, "perhaps no factor affected child life more than the growth of cities," Arthur Schlesinger writes in *The Rise of the City,* assessing the various efforts made to restore to urban children part of childhood's "natural heritage of outdoor recreation."[35]

In the altered conditions of the city, the gentry children's authors saw their own childhood swallowed up, in effect. To the extent that they recognized in their childhood a necessary basis for their own values and world view, they saw their world endangered. Unable to locate childhood in the bustle, congestion, and confusion, both visual and moral, that seemed to characterize a city like New York, they saw their survival as a distinctive and social type threatened. The city could not provide the kind of environment that promoted and sustained the natural gentility that democratic social institutions depended on for their orderly continuity. In their children's magazines, gentry editors and authors reasserted the value of the older rural culture, even as it waned everywhere except in memory. At the same time, their stories betrayed their fear of and ambivalence toward the city through the terms invoked to describe it, in the moral and physical characteristics attributed to its inhabitants, and in their own inability to imagine any satisfactory way of insulating children or adults from its potentially degenerative influence. Only by periodically leaving the city, an expedient effectively denied those who most suffered from the corrosive conditions of the city, could the city's pernicious influence temporarily be reversed.

In the stories of urban life, the city takes several distinct, but equally unwholesome, forms. It is where the competition for social position is carried on and where fashion, ostentation, and extravagance feed and thrive. It is the locus for economic and social conditions that threaten adult health, family stability, and the physical and moral development of children. But more than anything else, it is a place where children are more vulnerable than they are in the country. This situation may be treated humorously, as in the case of "Dandy Lyon's Visit to New York," but most often it is not. The threat cannot be laughed away. During her childhood in rural Virginia, Rebecca Harding Davis recalled, crime was "an alien monstrous terror." A person was not forced then, as they are now "by daily friction with crowds, by telegraphs, railways, and morning papers, to take [crime] into his decent jog-trot life and grow familiar with it."[36] Crime is rarely alluded to in children's stories, but the threat of personal harm is apparent nonetheless. A boy may be cheated out of fifteen dollars by two confidence men; a small girl who insists on making friends in the wrong quarter of New York City is waylaid on the streets as she walks home and taken to a house where her hair is cut off to be sold.[37] In neither story are the consequences too serious. In typical change-of-heart fashion, both children learn the folly of overconfidence or disregard of parental advice; but in both instances the threat to each child is clear and unmistakable. Two stories summarize particularly well the dangers of the city for young people who entered it unsupported by family or friends—"Fast Friends" by John Townsend Trowbridge, which appeared in *St. Nicholas* in 1874, and "Milly Brewster's Pride" a *Youth's Companion* story published in 1888.[38]

"Fast Friends" describes the efforts of two rural youths, who meet by chance, to reach New York City and establish themselves there. One of the boys, George Greenwood, who bears considerable resemblance to Trowbridge himself, hopes to become a writer. The other boy, Jack Hazard, Trowbridge's hero in several other serials, has embarked on the American child's archetypal search for long-lost and dimly remembered relatives. At the outset, the boys' pockets are picked—an omen of what lies before them when they reach the city. An old gentleman intercedes when they are about to be put off the boat, and they manage to earn enough to pay for their tickets by performing before the other passengers. Thus they enter New York penniless and unknown and settle in a modest boardinghouse. There follows for the two boys a series of disappointments and frustrations, punctuated by efforts to victimize and exploit them. Accepting a fellow roomer's invitation to dinner, they end up in a gambling saloon. An employment agency they turn to is revealed to be a racket, cynically exploiting the unemployed. A man engages George to write some publicity but refuses to pay him when the job is completed. The boys work briefly for a minstrel-show promoter, but when business is slow, they are the first to be laid off. By this time they have lost their room and in order to eat are forced to pawn what few possessions they can spare. Under the emotional strain of their failure and lacking sufficient food, George becomes ill.

At this point Trowbridge resorts to the kind of phenomenal luck more characteristic of an Alger novel:

Jack Hazard discovers a small diamond in his pocket, deposited there accidentally by the pickpocket who had relieved them of their wallets on the trip to New York, and a series of subsequent coincidences enable them to solve their problems. Jack eventually returns to the country, leaving George to pursue his writing, now with some hope of success. The fortuitous discovery of the diamond suggests the difficulty of resolving in a plausible fashion the net of competition, isolation, and exploitation which ensnares Trowbridge's heroes. As a network of social relationships, the city is presented as composed of a series of men unattached to the moral and economic stability of family life, who are either weak, unscrupulous, or indifferent. Gentility is represented in the ineffective figure of an old man whose aid to the boys is minimal and monetary and who reappears only after the crisis is passed.

"Milly Brewster's Pride" gives the kind of inexorable logic to urban wage earning that the *Companion* usually reserved for the drunkard's progress. Milly, a young, motherless girl living with relatives, is too proud to take a job in her small town as a governess for a family of wealth and culture, which has fled the turmoil of city life. Rejecting the advice of her uncle and aunt, she decides to seek a job in Boston. Although the street air oppresses her when she arrives and she must take a room alone in a boardinghouse, she procures a good job as a seamstress. She resents having the status of a servant when she works in a customer's home, however, and quits to look for a job in a store. She finally manages to find a position, but the lower wages require that she move to cheaper quarters—a single, dark, close room. Her associates are similarly limited—"giddy, loud-talking, bold" shop girls. Grown thinner and paler, Milly loses this job and moves again, down another step, to a room without cooking facilities, where she does piece work—crocheting garments for stores. Engaged in inefficient handicraft, she cannot make enough to cover her rent and the meals she

eats in inexpensive restaurants. Like the boys in Trowbridge's story, she begins to sell her extra clothing to
make up the difference. By winter, she is out of clothes and
too weak to work; one day she collapses on the street while
out walking. A policeman revives her, and she is taken in by
an older couple who have moved to Boston from the country. In their home she finds much that reminds her of her
own home, but in spite of her ordeal, she is at first unwilling
to stay on as a servant. With the saving recognition that "*true
pride can't be degraded by honest labor,*" she finally
agrees.[39]

It is clear from the events of the story, however, that some
kinds of labor are more appropriate to a respectable girl
than other kinds. Milly is better off as a governess than as a
shop girl, and not just because she happens to be good with
children. The conditions of wage earning in the city coarsen
and blunt the individuals forced to endure them or else
attract those already morally adapted to bear them. As a girl
with evident sensitivity and grace, Milly can find her place
in the city only in a home that recreates the mood and
tempo of her former rural home. The life of the elderly
couple with whom she stays does not reveal manners and
values conditioned by the city. Instead, their style of life,
maintained in the face of the new social pressures which
characterize the city, reflects the conditions of country life,
which they recently left. Unassociated with the economic
struggle that nearly destroys Milly, they offer no satisfactory resolution to the problems of living and working in the
city.

In an earlier chapter, I suggested that the rural landscape
did not always nurture qualities of courage, self-restraint,
and independence. Nevertheless, the effect of country living on adults and children is nearly always regenerative in
these stories. There is a sympathy between nature and man.
One who acts in conformity with the moral order of the
universe is supported and sustained, for nature is

pervaded by that order—one law for man and thing. Thus, the wind momentarily dies in order that Phebe may light her warning bonfires; in another story, lightning flashes just as a girl on an errand of mercy approaches a ruined bridge; and several young heroes and heroines are guided in their isolation by the twin tutelary agencies of stars and moon.[40]

The city, man's created environment that testifies everywhere to his hand, is generally indifferent to a person's plight. Whether jungle or machine, the city is no home. Milly Brewster, as we have seen, is saved in the name of rural ways perpetuated in a family only recently moved to the city. Similarly, when Charlie Norton considers eating the fateful doughnut, he withdraws from the distracting bustle and clamor of Rome to a quiet garden, to the soothing rhythm, spaciousness, and peace appropriate to and necessary for quiet reflection.[41] The park provides the symbolic balance and moderation that are lacking in the city, which is characterized by extremes of noise, temperature, dirt, and social class. It cannot nurture or sustain the child's need for self-examination in a symbolic environment shaped by the moral law where outward form corresponds to inner spirit. In the country, the natural environment reveals moral law. In contrast, the city in these stories, seen as a man-made structure, reveals the disastrous results of undisciplined human nature. Seen as social relationships, the city is predatory, cynical, exploitative, and deceptive.

As the locus for social climbing—personal mobility in its most competitive and least attractive form from the gentry perspective—the city revealed and symbolized a lack of correspondence between merit and reward, which undermined gentry conceptions of social distinction. The dangers of status competition are illustrated in a *Youth's Companion* story, "The Pettingills" (1873), in which the young, impressionable daughter of a refined family is briefly deceived by the apparent wealth and fashionable foreign airs affected by a family moving in next door. Returning a call by Mrs. Pettingill, the girl's mother is able to pierce the facade of respectability and detect the new family's true social and moral status, which a veneer of sudden wealth and hastily acquired polite usages cannot conceal. The signs pointing to the Pettingills' actual status are revealing: untidy personal habits, an imperfectly concealed Cockney accent, and occasional grammatical errors suggest the emphasis given by the gentry to the forms of social expression and their sensitivity to incongruities of expression as well as their conviction that the smallest gesture was expressive of character. The discipline of the gentleman made polite manners and speech an organic expression of disciplined feeling. Errors in social forms revealed that the Pettingills were not gentry; they were instead former servants who had inherited money, changed their names, and, in the relative anonymity of a large city, were seeking to enter a social class that they admired but for which they were not yet fitted. Although they had been good servants once, they were now "totally unreliable and dishonest" and consequently unfit for association.[42] The social danger of the situation is potential in the impulsive romanticism of the girl who admires the Pettingills' dashing son—until his dissolute habits are revealed. The gentry mother's sensitivity to social nuances guarantees that her daughter will not be used to further the social ambitions of a parvenu family.

The effect of the city on individuals and families is presented quite directly in several stories. In Emily Huntington Miller's story "Links in a Chain" (1888), the city's heat, congestion, and lack of privacy have nearly exhausted four sisters who work to support their widowed, semi-invalid mother. Once well off, the family is trapped in a city house when the father dies, leaving an estate of worthless mining stocks. The story describes the women's sacrifices to escape the city for a short vacation in the country. They return to the city invigorated, but only temporarily: "I wonder how long it will last when we get back into the tread mill," one of them reflects, contemplating the monotony and the exhaustion that their work entails.[43] There is no balance in their struggle for a bare livelihood, which consumes all their energies and leaves them unrewarded and unfulfilled.

Similarly, in Mrs. Dodge's story, "The Family with Whom Everything Went Wrong" (1879), family life is virtually destroyed by conditions that are not specifically assigned to city life but were frequently used to characterize it.[44] The father works as a night editor, a position that effectively removes him from normal contact with his family. His schedule interferes constantly with the pattern of the rest of the family. The mother's preoccupation with fashion and status provides no sound basis for raising children, and the four children reveal various behavioral problems, which objectify the tensions and maladjustments present in their home life.

All of this is not to argue, of course, that these characteristics defined the late nineteenth-century cities in fact. Manifest in descriptive passages in the stories and latent in tone, characterization, and incident, these qualities were selectively appropriated for the purposes of fiction. These aspects of the city presumably drew and held the attention of gentry writers because they were perceived as threats (and could be manipulated in fiction as threats) to the values and assumptions that constituted the basis of their social reality and especially their definition of democratic possibilities.

The attributes assigned to certain urban classes also reveal the deleterious effects of the city. Two stories summarize particularly well the personal qualities attributed to the urban fashionable elite, with whom the gentry tended to be preoccupied. The first, Edgar Fawcett's

"A Country Cousin" (1885), appeared as a serial in the *Youth's Companion*.[45] Rachel, the country cousin, comes to live in her wealthy uncle's New York City home. Fresh from the Connecticut countryside, she possesses those qualities of sympathy, courage, dignity, and integrity that define the true lady, regardless of her cultural accomplishments. Juxtaposing her character against those of her fashionable kin, Fawcett proceeds to ring the changes on the destructiveness of urban living. Rachel's quiet thoughtfulness, frankness, and country-bred vigor contrast sharply with the selfishness, caustic teasing, and pallid listlessness ascribed to the divided and unhappy Marivale family. The pressures of Mr. Marivale's job leave him preoccupied and irritable during what little time he can afford to give his family. Similarly driven, Mrs. Marivale frets constantly over maintaining the family's social position. As parents, the Marivales cannot agree over the appropriate discipline for either their son or daughter; each parent favors one child above the other, and as a result the children are quarrelsome, rebellious, spoiled, and unhappy. From the outset, the reader is led to suspect that the family's wealth is not free from the taint of an earlier injustice to Rachel's father, who was Marivale's partner before his unexpected and untimely death. Gradually, however, the force of Rachel's character heals the splintered family relationships. To the daughter Blanche, the country girl is a "breath of fresh air" in the close, overheated rooms of the city. To Mrs. Marivale, Rachel is "a remedy," bringing relief from the combination of ennui and anxiety borne of her involvement in the endless social maneuvering that consumes her days.

It is Rachel who detects and frustrates an attack on the family property, a plot by the butler and maid to loot the family safe. Later she generously forgives her uncle for the earlier wrong to which he finally confesses—a wrong that led to the premature death of Rachel's father and the disintegration of her immediate family. Her capacity to freely forgive the act that destroyed her own family is the final measure of her character. The morally reconstructed Marivale family, purged of its guilt and its false values, takes the country girl to its collective heart.

Rachel is a natural lady rather than a cultivated one.[46] She makes little pretense of learning; her moral vigor is associated with the harmony and natural beauty of her Connecticut home. Rachel's values, her natural gentility, are clearly superior to the languid airs, the heartless sophistication, and the moral confusion produced by the noisy, jarring, hothouse existence of her urban relatives. Social position gained at the expense of honor and character and success measured solely in terms of dollars undermine the family. Founded in this case on injustice and subjected to the extremes of city life, the fashionable family cannot transmit useful values to the young. Preoccupied with competing for status and money, the Marivale family is no longer a source of social continuity or a means to preserve and transmit a viable sense of social order. Insulated from nature, fashionable city life lacks balance, moderation, and meaning. In striving for the wrong things, the Marivales are on the verge of destroying themselves until they are confronted by a persuasive alternative way to order their lives. Rachel not only reunites but protects the family, for her moral perception exposes the servants' treachery. The Marivales, adept at keeping up a front themselves, have lost the ability, Fawcett seems to suggest, to penetrate the false appearances created by others—even when their money, their constant concern and the basis for their social position, is at stake.

In a series of stories for *Our Young Folks*, Harriet Beecher Stowe followed the lives of two girls, one born into a wealthy and fashionable New York City family, the other raised in a New England farm home. The latter child, christened Pussy Willow, has the gift of "always seeing the bright side of everything."[47] Less fortunate is Emily Proudie, whose birth in a splendid New York townhouse was not attended, as Pussy Willow's was, by any natural spirits bearing gifts. As a result, Emily "grew up . . . to be a fretful, discontented little girl."[48] In "Emily's New Resolutions" (1868), Mrs. Stowe brings the two girls together. Emily is sent to the country to seek her health, and it is clear what Mrs. Stowe blames for the girl's debilitation. The pace and rhythm of city life, the lack of moral and physical exercise, and the absence of a worthwhile motive for living have made Emily unfit for any useful activity. Her fashionable clothes, the hot, indoor air of the city, and her habitually staying up late at night have robbed her of any promise she might have had.

In the country, however, she quickly improves. With renewed health comes insight, and Emily recognizes and appreciates Pussy Willow's gift for brightening the lives around her. "With health and strength and cheerfulness came a sort of consciousness of power, and a scorn of doing nothing."[49] From the vantage point of her new health and perceptions, Emily realizes that there is no reason for her to be lazy because she is rich, and she sees that being poor entails no insurmountable deprivation or inconvenience for Pussy. She resolves to return to New York but not to her former style of life: "I know now what life is, and what health is worth, and I'm not going to waste it" by going to "Germans," she resolves.[50] There will be no more tight corsets, no more operas and late nights for the new Emily. She and Pussy, who accompanies her to New York, embark upon an ambitious program of self-culture and volunteer service through which Emily proves, to Mrs. Stowe's satisfaction, that "a temperate, sober, healthy, useful life might be led even in the higher circles of New York."[51] Temperance, seriousness, health, and service, traditional attributes of the lady, are just those qualities most threatened by adopting the customs and conventions of the fashionable, wealthy, urban elite. Such a life, Mrs. Stowe suggests, jeopardizes one's health, character, and capacity for serving others, unless its degenerative tendencies are recognized and vigorously resisted.[52] From the perspective of Europe, an American expatriot summarized gentry criticism of fashionable society: "No sadder pictures of moral ruin and degradation could be drawn from the lowest quarters of the city, than from the palaces of Fifth Avenue."[53]

Another group of stories set in the city deals with the problem of poverty, the other extreme of urban conditions to which the gentry authors responded. The uneasiness with which the subject was approached may be judged from the opening paragraph of "The Ash-Girl" (1876):

> I am going to tell you a story about a little girl who lived in a miserable, lowly place, among poor untaught people, who left her to take care of herself. She saw a kind of life from which your parents would shield you with loving tenderness. I shall have to repeat the language she used, and perhaps, tell you of some of the things she saw and heard; but if you will read my story carefully to the end, I do not believe it will hurt you. I hope rather it will make you think, when you see little street-sweepers, beggars, or poor children, that there may be hidden away under all their rough exterior, tender warm feelings, and hearts that are taught through suffering to be pure and true.[54]

Aside from a little slang and the loneliness of an abandoned child, "The Ash-Girl" successfully avoids portraying the plight of the urban poor, however.

If the ill effects of fashionable society could be alleviated by a trip to the country and the discipline of plain living and high thinking, the plight of poor children abandoned or exploited in the city failed to yield as readily to the gentry

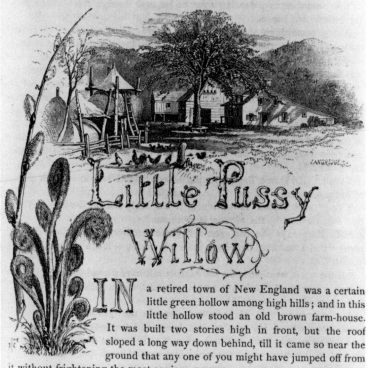

Little Pussy Willow

IN a retired town of New England was a certain little green hollow among high hills; and in this little hollow stood an old brown farm-house. It was built two stories high in front, but the roof sloped a long way down behind, till it came so near the ground that any one of you might have jumped off from it without frightening the most anxious mamma.

As I have said, this house stood in a little hollow formed by ever so many high hills, which rose around it much as waves rise around a little boat in stormy weather; they looked, in fact, like green waves that had been sud-

Harriet Beecher Stowe, "Little Pussy Willow."

CATHERN AND THE LADY.

Lucy G. Morse, "The Ash-Girl," *SN* 3 (1876): 391.

imagination. In a story by Harriet Prescott Spofford, for example, a young girl contributes to the support of her family by acting in a theater. The children of a well-to-do family become interested in Rosalie and, when they learn of her poverty, want to help her. They find, however, that there is no very effective way to express their concern. A gift of money from them will not help her for long. Rosalie cannot live with them because she would have to abandon the family which depends on her. Finally, it would be unwise even to invite her to visit them lest she become discontented with her own home. Rosalie's economic problem is temporarily solved when her quick-thinking and courage prevent a disaster as a theater set catches fire during a performance. A collection is taken up and given to her.[55] Private charity is frequently the acceptable response to the plight of a single child, but an entire family cannot be incorporated into the nuclear gentry family as readily as one child can be—and frequently is—in these stories.

Except for bringing the abandoned child into a family or taking him out of the city, there seems to have been only one other satisfactory alternative available—killing the young fictional charge. Intense, though seldom prolonged, suffering and even injury to children are not uncommon in the gentry literature for children. But only very rarely—in the death of the boy who persisted in running off to sea, in the murder of the boy who warned the mining engineer, and in the child's fatal injury which disciplined a family—do children die in these stories.[56] In each of these three instances, there is a threat to social order, which is abruptly terminated but not resolved. The lure of adventure, labor unrest, and parental inadequacy did not yield readily, in imagination, to the discipline basic to the gentry code. To these three threats to order and continuity may be added the problem of the urban poor. At its worst, their plight is symbolized by a ragged child exposed to winter in the city. In Abby Morton Diaz's "The Little Beggar Girl" (1867),

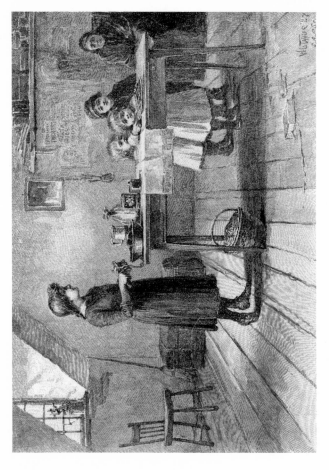

Harriet Prescott Spofford, "Little Rosalie," *SN* 15 (1888): 497.

these circumstances lead to the girl's death from exposure.[57] "A Modern Cinderella" ends on a similar note. The efforts of a genteel family to rescue an orphan girl from a woman who is viciously exploiting her fail when the girl is apparently abducted.[58]

In several other stories, however, the familiar pattern of removal from the city solves the problem. For example, in "Cash" (1868), ten-year-old Frankie Cash loses his father and is forced to quit school in order to help support his mother and the family's two other children. He finds work in a New York City department store, but it is clear that the people with whom he works exert potentially corrupting influence and that the pace of the work will eventually break him. Still, he perseveres: "It is a good thing not to give up easily when one is striving in a good cause."[59] In the summer, however, Cash becomes ill and can no longer work. The doctor who treats him finds the boy another job and eventually, after the death of the youngest child, helps the family move to the country. There Cash works for the doctor, and his mother and sister find machine work even more plentiful than in the city. Such work is more easily borne in a rural setting. As in "Milly Brewster's Pride," urban working conditions are shown to be incompatible with gentry values. The combination of vulgar associates and exhausting labor, which dulls the mind, are a constant threat to the young boy who recalls his father's injunction to grow up a gentleman.

Similarly, in Louisa May Alcott's "Little Pyramus and Thisbe" (1883), a poor, lame boy remains spirited despite his deprivations.[60] One day he discovers that behind the wall of the narrow court on which he lives, there is a beautiful garden and a little girl who takes an interest in him. The children have a reciprocal influence on each other, and eventually the girl's father, an artist, takes the boy to Italy to study painting. At one point in the story, it is suggested that the boy might become a shoe-mender, but just as

Frankie Cash was more suited to becoming a doctor's assistant, Miss Alcott's hero is better off studying to be an artist, a vocation that promises possibilities for cultivation not readily available to the humble cobbler, however financially successful.

The city, then, is seldom accepted on its own terms in the gentry literature for children. It is a place of social and economic extremes, capped by a listless and parasitic social elite and ballasted with a depressed and fragmented poor. Within limits, individuals in both classes may be reached by gentry figures, but rarely can this meeting be sustained in the city itself. It is usually necessary to withdraw to the country in order to make the conversion stick. Like Antaeus, the gentry figures in these stories depend for their strength on the rural conditions which nurtured them. In the city, they maintain their moral and physical balance only with great difficulty and effort. Cut off from the "earth element" by pavement, stairs, and elevators, "families run out in a generation or two of city life, unless there is a constant, regular recourse to the country for more vitality."[61] Homeless in the city, they periodically go home to the country or leave the city altogether. "To those who have been reared by the sea," Lucy Larcom writes in *A New England Girlhood*, "a wide horizon is a necessity, both for the mind and for the eye."[62]

A young subscriber who wrote to *Our Young Folks* touched the heart of the matter with poignant naiveté. She liked the new feature "Our Young Contributors," she said, and wanted to try writing for it, but she had spent her life entirely within the boundaries of the city. She had no beautiful scenery to describe and no adventures of even the most prosaic kind to relate. In reply to her letter, the editors could only assure her that the city was filled with scenes and experiences of interest. This was undoubtedly true, and as apparent to the editors of *Our Young Folks* as it was to the *Youth's Companion* staff when, two decades later, they called for stories to capture the drama of the teeming urban masses. On the basis of the sampled stories, however, it is apparent that the city inhibited those gentry authors who took it as their subject. They fled the city in imagination as many fled it in fact during the summer months. When they remained in the city, they imagined a quiet country garden or maintained the close family ways of an older, quieter remembered time.

It is not enough to regard these manifestations of rural values as nostalgic throwbacks to a nonexistent golden age, a tender-minded retreat from reality into a remembered world which in fact had never existed. This is a false view which distorts and cheapens the very real anguish revealed in these stories. Social order is always a precarious thing; it was especially so in nineteenth-century America where a viable order based on agrarian values had been an impressive, if short-lived achievement. To be faced with the need to legitimate urbanism and industrialism was a difficult task, especially since no strong or established intellectual tradition defending urban living could be readily invoked. In the face of aggressively competitive systems of organizing human endeavor and rewarding behavior, these writers could only attempt to shore up their own world with words. These were not uncourageous men and women, timidly confronting a real world that, we may now like to think, held out possibilities for a far richer life—if only those possibilities could be willed into expression. To know what ideals are needed and to envision what consequences for behavior flow naturally from them is not always to be able to articulate those ideas, to make them persuasive, or to translate them into programs. It is not at all clear that, even now, we will do what must be done for our cities and for our environment.

6

Strategies for Reassurance in an Age of Insecurity

> There is a "best" to be got out of everything;
> but it is neither the best of place or possession,
> nor the chuckle of the last word.
>
> Mrs. A. D. T. Whitney, "A
> Summer in Leslie Goldthwaite's Life."

In the several popular children's periodicals on which this study has concentrated, the gentleman and the lady are more than ideals by which to measure character, more than models by which to guide the difficult and precarious passage from childhood to adulthood, more too than social types capable of moderating satisfactorily the competition between free men in an open society. The gentry ideal also constitutes a defensive stance appropriate to an unsettled, precarious world; it presupposes a definition of experience that explains the significance of events and gives meaning to pain and suffering. In this sense, a story in *St. Nicholas* or the *Youth's Companion* was, as Robert Frost once defined poetry, a momentary stay against confusion. Blending Christian piety and gentry discipline, the children's authors repeatedly demonstrated in their fiction that misfortune was both test and opportunity. Those who were sound

146

proved and renewed their strength in adversity; those not yet converted were given an opportunity to learn the immutable laws that underlay their being. The beginning of wisdom lay in the recognition that the world is a school for character; this was one of the few certainties in an uncertain world.

During the Gilded Age, the ideal of the gentleman appeared to be jeopardized by several social factors. These challenges demanded interpretation and explanation if the gentry ideal was to be conveyed with its meanings intact to another generation. Rapid social change can undermine traditional systems of values unless vigorous efforts are made in the process of socialization to demonstrate the efficacy of the old ways. Moreover, as Professor Keller points out, both hereditarian and nonhereditarian elites "are vulnerable at exactly the same point: the link between the generations."[1] Recruitment is a constant necessity for elites; the plausibility of the socially objectivated world of a given elite must be effectively transmitted to and internalized by a younger generation. Economic insecurity—the possibility of downward social mobility—was an unsettling reality in the lives of many late nineteenth-century Americans. The isolated nuclear family—the predominant form and, in much social theory of the period, the basic social building block—was vulnerable to this pervasive threat as well as to illness, accident, and especially death, which threatened the stability of the individual family and hence its all-important capacity to transmit values to the young.

Given these pressures on the gentry, a group which put considerable emphasis on family nurture, we would expect to find in the fiction they produced considerable evidence of a deeply felt sense of precariousness in American society. This is, in fact, the case. Much of the fiction may be seen as strategies of explanation, justification, and reassurance. Legitimation may take the form of didactic statements in the stories or it may be implicit in the formulas, which act out the triumph of gentry values over the various actions or conditions threatening to disrupt social order. The business of living is a dangerous one; running through the stories is the assumption that the child must be trained to be careful as early as possible lest he needlessly, if innocently and unwittingly, endanger himself and others. Even in *St. Nicholas,* where toads were seldom seen and snakes were forbidden, writers of domestic fiction referred to the real world with appropriate seriousness. Louisa May Alcott's Mrs. Minot, who defines the moral center of "Jack and Jill" (1879), expresses this attitude perfectly when she warns, "Our actions are in our own hands, but the consequences of them are not. Remember that . . . and think twice before you do anything."[2] Foresight, self-discipline, and constant vigilance were necessary, children were shown, if one was to avoid the subtle dangers that hedged the lives of even the very young. The devil might no longer lurk, a constant peril to the unwary; still, these stories taught a prudence grounded in a sense of hovering threat. If the agency of that threat no longer took the traditional form of Satan, it was more diffuse, perhaps more inexplicable for being disembodied. "Our heavenly Father has told us that every step of our way is unsafe," a child is reminded in an early *Youth's Companion* story.[3]

In another *Youth's Companion* story, two girls play what seems to them a harmless practical joke on an impressionable playmate. The result is a terrifying experience for the victim, which precipitates a nearly fatal attack of brain fever and provides a sobering lesson for the two girls who thoughtlessly took advantage of their friend's credulity.[4] In other stories, carelessness, the attitude so warned against, frequently leads to serious results. Everyone, the small child not excepted, walks a narrow line; a rash act can lead precipitously to danger, humiliation, and suffering. If the relationship between deviance and consequence seems to us utterly disproportional, it suggests again the concern with which the gentry viewed the failure to consider the consequences of one's actions.

Both personal and economic equilibrium in these stories frequently seems to be fragile. Sudden disaster lurks everywhere. In Thomas Bailey Aldrich's "Story of a Bad Boy," which first appeared in *Our Young Folks* (1869), a merry outing of boys unattended by adults turns to tragedy in the time it takes for one of the boys to check on a boat's moorings. By the time his companions realize he has been gone overlong, the child and the boat have drifted beyond swimming distance, and an approaching squall has raised a dangerous chop on the water. The boy is drowned in the storm.[5]

Perhaps the most explicit statement of the pervasive sense of precariousness to be found in the periodicals sampled is "Two Ways of Telling a Story" (1866) by Jean Ingelow, the author of "Vale of Childhood" and an English correspondent of Lucy Larcom.[6] Although the story is set in England, the moral was undoubtedly perceived as having a wider geographical relevance. A young midshipman, described as "thoughtless" as well as gentlemanly, is returning home after a year at sea. The title's "two ways of telling a story" refers to the boy's very limited perception of events during his journey home in contrast to the author's wider perspective as an experienced adult. Early in the story, Miss Ingelow reveals that a man intent on robbing the young midshipman is stalking him. The boy reaches home safely, however, preserved by a series of providential coincidences. Although the midshipman remains oblivious to his danger, the reader fears for his safety throughout the story. "Some few dangers we are aware of," Miss Ingelow warns, "and we do what we can to provide against them; but, for the greater portion, 'our eyes are held that we cannot see.' "[7] This is not a situation to be feared, the author hastens to reassure her young readers:

It is not well that our minds should be much exercised about these hidden dangers, since they are so many and so great that no human art or foresight can prevent them. But it is very well that we should reflect constantly on that loving Providence which watches every footstep of a track always balancing between time and eternity; and that such reflections should make us both happy and afraid,—afraid of trusting our souls and bodies too much to any earthly guide or earthly security,—happy from the knowledge that there is One with whom we may trust wholly, and with whom the very hairs of our heads are all numbered.[8]

The religious tone is more pronounced in this example than is ordinarily the case in the domestic fiction; if there was any "earthly security," it lay, of course, in the self-discipline of the gentlemanly ideal. A final example from a *Youth's Companion* story may be cited.[9] In "Scraping an Acquaintance" (1888), a young lady foolishly allows herself to become acquainted with a stranger, a young man, while traveling by train. Although he is dressed as a gentleman, the wild gleam in his eye provides the conventional hint of his true character. When his villainous nature is finally revealed, the girl learns from her experience that "life beyond the sheltered home nest, and from under her mother's protecting wing, was full of unimagined dangers. These she began to arrange from out the bewilderment of her mind into two classes. The ones we cannot foresee, where we can only be thankful if we are preserved, and the dangers which come to us through doors opened by our own folly and indiscretion."[10] Even quite a young child could learn to recognize, and thus exercise some control over, the latter dangers; in contemplating the possibility of unforeseeable dangers, one could only seek comfort in the thought that no event was wholly meaningless or destructive. Every event taught some valuable lesson.

The pattern of broken homes apparent in the domestic fiction and the preoccupation (noted in chapter 5) with the social competition of fashionable society also point to the pervasive sense of precariousness underlying gentry fiction for children. The importance of the family as the basis for social organization suggests that the broken home might readily serve as a symbol for a deeply felt sense of social instability. The principles of the gentry were located less immediately in a sacred or cosmic order—quotations like Miss Ingelow's notwithstanding—and more in a style of life and in particular regional cultures. Both were under attack as the century waned. The rural culture was transformed by developments in communication, transportation, and agricultural technology, and fashionable society proved to be a powerful competitor, as Professor Schlesinger's graceful essay on etiquette books, *Learning How to Behave,* suggests.[11] A variety of forces combined to produce the sense of social instability and vulnerability which issued directly in the kind of statements noted above and indirectly in patterns of incident, reward, and resolution.

Given this feeling of social instability, the formulas present in domestic fiction for children may be seen as aiming to reassure a new generation of the efficacy of gentry values in meeting specific threats to social order at the same time that the formulas reaffirmed the writer's own commitment to those values. In previous chapters I have suggested the emphasis in these stories on dramatizing the effects of careless behavior, the consequences of which individuals could learn to control by curbing their impulses. But as the young lady cited earlier learned, there are dangers the individual cannot foresee or prevent. Principal among these are the consequences of elite competition, economic competition, and the general vulnerability of the family as a social unit and of its members as individuals. Children's authors might not say, with Job, that man is of few days and full of trouble, but they chose not to ignore the possibility of sudden accident, illness, and even death.

We have already seen that fashionable society appeared as a devitalized elite pursuing an aimless, unhealthy, and parasitic life style. In "A Country Cousin," cited in the previous chapter, the fashionable cannot even guard themselves from the treachery of their own servants.[12] In this instance, fashionable life appears to be self-defeating and in danger of being unable to perpetuate itself. "A Country Cousin," and other stories like it, appears to promise the reader that the values of self-discipline, moderation, and service which characterize the gentleman are productive of a more effective social order than the tempting, but ultimately useless, values and manners of the nouveau riche. Since the threat of the fashionable elite was examined in the last chapter, we may take up the other principal matters that needed legitimation: problems of economic mobility and family vulnerability. Both conditions were explained and interpreted to children in the gentry children's magazines.

Experience is a school for character: a basic form of legitimation found in the stories is the definition of life as an educational process. Accidents, disappointments, suffering, even death, occur for reasons that may be obscure, but these events can teach the virtues necessary for the establishment and maintenance of a satisfying individual life and a stable society: "We can't see why the trial was sent," a mother explains in one story, "but perhaps it was to make you patient and full of charity for others. You may depend upon it as the truth, that 'The sorrows of your youthful day / Will make you wise in coming years.' "[13] Perfectly representative of this explanation of youthful tribulation is Louisa May Alcott's serial "Jack and Jill."[14] Set in Concord, or New Harmony as it is called in the story,

"Jack and Jill" describes the changes that occur in four families in the aftermath of a sledding accident in which Jack Minot, a boy of thirteen, breaks a leg and "Jill," his friend Janie Pecq, badly sprains her back. Both children are confined to their beds as a result of the accident and, until late in the story, are under the constant care of their mothers as they recuperate. Forced to confront the consequences of their folly and to appraise their faults as these are revealed in the circumstances of their painful convalescence, they learn "that cheerfulness can change misfortune into love and friends; that in ordering one's self aright one helps others to do the same; and that the power of finding beauty in the humblest things makes home happy and life lovely."[15] Throughout her tale, Miss Alcott shows that the basis for "ordering one's self aright" is the familiar gentry discipline. For instance, Mrs. Pecq, Janie's mother, specifically wants her daughter to be a gentlewoman, and Mrs. Minot is the quintessential lady, whose qualities Calvert summarized: "Ladyhood is a something of still finer quality, woman's sensibilities being more tender, her aspirations more generous, her whole nature more diffusely and delicately dyed with beauty."[16]

When one of the most promising young men in New Harmony dies from a sudden illness, the metaphor of education is explicit in explaining and interpreting the unexpected tragedy. Nature consoles his grieving friends, including Jack and Jill. They realize "that their friend was not lost, but gone on into a higher class of the great school whose Master is eternal Love and Wisdom."[17] True, the master's purposes are often inscrutable, but a sudden tragedy that might suggest the precariousness of all life is muted, softened, and made familiar by Miss Alcott's careful interpretation of it. The world is a diverse but not unordered classroom, and everything, from a sledding mishap to a fatal illness, is directed toward the perfection of character and of the society which nurtures it. As the cycle

Louisa May Alcott, "Jack and Jill," *SN* 7 (1879): 453.

of a year ended for Miss Alcott's children, they "stepped out of childhood into youth, and some of the experiences of the past months had set them thinking, taught them to see the use and beauty of the small duties, joys and sorrows which make up our lives, and inspired them to resolve that the coming year should be braver and brighter than the last."[18] The preoccupation with death and injury in "Jack and Jill" and the intense effort to explain and justify the experiences undoubtedly reflects, in some measure, Miss Alcott's own grief at the illness and subsequent death of her sister May in December 1879, as "Jack and Jill" was being written.[19]

The identification of life with education emphasizes again the impossibility of moving very far from the instructional element in a literature for children dedicated, even in part, to displaying moral truth. If pleasure became the primary intent, the children's literature produced by the gentry tended to take the form of fantasy. It is not surprising that in *St. Nicholas* fantasy increasingly displaced domestic fiction in the 1880s, given the importance Mrs. Dodge placed on pleasure in children's reading. On the other hand, if the world is a schoolhouse, the change-of-heart formula, which stresses altered perception in response to personal experiences, is the form most appropriate for fiction, and it is the more common formula that guided the production of gentry children's literature.

Downward mobility as a specific threat to individuals or families was justified and explained in several ways. Consistent with the assumption that life is a process of education, poverty or economic insecurity frequently provide opportunities to learn certain truths. Specifically, individuals are led to recognize that reward follows character and that the values of gentility provide the best means of organizing and interpreting endeavor in a precarious world. Reward is made relatively independent of social class since it cannot be adequately measured in monetary terms or readily related to a particular standard of living and consumption.

Second, the basis for happiness is not necessarily an elevated social position, measured against a standard of wealth, but rather a place in society suited to a person's talents: "It is not always by rising in life that safety and success are to be secured. It is rather by finding in this struggling world where we can accomplish best that which it is in our power to do, even if that be of a humble kind."[20] As a writer for *Our Young Folks* suggests, "It is well to make the best of your surroundings."[21]

Daniel Ford's fear of industrial warfare and the bleak picture of economic competition painted in Rebecca Harding Davis's "Naylor o' the Bowl" (both cited in earlier chapters) suggest the gentry concern with the threat to social order implicit in competitive individualism.[22] In stories that raise the issue of competition and the possibility of downward mobility, individuals are shown to be successful not by displacing others but by creating opportunities for service that had not previously been discovered. Success generates opportunity; it does not create relative deprivation.

One of the best examples of this tendency occurs in "Nan: The New-Fashioned Girl," which appeared serially in *Wide Awake* (1876).[23] At the outset, the situation of the Norris family appears desperate, for the father, a bookkeeper, has been out of work for some time. The author soon establishes that Mr. Norris will never return to his job; he has become blind. The story is primarily concerned with one daughter, however. Nan, a negligent, careless girl of about fifteen, gradually learns, through hard work and the discipline of necessity, those attitudes, values, and manners that define the true lady. Despite his handicap, the father also helps to establish the economic security which finally replaces the poverty and insecurity with which the story begins. Mr. Norris and a younger friend patent an unspecified but useful device: "There was nothing very wonderful about it,—the wonder was it had not been thought of years ago. And it was not a mine of gold, nor anything of the sort; but it would be really useful to a great many people, and there would be a small income from it now, which would grow with every year."[24] Economic security, then, is not earned competitively at the expense of others' well being. Life may be a struggle in these stories, but it does not pit individual against individual or one social class against another in a ruthless struggle for survival. Necessity breeds invention quite literally; the ideal of service channels energy into activity that is both useful to society and sufficient for a family's needs.

The care with which the monetary reward is limited in "Nan: The New-Fashioned Girl" exemplifies the effort made in these magazines to avoid any appearance of the rags-to-riches formula. To risk arousing such expectations in children conflicted with basic gentry ideals. More important than the money earned by Mr. Norris's invention are his renewed courage and usefulness, Nan's wonderfully altered character, and the salutary process of hard work, which unites the family in the face of adversity. Such stories emphasize only a modest success if defined solely in terms of augmented purchasing power, for example. Wealth too often was seen to issue in selfishness and self-indulgence, in flamboyant display, and in pride of place. It tempted persons away from work, away from service, away from self-discipline—in short, away from the leadership by example which the gentry regarded as the gentleman's responsibility.

Not surprisingly, the fashionable elite is shown to be extremely vulnerable to the rigors of downward mobility as "Kate Oxford's One Talent" (1885), for example, demonstrates.[25] Like other *Wide Awake* stories, Kate's includes a measure of anti-New York City feeling that appears as a recurrent motif in Lothrop's Boston-based magazine. Kate is an orphaned New England girl living with relatives who are wealthy enough to have a summer house at Newport, a symbol of fashionable splendor. Kate, the author makes clear, however, remains unspoiled by this butterfly life; she "was *in* and not *of* this great gay money-spending world."[26] She is the familiar natural lady with an unusual interest—photography—which her aunt ridicules. When the Oxford firm is forced into bankruptcy, however, Kate's talent becomes the family's economic stay. She puts a cousin through college, but none of her uncle's sons have any business ability; their fashionable accomplishments are inadequate for earning a living, and the family disintegrates. Kate becomes the moral and economic support for those members of the Oxford family who remain in Newport. Fashionable society, which is the product of sudden, unearned good fortune, is shown to be at the mercy of equally sudden misfortune. Wealth is insufficient to nourish those qualities of character that enable a person to stand the cycle of boom and bust. The individual who is complacent and self-satisfied with a sudden rise in his earthly fortunes will be demoralized by the loss of his property. In contrast, the logic of gentry values made individual success relatively impervious to the business cycle and to unforeseen misfortunes, which might deprive the family of its male head and principal breadwinner. Given the pervasive economic insecurity of the stories and the emphasis on self-reliance, it is hardly surprising that women are generally presented as being extremely capable.

If life is a great schoolhouse, it is also a perpetual struggle. Activity is constantly emphasized in these periodicals. Problems are to be expected; but the courageous, the self-disciplined, and the strong-willed triumph over circumstances and become, in the process, stronger persons and better exemplars of gentility as a style of life appropriate to republican society, even if they do not live in Fifth Avenue chateaux and summer in Saratoga Springs.

The rigors of downward social mobility are everywhere softened in the gentry children's fiction. James Russell Lowell remarks, in a sketch for *Our Young Folks,* that "people have a trick in America of being poor one day and rich the next, or the other way";[27] children ought to recognize and accept this aspect of American life, which exempted no one from a life of discipline and labor. Stories of successful home industry exemplify the most common strategy adopted and dramatized in these periòdicals for countering economic insecurity. Such stories suggest the faith that everyone has a discoverable place of service in society—that interstices still exist abundantly for meeting others' needs. In the process, economic security and personal fulfillment go hand in hand with the ideals of service and production frequently encountered in the stories. Thus, as we've seen in John Townsend Trowbridge's "His Own Master," Jacob resolves to become an iron master rather than seek a clerkship after he is inspired by a visit to his uncle's iron works.[28]

A variety of examples from the other periodicals support the contention that economic security was often established on the combined basis of small productive enterprises, on character, and on a modest definition of success. Ultimately outward circumstances are regarded as the expression of inward character. The individual triumphs as he demonstrates his courage, self-reliance, integrity, and usefulness. The gradual success achieved in "The Boy Who Worked" or in "Jack's Treadle" (cited in earlier chapters) are typical.[29] In the former, it will be remembered, a boy slowly acquires an education and the interests of a gentleman and eventually rises to an editorship. In the latter, Jack works as a printer to support his mother while he acquires an education. His activity exemplifies a lesson of the story: "Whatever is in a man, is put there for some use."[30]

The peculiar problems faced by young women forced by circumstances to support their families are exemplified in the story "Losing Caste" (1873), in which a young woman rejects the two most socially acceptable opportunities available to her—teaching school or giving music lessons—and goes to work in a retail store.[31] Similarly, in "What Came of Making Pickles" (1873), a young wife with two children and an ill husband scandalizes her socially conscious (i.e., fashionable) stepmother by personally soliciting orders for homemade pickles in Boston hotels and groceries.[32] When her husband recovers, however, she turns the thriving business over to him and returns to her proper role as mother—proper, that is, within the gentry system of values. The intended function of reassurance is made explicit at the conclusion of the story. Engaging his readers directly, the author tells them that he was not merely dramatizing the maxim "where there's a will there's a way;" the outlines of the story he has told are true. The individuals concerned made "not a little money"—a rare instance of an emphasis on money. The line between fiction and reality dissolves; the story not only could happen but did happen, is therefore more real, and presumably more likely to happen again than if the events had merely been imagined.

In "How Miss Chatty Earned a Living" (1876) by Ella Farman, editor of *Wide Awake,* a middle-aged, unmarried woman is suddenly left alone with no means of support when her parents die.[33] She decides not to teach school since she is unaware of newer, more effective teaching methods, but she wants to do something for children. After rejecting several other ideas, Miss Chatty decides to become a doll doctor and soon finds that she has a business lucrative enough to permit her to remain in her parents' house. In a similar story by Miss Farman, "Kitty's Happy Thought"

(1878), a child's idea helps bring stability to a family weakened by an improvident father.[34] Kitty, a girl of ten, sews overalls until she gets the idea of raising strawberries for profit. As she works hard at this, her father gradually becomes accustomed to staying at home. Kitty's idea not only provides a basis for the family's economic success but also the basis for recreating the family itself. The family business, although threatened by major social changes of the period, such as the rise of corporate business, remains the solution in many stories to the problem of economic insecurity.

The efficacy of individual exertion is central to the reassurance voiced in these stories, but in the city such exertion did not yield the expected results. "Links in a Chain" (1888) by Emily Huntington Miller exemplifies a familiar pattern.[35] A mother and four daughters are left in the city when the husband dies. As so often is the case in the domestic fiction, Father is noteworthy only for having left the other members of the family exposed to the rigors of competitive individualism. All four daughters work in the city and are exhausted by their labor at day's end. Mrs. Miller likens the city to a chain of reciprocal relationships and obligations but fails to be convincing, for it is only in the country that a friend remarks, "I suppose we are all put in [as links in a chain], if we only really believed it."[36] The city apparently threatened the ideal of individual exertion just as it threatened other aspects of the gentry synthesis.

The kind of economic instability so far examined is closely allied with, indeed it is frequently caused by, family instability, most often the loss of the father. The broken family, a common pattern in the children's periodicals, is at once a symbol of the precariousness of society and a threat that had to be faced directly. The broken family is often the precondition but rarely the final condition in examples of either story formula.

The nuclear family dominates the social landscape of the

domestic fiction. Except for its occasional use as a setting, the school is not a prominent social institution, and the church is almost invisible. Although the nuclear family seldom is made to seem part of a complex web of social, political, and economic interdependencies, it is shown to be highly vulnerable nevertheless. Owing to the dominant economic role of men in nineteenth-century American society and the relatively limited opportunities for employment open to women, the death or serious illness of the husband frequently meant a radically revised standard of living. Moreover, the relative isolation of the nuclear family and the vastly reduced importance of other institutions capable of carrying and transmitting basic social values placed an enormous moral responsibility on parents, particularly the mother. Thus, her death, or her misguided penchant for fashion, readily becomes symbolic of the loss of moral direction in a family. The vulnerability of the family is perhaps most dramatically symbolized by its precarious economic position. But other, more subtle dangers are equally real. The family is not proof against invasion and subversion by cheap and vulgar literature; it may be jeopardized by ignorance, selfishness, or alcohol.

Serious natural misfortunes that suddenly threaten to overwhelm a family are relatively rare in the magazines considered in this study. The accidents, storms, or fires which do occur, however, are carefully contained in a fictional framework that mutes the danger and terror of the situation. Often these misfortunes serve as a context for demonstrating the superiority of character to varying degrees of disaster. In "The Wrong Coat" (1883), a boy who barely escapes a forest fire which claims the rest of his family is further tested when he finds and elects to return forty dollars mistakenly left in the pocket of a coat that was part of a relief shipment to the fire's victims.[37] The boy's honesty earns him the friendship of the coat's owner and the offer of a job. Character is tested but emerges from the ordeal stronger than before.

The possibility for individual happiness in this literature is seldom diminished since it rarely finds its measure solely in dollars wrung from others in a competitive scramble. The economic vulnerability of the individual unfortunate enough to sustain injury or to lose a father or entire family becomes less disturbing in the context of such stories, and the individual is assured a useful place and a measure of personal fulfillment in the social order. The incident which, from a child's limited perspective, represents a personal catastrophe, a diminution of freedom, or a loss of pleasure becomes an instructive experience under the guiding perspective of a gentry adult. If met and mastered, these crises teach that fortitude and good cheer, maintained even under the most trying personal circumstances, may provide an example and inspiration for others and that, in a universe of order, nothing happens except for the best. Out of temptation and tribulation come character, self-knowledge, and independence—and these never lack their appropriate reward. Such is the reiterated lesson of the fiction.

Similarly, readers are assured that fraud and malice, whatever the source or degree, are ultimately unsuccessful. The spoiling hatred of an embittered farm hand,[38] an armed robbery that shatters the peace of an innocent rural retreat,[39] or the vicious attack of a drunken husband on his wife and invalid son[40] suggest that, stripped clear of their dramatic contexts, particularly ugly examples of personal violence can be found even in these carefully laundered magazines. None of the stories are resolved through violent confrontation, however. That each of the central characters is a woman affords only a partial answer. Generally violence is not presented as an effective response in any story, and even anger tends to be rare and ineffective, a failure of self-control. In an instance when a young gentleman is about to grapple with a burglar, the latter turns out to be a harmless Irish servant known to the boy.[41] In two stories in which guns might have been used in self-defense, the conflict is resolved without shooting. Violence does resolve a story in which a man seeks to revenge himself upon a minister who testified against him in court. The man is prevented from hanging the minister by a young Negro to whom the minister has given a home.[42]

An incident in Aldrich's *Story of a Bad Boy* suggests the uneasiness with which gentry authors viewed conflict. A snowball fight begins with an amicable parley between the leaders of the two groups of boys, The two sides are clearly drawn along lines of social class. At first, the battles are governed by rules to which each side carefully adheres. Despite these rules, the spirit of competition recognizes no bounds: "As the winter wore on, the war-spirit waxed fiercer and fiercer." Soon snowballs are being frozen or ballasted with rocks, and boys are injured. As the rules are increasingly disregarded, the battles become more intense until the adult community is forced to halt the activity by sending in constables to separate the two groups. Conflict between the two groups, it would seem, cannot long be restrained, even by rules mutually agreed upon. The social importance of self-discipline is evident again, and it is worth noting that the only problem discussed in each of nine child-rearing manuals published during the period 1865-1874 was the problem of controlling personal aggression.[43]

The dominant change-of-heart pattern offered readers a considerable measure of reassurance. An ill-considered decision or an inappropriate value may involve an individual in a humiliating or painful experience, but events almost always force him to recognize his mistake and to perceive what he ought to do. Few decisions are presumed to lead ineluctably to disaster. Resorting to alcohol is a most important exception, however. The victim's first drink almost invariably defines an inescapable pattern of personal degradation and disaster.[44] The rare individual who manages to escape the clutches of demon rum pays for his past with considerable suffering—the loss of a foot in one instance, for example.[45] An ill-advised and hasty decision to marry similarly initiates an irreversible chain of events—but without the implication of a necessary physical and moral degeneration. The young couple who foolishly elope in "The Best of a Bad Bargain" (1873) eventually achieve an economic sufficiency, but the physical and emotional cost is high.[46] Answering a marriage advertisement in a newspaper, an even less judicious decision, precipitates a commensurately harsher result.[47] The young woman finds herself married to a widower with six children. "What can't be cured must be endured" is the small comfort she must accept for her ill-considered choice. There is no legitimate way to reverse the decision and its subsequent consequences. Divorce, not surprisingly, has no place in the gentry children's literature of the period. A bad marriage was one of those dangers that presumably could be foreseen and avoided.

Precisely because gentry values could be learned and because the individual was considered responsible for his actions, radical improvement in character was always possible. Neither habit, heredity, nor environment inevitably gripped or molded character. The individual's capacity for moral perception and for choosing appropriate behavior are everywhere acknowledged. Further, since life is fundamentally an educational process, no stigma attaches to earlier, less attractive behavior. The acting out of these principles in the fictional context might reassure the reader of his innate capacity for moral improvement; the possibility of reversion to earlier habits is not hinted or examined. Life was precarious enough without suggesting that virtue achieved might subsequently be lost. Stories either demonstrated the sufficiency of virtue—or dramatized the rite of passage.

It should be clear, finally, that these stories, conceived as reassuring examples, were particularly relevant for the young ladies who doubtless comprised the majority of readers, as their mothers dominated the audience for fiction generally. Preponderantly written by women, the stories dramatize and reiterate the lady's ability to cope with adversity and to do so with grace and good cheer. The stories encourage their young readers to expect occasional disappointment, even hardship, and to find the solution to these trials in self-discipline, competence, and vigorous effort. The image of the lady as a pale, delicate, neurasthenic being, no matter how cultured or aesthetically sensitive, had no place in the gentry children's magazines. Mother was a lady—vigorous, decisive, strong, though never self-assertive. It is true that her primary place was the home; yet many stories reveal a realistic recognition of the vulnerability of the nuclear family, even if the eventual salvation proposed in a given story seems far-fetched to us. Since character was not evaluated in terms of money, however, the lady ought to have been less prey to that dissatisfaction which often inheres today in the role of "housewife" in a society which has largely abandoned any standard of value save that of the dollar. In light of the family's economic insecurity, authors emphasized the lady's competence to support a family if the loss of a husband made it necessary. Although the solutions proposed—often a kind of home handicraft—do not strike us as radical or liberating, there can be little question of the authors' basic intention: to define the highest type of womanhood as a blend of gentleness and strength, capable of nurturing democracy's children and, when necessary, of preserving the family economically as well as spiritually. Conversely, the gentleman was compounded ideally of strength tempered by gentleness and sensitivity to the feelings of others.

Amid the growing tensions and unrest of the last quarter of the nineteenth century, the fiction of the popular children's magazines created a world of comparative serenity and especially of order. It is a domestic world peopled by familiar figures and organized around familiar relationships. Whatever the physical setting may be, the moral setting remains that of the parlor, the garden, and the kitchen. It is a world not without its own anxieties, even terrors, but these are kept tightly leashed. The order of the family prefigures that social order which, it is assumed, would result from the interaction of freely competing gentlemen. In the family, love and mutual respect, exemplified in gracious manners and thoughtful concern for the welfare of others, replace patriarchal domination. The wisdom of experience takes the place of autocratic whim as a basis for authority. The isolated boy on a journey of self-discovery in these stories is never Huck Finn, encountering one unsatisfactory family after another. And in the end the Jacks and the Jacobs never light out for the territories, fugitives from a civilization formed in the image of the gentry family.

7

The Precariousness of the Gentry Ideal

> We shall see good days, when our children
> start from the true home feeling, and a sacred
> memory joins hands with a brave and cheer-
> ful hope. Our good old mothers thought so;
> and our books are good as they repeat their
> wisdom and renew their love.
>
> Samuel Osgood, "Books for
> Our Children"

In an important essay a dozen years ago, in which he undertook to redefine the field of American social history,
Rowland Berthoff wrote: "Well before the end of the century, it became abundantly clear that the industrial revo-
lutionaries had produced an American social order almost without parallel in the modern world. A self-made
plutocracy recognized little responsibility for the working classes, the latter repudiated whatever common interest they formerly felt with their employers, ethnic groups
regarded each other with little sympathy, the farming
regions resented their exploitation by businessmen and
bankers, and individuals in general acknowledged few social duties except to themselves, their families, and their

narrow interest groups."[1] Within the constraints imposed by their assumptions about fiction, about childhood, and about the bases for social order in a democracy, the writers discussed throughout this study responded to this disintegration. It is true that they sought stability in relationships that, in retrospect, appear deeply conservative. Yet the ideals professed in the gentry children's magazines had much in common with Progressivism, as John Morton Blum has pointed out, and with what Berthoff calls its "gospel of mutual responsibility."[2] And when Jane Addams confronted the Pullman strike in her essay "A Modern Lear," she found in Shakespeare's tragedy of family relationships a dramatic analogue, which permitted her both to discover meaning in the explosive Pullman situation and to offer a solution—a just regard by both parties for the reciprocal obligations that bound them.[3] This proposal hardly makes for a sharp division between, say, Daniel Sharp Ford and the founder of Hull House, at least in this instance.

Before the turn of the century, the forces of social reintegration were feeble, and much of the reform that was to follow was conservative.[4] Whatever its evident shortcomings, the ideal of the gentleman that shaped this children's fiction—and that was modified by the economic and ideological demands made of it—was basically a generous and responsible one. Traditionally, the gentleman was a free man, dependable in moments of crisis, confident of his judgment and instincts, and possessed of the courage to resist compromising his principles in the face either of merited praise or unmerited censure.[5] This was not a freedom defined by the absence of all restraint, and in the periodicals it was clear that freedom and responsibility are intimately related. *"Whosoever would reign, let him serve,"* the Biblical precept invoked by George Henry Calvert to exemplify and interpret the social implications both of Christianity and gentility, serves equally to summarize the basis for action urged on children in the gentry periodicals.[6] The promise of democracy held out to children in this literature is not liberty to do as one pleases but the opportunity to become what one could be by accepting responsibility for service within the discipline of self-culture.

As exemplars of freedom and duty dedicated to public service, the gentleman and the lady were expected to wear their responsibilities lightly and with good humor, for freedom is diminished if duty becomes burdensome. Good cheer in the face of adversity is counseled throughout the domestic fiction in these children's periodicals. Children are instructed to bear misfortune with goodwill; in the words of Miss Alcott, "Cheerfulness can change misfortunes into love and friends."[7] And as we have seen, the stories insisted on the necessity of, and the personal fulfillment to be found in, generosity, active self-sufficiency, and a courage that at times seems almost stoic: "*To be able to bear*; perhaps this was it*," one young lady muses as she seeks the meaning of the lives of those less well off than herself. Their capacity to endure "was greater, indeed, than any outer grace."[8]

To endure, and hopefully to prevail, by means of courage and goodwill and to cherish life for its possibilities are the lessons taught in the periodicals. "The world is for endeavor; the world is the flint, the will of man the steel," Trowbridge wrote in the preface to his autobiography, echoing Emerson; and this is the basic creed that his Father Brighthopes preaches.[9] As it appeared in these periodicals, the ideal of the gentleman was neither flamboyant nor colorful; it was a compromise, an effort to preserve, in harmonious balance, the democratic ideal of the free individual and the hope for an orderly democratic society. The gentry writers sought to acknowledge the just demands of both and to avoid regarding the free individual as inevitably engaged in conflict with a society from which he was more or less alienated. Theirs was a courageous effort, even if it proved to be beyond the powers of most of the authors to dramatize their world very persuasively. If these stories descend, on occasion, to the maudlin, the trivial, and the pathetic, they nevertheless reveal the conviction that democracy is ill served by deifying either the individual or society.

At best, the ideal they sought to convey was a fragile one in a world increasingly hostile to its realization, at least in the form in which it was given expression in the popular children's magazines. There is irony, perhaps, in stressing production without providing any model for consumption consistent with the gentry values. Despite the emphasis on hard work and productivity, the stories provide little sense of the right uses of the material rewards such activity might provide, even in moderation. This is only to say that however much the gentry looked to fiction to provide guidance or to dramatize morally acceptable behavior, the popular conventions could be stretched only so far. The gentry had few fictional forms available through which to present an ethic of consumption.

Far more important in defining the instability of the proffered ideal, however, is the shift in the social sources of moral authority that was taking place in the latter part of the nineteenth century, a process which Thomas C. Cochran has called "the inner revolution."[10] An old world of fixed principles, a stable cosmic order thought to lie beyond time and mutability, was being undermined; a new world characterized by flux was being discovered and persuasively articulated. A major assumption central to that increasingly precarious world view and to the moral order on which the children's fiction was grounded is perfectly summarized in a quotation from Mrs. A. D. T. Whitney's story for *Our Young Folks,* "A Summer in Leslie Goldthwaite's Life" (1866):

[Leslie's aunt] took for granted that her children were
born with the same natural perception as herself; that
they could recognize, little by little, as they grew into it,
the principles of the moral world;—reason, right,
propriety,—as they recognized, growing into them, the
conditions of their outward living. She made her own
life a consistent recognition of these, and she lived
openly before them.[11]

But the new order, symbolized most potently and starkly
by Darwinian theory, contravened the basic assumption of
natural order on which the old view depended. The correspondence theory that served to mediate between the world
of apparent change and the underlying stable order of the
universe would be called into question. Near the end of
Mrs. Whitney's story, one of Leslie's fashionable friends, a
high-spirited girl with the arresting diminutive "Sin," begins to grasp those changeless moral principles waiting to
be perceived and asks, "Why is it that things seem more sure
and true as soon as we find out we can make an allegory to
them?"[12] She is told that it is not fallible human perception
that creates the allegory. One-half of the correspondence
already exists, rooted in the nature of things, waiting to be
grasped by the intuitive imagination of a suitably prepared
and chastened individual. The word *is* made flesh and
needs only the individual's altered perception to reveal its
presence and to make actual what until then was only potential in that person's experience.

A little later, while watching a sunset with Leslie and
other friends, Sin Saxon's attention is drawn to the others in
the group as they stand silhouetted against an arch in the
mountains. The arch, in turn, is outlined against a cliff, and
beyond it the mountains are ranged against the splendor of
the setting sun. Remarking the scene, her companion establishes one correspondence or interpretation: people must
have steps to climb, even in imagination. The girl

herself perceives another meaning: the ordered elements of the scenery suggest a principle of gradation that holds true for individuals as well.[13] At the top, she sees, are the lady and the gentleman. Thus flooded with awe at the beauty of the scene, Sin is led unerringly to a perception of the natural order, to a recognition—that has the irresistible force of revelation—of the necessity for constant individual striving, and to the understanding that character constitutes the basis for the only genuine hierarchy among individuals. Rightly understood, life in a democracy is an opportunity to achieve character; the principles that nurture and sustain it are manifest in the natural world, especially, it would seem, in the mountains of New Hampshire and Vermont.

The assumptions basic to the world view in this story, as well as in a story such as Miss Alcott's "Jack and Jill," might be summarized by the following paradigm. The world of nature, for all its outward appearance of change, mutability, and occasional meaninglessness, is really stable, orderly, and coherent and can be apprehended as such by man, even if not in all its manifold detail. Man, similarly, has his inner hidden being and his overt behavior. In theory, the concepts of the gentleman and the lady mediated between this inner reality and the outer appearance. The gentleman was, in truth, what he presented himself to be. His disciplined manners and speech, his gestures, tastes, and sympathies had the force of instinct and were the perfect, organic expression of disciplined being. Similarly, to the prepared and sensitive individual, the rocks and rills and templed hills revealed the laws of creation, of which the visible elements of nature were but the husk. The relationship between man and nature, finally, was conceptualized, as we saw in chapter 5, as one of nurture and discipline. To nature was transferred much of the discipline that otherwise would have fallen to parents, and particularly to the mother, to administer. But if deviance led ineluctably to certain consequences rooted in the nature of things, the erring child might return to the loving embrace of the family, chastened by his recognition that the laws he had transgressed by his selfishness or disobedience were not merely arbitrary parental whim but were given in the world. Nature mediated, expressed, made manifest the moral law that defined and ordered creation, and gentility provided the perspective from which to see moral law in a White Mountain sunset. Such a paradigm could remain plausible only so long as these accepted relationships between appearance and reality remained plausible. It was the fate of the generation of children's authors writing during the Gilded Age to attempt the difficult, and as it turned out largely unsuccessful, task of shoring up a view that appeared increasingly implausible as the social authority of scientific knowledge waxed stronger.

The theories of evolution undermined the critical relationship expressed in the idea of natural correspondences. Random mutation, as an explanation for phylogenic change, struck at the heart of the belief in a stable universe and in a design discoverable, in principle, in the organization and structure of the creation. Beneath the shifting forms of nature, evolutionists claimed, lay chance variation, not the creator's express design. The lessons taught by contemplating the evolutionists' doctrine did not fit well with the lessons taught by White Mountain sunsets. Where were freedom, responsibility, and the hard-earned lessons of suffering if man was finally and merely the sport of chance, buffeted by forces beyond his control? He was, as we have come to learn, homeless—and in a far more radical fashion than the gentry feared as they contemplated the conditions of urban living.[14]

The ideal of the gentleman, as it organized gentry children's literature, was jeopardized too by the authors' inability to imagine children maturing naturally in the city and by their inability to discover rewards that were congruent with the gentry ideal and also widely appealing. What was needed was a dramatic, symbolic equivalent to money and fashionable status. Character, insight, and economic sufficiency paled, it can be imagined, in comparison with the rewards garnered by the plucky, indomitable boys of the dime-novel and story paper traditions. In this regard, it is not surprising perhaps that one of the most popular late nineteenth-century juveniles was Frances Hodgson Burnett's *Little Lord Fauntleroy*, a *St. Nicholas* serial, in which perfect character receives its commensurate reward—a magnificent English estate.[15] The young Cedric, nourished by the frugal conditions of his early childhood ("the useful lesson of *doing without*," Miss Larcom calls it) and by the spirit of republican institutions, returns to his birthright as an English gentleman, prepared to manage his ancestral estate with perfect courtesy and compassion. The American, so long uprooted, regains at last what Hawthorne called "Our Old Home." The dream that tantalized Hawthorne, Cooper, and others thus found its apotheosis in little Cedric Errol, the boy-man—lace collar, velvet suit, love curls, and all. By comparison, *The Adventures of Tom Sawyer*, which also ends with the bestowal of a fortune, seems far less satisfying. What, after all, can one do in Hannibal-St. Petersburg with "a dollar for every weekday in the year and half of the Sundays"?

As it had been for generations of Americans, it was the fate of many children's writers of the period to have left home at an early age, only to discover as adults that mobility, success, and progress had robbed them of a symbolic resting place. When Rebecca Harding Davis returned to the West Virginia farm of her childhood, the orchards, wheat fields, and woods where she had played as a child were gone, replaced by a grassless plain littered with the debris of the burgeoning oil industry—with derricks, hogsheads for the oil, and the shops and crowded saloons of a boom town.[16] Together with one of the stories that best reveals the integrating power attributed to the gentry ideal, "Naylor o' the Bowl," Mrs. Davis contributed another story to *St. Nicholas,* which suggests one form the failure of the gentry vision might take. "The Enchanted Prince" (1873) also appeared in the first volume of *St. Nicholas,* indicating perhaps the degree to which many of these stories were responses to the authors' own uncertainties and their need to reaffirm continually the gentry values.[17]

Bob, the hero of Mrs. Davis's story, appears to be an ordinary boy who grows up in a grimy mill town, becomes a grocer, marries, and has several children of his own. Although his life seems only to be a round of uninterrupted dullness, he is neither unhappy nor bitter at his modest fate, for he knows that he is, in reality, a prince who has been enchanted.[18] He recalls his real life with pleasure and acts kindly toward his family because of it. The American mill towns spawned by the reckless exploitation of natural resources are only a cruel enchanter's spell, cast on a great forest, its banished king, and his son. Unlike a traditional fairy story, however, no beautiful princess awakens the grocer-prince with a kiss and restores him to his birthright of freedom and authority. Such a story is not typical of *St. Nicholas,* of course, and the mill towns could hardly be explained or legitimated very satisfactorily as the work of vindictive magicians. What "The Enchanted Prince" suggests is the increasing difficulty the gentry would experience in transmitting their version of self and society, given the urbanization and industrialization of American society.

Evolution challenged eternal law; the gentleman was less and less a force in politics as the Gilded Age wore on; and as the cities grew, the quality of rural life declined while that of urban life remained deplorable. Although it had become apparent decades earlier that a state church was not an essential factor in the maintenance of social order, those who wrote for and edited the magazines selected for this study were unable to countenance an analogous cultural pluralism. Culture was a body of great literature and, to a lesser extent, great art and music. The classics conveyed moral knowledge and revealed the truths of human nature and the lessons gleaned from centuries of experience. Had they been able to divorce the ideal of the gentleman from this notion of culture, they might have been able to say, with William James, that one ought not

> to be forward in pronouncing on the meaninglessness of forms of existence other than our own; and [the recognition that life is shot through with meanings to which we are insensitive] commands us to tolerate, respect, and indulge those whom we see harmlessly interested and happy in their own ways, however unintelligible these may be to us. Hands off: neither the whole of truth nor the whole of good is revealed to any single observer, although each observer gains a partial superiority of insight from the peculiar position in which he stands.... It is enough to ask of each of us that he should be faithful to his opportunities and make the most of his own blessings, without presuming to regulate the rest of the vast field.[19]

As it was, the arbiters of culture identified the principles of disorder evident to them in sensational fiction, for example, with the potential for social disruption existing among the classes which patronized that fiction. The crimes committed by boys who admitted to devouring dime novels demonstrated to their satisfaction that the fear of such reading was no idle fancy. In the end, the ideal of freedom that informed the image of the gentleman was betrayed by an ideal of culture that conflicted with mass reading patterns. If good literature improved character, bad literature, by the same logic, threatened deleterious social consequences. The pressure on gentry authors to maintain an acceptable moral stance in their fiction was, as we have seen, extremely strong. Assessing the self-imposed censorship of such publishing firms as Scribner's and Harper's during the Gilded Age, Donald Sheehan concludes that they were more likely to accept manuscripts embodying radical economic or political ideas than manuscripts that contained attacks on orthodox religious beliefs and traditional moral values, especially the sanctity of marriage vows.[20] Above all, the vows that established and sustained the family were not to be threatened.

It remains to be asked what happened to the lady and the gentleman in American life and in its children's literature. *St. Nicholas* and the *Youth's Companion* continued well into this century, the former until 1939; and we remember that as late as 1900, E. A. Ross regarded the social type of the gentleman as still constituting a powerful public symbol.[21] To the extent that the gentry elite overlap with the genteel tradition in American letters in the last decades of the nineteenth century, the demise of that tradition may serve to date the end of the former. It seems generally agreed that the genteel tradition, however it is defined, did not survive World War I. Howard Mumford Jones defines it as "the fusion of idealism with craftsmanship that dominated high culture in this country from 1865 to 1915." He does not attempt to explain the factors that combined to destroy that fusion, although he hints that the rise of irrational psychology, symbolized by Freud, was one such factor.[22] In the most recent work on the genteel tradition, *A Genteel Endeavor,* John Tomsich narrowly defines the group in terms of eight prominent literary men and argues that their genteel endeavor—not quite a tradition as it turns out —died with the last of the group in 1904, a casualty of the forces of immigration, industrialization, and urbanization that were transforming the nation.[23] Writing in 1935, Henry Dwight Sedgwick, whose younger brother Ellery had been an editorial assistant to Daniel Ford and later editor of the *Atlantic Monthly,* identified the factors that seemed to have led to the virtual elimination of the gentleman as an influential social type.[24] The principal ones, Sedgwick thought, were science, democracy, business, specialization, humanitarianism, and success.

As for children's literature, there is evidence to suggest that a new type of hero, the prep school athlete, embodied many of the same traits of character that earlier stories had urged in terms of the gentry ideal. Fred Erisman, for example, concludes that in the school and sports stories of Ralph Henry Barbour, a prolific contributor to *St. Nicholas* at the turn of the century, character is equated with physical prowess, and sportsmanship becomes the measure of honesty and teamwork.[25] Courage, integrity, and reliability are valued traits, as they are in the gentry stories examined in this study, but the social type in which the traits are organized and expressed is different. The games of football and baseball appear to function in these school and sports stories as social microcosms in much the same way that the institution of the family functions in the earlier stories. Self-control and the ideal of service undergo subtle but unmistakable shifts in emphasis as they become the qualities necessary for smoothly coordinated teamwork and winning seasons on the grid-iron or diamond.

If E. L. Godkin was correct, gentlemen as a class had lost political influence by the middle of the nineteenth century; and it seems clear now that the cultural influence of the genteel tradition had greatly diminished by the outbreak of World War I. In the field of children's literature, however, the principles articulated by Mrs. Dodge in undertaking the editorship of *St. Nicholas* and by Caroline Hewins in selecting and recommending books appropriate for use in schools and public libraries have continued to shape the production and evaluation of quality children's literature in the twentieth century. First, the structure of historical interpretation of the development of children's literature offered in textbooks today differs in no substantive way from interpretations written at the turn of the century.[26] Second, the friendship begun in 1896 between Miss Hewins and Anne Carroll Moore, who is still regarded as a model critic of children's literature, suggests that a study of recruitment patterns, personal relationships, and influence in the training of children's librarians would demonstrate the enduring influence of a relatively small group of New England ladies.[27] The possibility of strong continuing influence of gentry ideas in the field of children's literature may help to explain why twentieth-century writers considered most significant by modern critical standards have contributed so little to children's literature and why, institutionally, the teaching of children's literature is largely divorced from, or barely tolerated in, departments of English. But it lies beyond the scope of this study to pursue these matters further.

If, in conclusion, we raise the question as to the predictive value of the generalizations advanced in this study, we raise a question that can finally be answered only empirically. Certainly it was my intent that the generalizations presented in this study have predictive value for children's literature issued under gentry auspices during the Gilded 'Age but not examined in the course of the research for this book. An examination of biographies for children written by George M. Towle, Elbridge Streeter Brooks, Sarah Bolton, and others suggests that the generalizations about valued character traits and the centrality of the gentleman and lady hold true for these works as well.[28] It should be clear, moreover, that the emphases evident in the periodicals considered are consistent with the concept of discipline that Howard Mumford Jones argues constitutes the heart of the genteel tradition. Whatever the world weariness that weighed down the souls of the genteel figures studied by John Tomsich and that was aired in their private correspondence with each other, the essentials of gentry discipline were presented to children as values sufficient to realize the promise of American life.

Abbreviations

OYF: *Our Young Folks* (Boston: Ticknor and Fields, 1865-1872)

RM: *Riverside Magazine for Young People* (Boston: Houghton and Osgood, 1867-1870)

SN: *St. Nicholas* (New York: Scribners, 1873-1939)

WA: *Wide Awake* (Boston: Lothrop, 1875-1893)

YC: *Youth's Companion* (New York: Perry Mason, 1827-1929)

Notes

Introduction

[1]Owing to its long and complicated history, the term "culture" is used in a variety of ways. Although no single definition of culture prevails absolutely even among anthropologists, there does appear to be wide agreement on a number of points according to Yehudi Cohen, ed. *Man in Adaptation: The Cultural Present* (Chicago: Aldine, 1968), pp. 7-12. Whether culture properly refers only to cognitive systems, as some anthropologists insist, is a point better left to theorists in that field. It seems clear, however, that an essential aspect of a given way of life is the "cultural knowledge" that orders, informs, and gives meaning to behavior; it is what Clifford Geertz has called the "set of control mechanisms—plans, recipes, rules, instructions—for the governing of behavior," in his essay "The Impact of the Concept of Culture on the Concept of Man," in Cohen, ed., *Man in Adaptation*, p. 24. This cultural knowledge is a body of shared meanings specific to a particular group, which functions to define an environment and to relate individuals to that environment and to their fellow men. Since it is the perceptual-conceptual system of a group that defines the meaning of its members' actions, human behavior is intelligible in terms of that system. Geertz is essentially correct when he says of the cathedral at Chartres: "To understand what it means, to perceive it for what it is, you need to know rather more than the generic properties of stone and glass and rather more than what is common to all cathedrals. You need to understand also—and, in my opinion, most critically—the specific concepts of the relations between God, man, and architecture that, having governed its creation, it consequently

embodies." Geertz, "Impact of the Concept of Culture," p. 27.

The emphasis on cultural knowledge advocated here directs our attention primarily to what passes for knowledge, to what has meaning and value—and in what terms—for particular groups of people living in different times and places; and the emphasis acknowledges the probability that these characteristic structures of meaning will vary greatly from one group to another.

For efforts to define the significance of the concept of culture for American studies, see especially Richard Sykes, "American Studies and the Concept of Culture: A Theory and Method," *American Quarterly* 15 (1963): 253-70, and Seymour Katz, " 'Culture' and Literature in American Studies," *American Quarterly* 20 (1968): 318-29.

[2]James Spradley, *Culture and Cognition* (San Francisco: Chandler, 1972), p. 21.

[3]In the history of children's literature, one generation's "realism" is the next generation's "didacticism." See John Rowe Townsend, "Didacticism in Modern Dress," in Sheila Egoff, G. T. Stubbs, and L. F. Ashley, eds., *Only Connect* (Toronto: Oxford University Press, 1969), pp. 33-40.

[4]Cf. Alexander C. Kern, "The Sociology of Knowledge in the Study of Literature," *Sewanee Review* 50 (1942): 505-14.

[5]For an examination of the biological determinants of culture, see Eugene d'Aquili, *The Biopsychological Determinants of Culture* (Reading, Mass.: Addison-Wesley, 1972). Peter Berger and Thomas Luckmann discuss the process of socialization at length in *The Social Construction of Reality* (Garden City, N.Y.: Doubleday, 1966), pp. 129-84.

[6]Berger and Luckmann, *The Social Construction of Reality*, p. 31.

[7]This study is based on fiction sampled from five children's periodicals: the *Youth's Companion*, *Our Young Folks*, the *Riverside Magazine for Young People*, *St. Nicholas*, and *Wide Awake*. Narrative fiction having a contemporary setting was selected, first, from every third year of publication, beginning with the initial volume. The exception to this is the sample drawn from the *Youth's Companion*, starting with v. 46 (1867). In the case of monthly magazines, stories were selected from every other issue, beginning with the first. Thus, in the case of *St. Nicholas*, the sample begins with the issue of November 1873, followed by January, March, May, etc., of 1874; November, January, etc., of 1876/77,

through v. 15 (1888). The *Youth's Companion*, a weekly, was sampled on the basis of the first issue of each month. In every case, all fiction in an issue was included in the sample. Serials begun in sampled issues were read in their entirety.

[8]A. I. Hallowell, *Culture and Experience* (1955; reprint ed., New York: Schocken, 1967), p. 76.

Chapter 1

[1]Margaret Sangster, who helped edit a number of magazines, including *Hearth and Home, Harper's Young People,* and *The Ladies' Home Journal,* provides a glimpse of this aspect of the cultural elite in *From My Youth Up* (New York: Fleming H. Revell, 1909), pp. 227*ff.*

[2]There are few figures available, but Goldie Merrill cites as representative an instance in which 13 percent of the contributors to a children's periodical produced about 40 percent of the material. "The Development of American Secular Juvenile Magazines: A Study of the Educational Significance of Their Content" (Ph.D diss., University of Washington, 1938), p. 9.

[3]Betty L. Lyon, "A History of Children's Secular Magazines Published in the United States from 1789 to 1899" (Ph.D. diss., Johns Hopkins University, 1942).

[4]Ibid., pp. 381-87.

[5]Quoted in Lovell Thompson, ed., *Youth's Companion* (Boston: Houghton Mifflin, 1954), p. 1124.

[6]Lyon, "A History of Children's Secular Magazines," pp. 372-74.

[7]Ibid. See also John C. Crandall, "Patriotism and Humanitarian Reform in Children's Literature, 1825-1860," *American Quarterly* 21 (1968): 3-22 and Merrill, "The Development of American Secular Juvenile Magazines," p. 3.

[8]Lyon, "A History of Children's Secular Magazines," p. 375.

[9]Ibid., p. 376. See also Henry Steele Commager, "When Majors Wrote for Minors," *Saturday Review of Literature* 35 (May 10, 1952): 10-11. Commager makes much of the fact that the period's most gifted writers contributed to *St. Nicholas,* but a systematic reading of its files suggests that the bulk of the material came

from the pens of writers whose names have long since ceased to be familiar.

[10]Quoted in Raymond Kilgour, *Lee and Shepard: Publishers for the People* (Hamden, Conn.: The Shoe String Press, 1965), pp. 61-62.

[11]Hellmut Lehmann-Haupt, *The Book in America,* 2d ed. (New York: Bowker, 1951), pp. 146-47, 153-69; Frank Luther Mott, *A History of American Magazines* (Cambridge: Harvard University Press, 1938-1957), III: 6.

[12]William Charvat, "The People's Patronage," in Matthew Bruccoli, ed., *The Profession of Authorship in America 1800-1870* (Columbus: Ohio State University Press, 1968), pp. 298-316; Charles A. Madison, *Book Publishing in America* (New York: McGraw-Hill, 1966), p. 53.

[13]Lehmann-Haupt, *The Book in America,* p. 212.

[14]Donald Sheehan, *This was Publishing: A Chronicle of the Book Trade in the Gilded Age* (Bloomington: Indiana University Press, 1952), p. 7.

[15]Ibid., pp. 8-9, 15.

[16]Lehmann-Haupt, *The Book in America,* p. 212; Madison, *Book Publishing in America,* pp. 49-50.

[17]Quoted in Sheehan, *This Was Publishing,* p. 16.

[18]Ibid., pp. 26-27.

[19]Quoted in Madison, *Book Publishing in America,* p. 50.

[20]Sheehan, *This Was Publishing,* p. 104.

[21]William Charvat, *The Origins of American Critical Thought* (Philadelphia: University of Pennsylvania Press, 1936).

[22].Quoted in Thompson, *Youth's Companion,* p. 1123.

[23]John Townsend Trowbridge, *My Own Story* (Boston: Houghton Mifflin, 1903), p. 326.

[24]Mott, *A History of American Magazines,* II: 206; Lyon, "A History of Children's Secular Magazines," p. 66. Ford was assisted principally by Hezekiah Butterworth (1870-1886), by Butterworth and Edward Stanwood (1887-1894), and by Stanwood until 1899. Editorial assistants included James Parton, George M. Towle, J. H. Woodbury, William H. Rideing and J. L. Harbour in the 1870s and M. A. deWolfe Howe and Ellery Sedgwick in the 1890s.

[25]Lyon, "A History of Children's Secular Magazines," p. 67.

²⁶Quoted in Ray Stannard Baker, *American Chronicle* (New York: Scribner's, 1945), pp. 70-71.

²⁷Ibid. See also Mott, *A History of American Magazines,* II: 271*ff.*

²⁸Lyon, "A History of Children's Secular Magazines," pp. 67-68.

²⁹Mott, *A History of American Magazines,* II: 262, 269-71; among those who contributed frequently to the *Companion,* as well as to other quality children's periodicals, were Louise Chandler Moulton, C. A. Stephens, Rebecca Harding Davis, Edward Everett Hale, Ruth Chesterfield, Sophie May, Harriet Beecher Stowe, Louisa May Alcott, John Townsend Trowbridge, Sophie Swett, Sarah Orne Jewett, Olive Thorne Miller, Rose Terry Cooke, Lyman Abbott, and Frank Stockton. Additional names are noted by Lyon, "A History of Children's Secular Magazines," p. 68-69.

³⁰Mott, *A History of American Magazines,* II: 266-68.

³¹J. L. Harbour, "How Ford Hall Came to be Built," in George W. Coleman, ed., *Democracy in the Making* (Boston: Little, Brown, 1915), p. 10. In 1925, with circulation down to 300,000, the *Companion* was purchased by the Atlantic Monthly Company headed by Ellery Sedgwick and M. A. deWolfe Howe, two former editorial assistants of Ford's.

³²Rebecca Harding Davis, *Bits of Gossip* (Boston: Houghton Mifflin, 1904), p. 221.

³³Harbour, "How Ford Hall Came to be Built," pp. 10-13; "Daniel Sharp Ford," *Dictionary of American Biography,* VI: 513-14.

³⁴Alice M. Jordan, *From Rollo to Tom Sawyer* (Boston: Horn Book, 1948), pp. 116-20; Lyon, "A History of Children's Secular Magazines," p. 299.

³⁵Horace Scudder, *Henry Oscar Houghton* (Cambridge, Mass.: Riverside Press, 1897), pp. 89-91.

³⁶Lyon, "A History of Children's Secular Magazines," p. 299; Jordan, *From Rollo to Tom Sawyer,* pp. 114-16.

³⁷Quoted in Alexander Allen, "Horace E. Scudder: An Appreciation," *Atlantic Monthly* 91 (1903): 550.

³⁸Ibid., pp. 550-51, 557.

³⁹Quoted in ibid., p. 557. Scudder's contribution to American letters is briefly remarked by Howard Mumford Jones, "The Genteel Tradition," *Harvard Library Bulletin* 18 (1970): 14.

⁴⁰Allen, "Horace E. Scudder," p. 556.

[41]Charles E. Samuels, *Thomas Bailey Aldrich* (New York: Twayne, 1965), p. 15.

[42]Scudder, *Henry Oscar Houghton,* p. 92.

[43]W. S. Tryon, *Parnassus Corner: A Life of James T. Fields* (Boston: Houghton Mifflin, 1963), p. 228.

[44]Lyon, "A History of Children's Secular Magazines," pp. 271-72.

[45]Jordan, *From Rollo to Tom Sawyer,* p. 123.

[46]Trowbridge, *My Own Story,* p. 317; Lyon, "A History of Children's Secular Magazines," p. 276. Samuel Osgood was probably referring to *Our Young Folks* when he said that "the authors who figure on the list of contributors to our leading juvenile magazine need not hide their heads before any staff of contributors to any periodical in the country." "Books for Our Children," *Atlantic Monthly* 16 (1865): 733.

[47]John Morton Blum, *Yesterday's Children* (Boston: Houghton Mifflin, 1959), pp. xiii-xxiii.

[48]Tryon, *Parnassus Corner,* p. 290.

[49]Lucy Larcom, *A New England Girlhood,* ed. Charles T. Davis (1889; reprint ed., New York: Corinth, 1961); "Lucy Larcom," *Dictionary of American Biography,* X: 614.

[50]Larcom, *A New England Girlhood,* p. 246.

[51]Ibid., p. 209.

[52]Ibid., p. 13.

[53]Ibid., pp. 208-9.

[54]Trowbridge, *My Own Story,* pp. 9-15. See also *Dictionary of American Biography,* XVIII: 655-56, and "Some Recollections of My Boyhood," *Youth's Companion* 61 (October 4, 1888): 477-78.

[55]Trowbridge, *My Own Story,* pp. 26-30, 338. Of his encounter with Emerson's work, he recalled that "it was more like the old-time religious conversion or change of heart than anything I had ever before experienced. . . . [The essays] inspired me with self-trust; they reinforced my perceptions, and opened new vistas of ideas. . . . They caused me to make vows to truth, to purity, to poverty. . . ," p. 339.

[56]Ibid., pp. 32-99, 132.

[57]Ibid., pp. 135-36, 158, 192-96.

[58]Ibid., pp. 233-55.

[59]Quoted in Kilgour, *Lee and Shepard,* p. 226.

[60]Madison, *Book Publishing in America,* p. 143.

[61]Mott refers to Holland as the most successful editor of the period 1865-1885. Mott, *A History of American Magazines,* III: 23.

[62]Madison, *Book Publishing in America,* pp. 89-90; Samuel C. Chew, ed., *Fruit Among the Leaves* (New York: Appleton, 1950), pp. 68-79.

[63]Jordan, *From Rollo to Tom Sawyer,* pp. 132-41; William Webster Ellsworth, *A Golden Age of Authors* (Boston: Houghton Mifflin, 1919), pp. 88-99; Lyon, "A History of Children's Secular Magazines," pp. 296-98, 318; Chew, *Fruit Among the Leaves,* p. 132.

[64]"Mary Mapes Dodge," *Dictionary of American Biography,* V: 351.

[65]Ellsworth, *A Golden Age of Authors,* p. 89; Chew, *Fruit Among the Leaves,* pp. 136-38; Jordan, *From Rollo to Tom Sawyer,* pp. 133-35.

[66]Edward Everett Hale, "An American Publisher," *Lend a Hand* 9 (1892): 261.

[67]Lyon, "A History of Children's Secular Magazines," p. 238; Mott, *A History of American Magazines,* III: 508-9.

[68]Hale, "An American Publisher," 254.

[69]Ibid., p. 263.

[70]Ibid., p. 258. Hale's own moralism found expression in four terse rules: "Look up and not down, look out and not in, look forward and not back, and lend a hand." Quoted in Sangster, *From My Youth Up,* p. 284.

[71]"Daniel Lothrop," *Dictionary of American Biography,* XI: 423-24.

[72]Lyon, "A History of Children's Secular Magazines," pp. 302-4.

[73]Budd Leslie Gambee, Jr. *Frank Leslie and His Illustrated Newspaper, 1855-1860* (Ann Arbor: University of Michigan Press, 1964), pp. 1-16.

[74]Ibid., pp. 15-24. See also Madeline Stern, *Purple Passage: The Life of Mrs. Frank Leslie* (Norman: University of Oklahoma Press, 1953).

Chapter 2

[1]See, for example, Fr. Ronald Knox, "Introduction," in *The Best*

Detective Stories of the Year: 1928 (London: Faber & Gwyer, 1929), pp. vii-xxiii, and Marie F. Rodell, *Mystery Fiction: Theory and Practice* (New York: Duell, Sloan and Pearce, 1943).

[2] Ray Stannard Baker, *American Chronicle* (New York: Scribner's, 1945), pp. 69-70.

[3] Ibid. See also [The editors of *The Youth's Companion*], "Editorial Talks with Contributors," *The Writer* 9 (1896): 143-45.

[4] R. Richard Wohl, "The 'Rags to Riches Story': An Episode of Secular Idealism," Seymour M. Lipset and Reinhard Bendix, eds., *Class, Status and Power* (Glencoe, Ill.: Free Press, 1953), pp. 388-95; John Cawelti, "From Rags to Respectability: Horatio Alger," in *Apostles of the Self-Made Man* (Chicago: University of Chicago Press, 1965), pp. 101-24; Michael Zuckerman, "The Nursery Tales of Horatio Alger," *American Quarterly* 24 (1972): 191-209.

[5] John Cawelti, "The Concept of Formula in the Study of Popular Culture," *Journal of Popular Culture* 3 (1969): 381-90. A somewhat expanded discussion of the formula concept, together with an analysis of the western formula, is available in Cawelti's *Six-Gun Mystique* (Bowling Green, Ohio: The Popular Press, 1970).

[6] Cawelti, "The Concept of Formula," p. 388. The concept of formula serves, first, as a rudimentary theory. It defines the elements appropriate for analysis and in this respect is conventionally literary in emphasis. The elements Cawelti identifies as significant are the familiar ones of setting, character, conflict, and resolution. Meaning is seen to be a function of the relationships, first, among the elements of a given work (thus preserving the structural integrity of that work) and, secondly, a function of a marked similarity between works. The concept of formula is also regarded as having explanatory significance. The popularity of certain formulas may be accounted for in terms of the social functions they perform. Given the scarcity of audience data, these functions remain speculative, especially since the content of the formulas admits of various plausible functional interpretations. Consequently, I have confined my discussion of function to the producers of children's fiction, on the assumption that the stories constitute better evidence for authorial than for audience behavior.

[7] Baker remarks in his autobiography that he had little diffi-

culty in adjusting to the limitations of the formula and soon felt quite free in them.

[8]The sociological literature on effect is summarized in J. T. Klapper, *The Effects of Mass Communication* (New York: Free Press, 1960) and in Wilbur Schramm and Donald Roberts, eds., *The Process and Effects of Mass Communication,* rev. ed. (Champaign: University of Illinois Press, 1971). See also: Warren Breed, "Mass Communication and Sociocultural Integration," in Lewis Dexter and David Manning White, eds., *People, Society and Mass Communications* (Glencoe, Ill.: Free Press, 1964), pp. 183-200.

[9]Peter Berger and Thomas Luckmann, *The Social Construction of Reality* (Garden City, N.Y.: Doubleday, 1966); Hugh D. Duncan, *Symbols in Society* (New York: Oxford University Press, 1968); Erving Goffman, *The Presentation of Self in Everyday Life* (New York: Anchor Books, 1959). The inherent instability of any given society reflects in large measure the principal given qualities of human life. Human behavior, compared with that of other animal species, appears to be relatively unstructured by biologically based imperatives. What serves man in place of instinct is culture.

[10]Berger and Luckmann, *The Social Construction of Reality,* pp. 129-84.

[11]Arnold van Gennep, *Rites of Passage,* trans. Monika B. Vizedon and Gabrielle L. Caffee (Chicago: University of Chicago Press, 1960). Bernard Wishy, in *The Child and the Republic* (Philadelphia: University of Pennsylvania Press, 1968), suggests a different analysis of late nineteenth-century children's fiction, noting the recurrence of three child types: the lovable, erring child; the pure child who is rejected by a corrupt world; and the child redeemer.

[12]Susan Archer Weiss, "Nellie in the Light-house," *SN* 4 (1877): 577-80.

[13]Louisa May Alcott, "Bonfires," *YC* 46 (January 9, 1873): 10.

[14]Margaret Bertha Wright, "Charlie's First Doughnut," *WA* 15 (1882): 295-99.

[15]Ibid., p. 298.

[16]"Vieux Moustache" [pseud. Clarence Gordon], "Charley Balch's Metamorphosis," *RM* 1 (1867): 106-12.

[17]Ibid., p. 110.

[18]Richard L. Rapson, "The American Child as Seen by British Travelers, 1845-1935," *American Quarterly* 17 (1965): 520-35.

[19]G. Hamlen, "When Book Meets Book," *WA* 23 (1886): 206-10.

[20]Ibid., p. 209.

[21]Mary Barker French, "Jenny, the 'Flying Fairy,' "*YC* 61 (August 30, 1888): 413-14.

[22]Marie B. Williams, "The Fatal Fire-hunt," *YC* 49 (February 3, 1876): 35-36.

[23]Rebecca Harding Davis, "Naylor o' the Bowl," *SN* 1 (1873): 65-69.

[24]"The Magician," *Frank Leslie's Boys' and Girls' Weekly* 3 (November 9, 1867): 21-22.

[25]Ibid., p. 21.

[26]Wohl, "The 'Rags to Riches Story,' " p. 390.

[27]Robert Wiebe, *The Search for Order, 1877-1920* (New York: Hill and Wang, 1967).

[28]Frederick Elkin, *The Child and Society* (New York: Random House, 1960), pp. 3-44. Cf. Berger and Luckmann, *The Social Construction of Reality*, pp. 129-84.

[29]Elkin, *The Child and Society*, p. 19.

[30]Ibid., p. 33.

[31]See, for example: Mrs. A. M. Diaz, "Jimmy's Dream," *YC* 49 (June 1, 1876): 174; S. S. Colt, "The Land of Short Memories," *SN* 7 (1880): 217-18; Walter Babbett, "How Conrad Lost His School-Books," *SN* 13 (1886): 514-17.

[32]Rose Terry, "Isabella," *OYF* 7 (1871): 346.

Chapter 3 [Portions of this chapter appeared in R. Gordon Kelly, "Literature and the Historian," *American Quarterly* 26, No. 2 (May 1974): 141-159. Copyright 1974, Trustees of the University of Pennsylvania.]

[1]Samuel Osgood, "Books for Our Children," *Atlantic Monthly* 16 (1865): 724.

[2]Ibid., pp. 730, 727.

[3]Josiah Gilbert Holland, "Fashion," in *Complete Works* (New York: Scribner's, 1897-1911), VIII: 142.

[4]See, for example, Louise Chandler Moulton, "My Little Gentleman," *YC* 46 (January 2, 1873): 1-2. Howard Mumford Jones and Richard Ludwig, in their *Guide to American Literature and Its Backgrounds Since 1890*, 3d. ed. (Cambridge: Harvard University Press, 1964), remark that much late nineteenth-century children's literature "was written within the Genteel Tradition in

the sense that the ethical and religious prepossessions of the cultural group were made the canons by which childhood was judged" (p. 133).

⁵Stow Persons, "The Origins of the Gentry," in Robert Bremner, ed., *Essays on History and Literature* (Columbus: Ohio State University Press, 1966), pp. 83-119; and *The Decline of American Gentility* (New York: Columbia University Press, 1973), which appeared as this book was going to press. Cf. Howard Mumford Jones, "The Genteel Tradition," *Harvard Library Bulletin* 18 (1970): 5-20, and John Tomsich, *A Genteel Endeavor: American Culture and Politics in the Gilded Age* (Stanford, Calif.: Stanford University Press, 1971).

⁶Quoted in Persons, "The Origins of the Gentry," p. 87.

⁷Ralph Waldo Emerson, "Manners," in *The Works of Ralph Waldo Emerson* (Boston; Houghton Mifflin, 1893-99), III: 120.

⁸Sarah N. Randolph, *The Domestic Life of Thomas Jefferson* (Cambridge: Harvard University Press, 1939), pp. 314-15, quoted in Edwin Cady, *The Gentleman in America* (Syracuse, N.Y.: Syracuse University Press, 1949), p. 91.

⁹Louis B. Wright, *The First Gentlemen of Virginia* (1940; reprint ed., Charlottesville, Va.: Dominion Books, 1964), pp. 6-9; Cady, *The Gentleman in America,* pp. 6-9.

¹⁰Wright, *The First Gentlemen of Virginia,* pp. 57-84.

¹¹Cady, *The Gentleman in America,* p. 17.

¹²Ibid.; Persons, "The Origin of the Gentry," pp. 93-95.

¹³This point is implicit in Persons, "The Origins of the Gentry," p. 94, and explicit in *The Decline of American Gentility.* The concept of functional elites used here is adopted from Suzanne Keller's study *Beyond the Ruling Class* (New York: Random House, 1963). In Professor Keller's view, elites are best defined as "effective and responsible minorities," which are functionally discriminated. These groups are "ultimately responsible for the realization of major social goals and for the continuity of the social order." Functionally defined strategic elites may be distinguished from a ruling class. Traditionally comprised of groups of families, the ruling class is better able to control access to the positions they hold and to convey those positions to their children than are members of functional elites.

Strategic elites contribute to social continuity by assuming responsibility for translating the functional prescriptions contained

in accepted social values "into workable rules." Two broadly
defined elite groups can be distinguished. One group is primarily
concerned with "the achievements of economic growth, political
stability, or scientific advance." A second group, the "integrative
elite," is primarily responsible for moral guidance and reassurance, for reaffirming and justifying adherence to certain values
believed essential to the social order, and for resolving tensions
that are inherent in the precariousness of social order and in the
inevitable frustration of individual desire. Each elite has a style of
expected behavior considered appropriate to and expressive of
its function, organization, and efficacy. Its life-styles may serve as
models for emulation, as ways of life that can focus, sustain, and
fulfill individual desire.

Under conditions of modern industrial society in which functionally discriminated elites have proliferated, there is inevitably
competition between them. At one level, it is a matter of competing for personnel. At another, it is a competition between styles of
organizing human activity that objectify different moral assumptions and expectations. This is precisely the situation which many
late nineteenth-century children's authors thought themselves to
be facing. Competing assumptions about moral order, desirable
character traits, the function of reading, and the bases of success
embodied in other forms of children's literature—popular story
papers or series novels, for example—appeared to make a mock-
ery of such presumed verities as the necessity for hard work and
self-control.

14"The Political Decline of the Perfect Gentleman," *The Nation*
5 (August 22, 1867): 153-54.

15Ibid., p. 154. Of the need for Christian gentlemen in politics,
see also Josiah Gilbert Holland, "The Gentleman in Politics," in
Works, X: 326-30.

16Persons, "The Origins of the Gentry," pp. 88-92.

17Dixon Wecter, *Saga of American Society* (New York: Scribner's,
1941), pp. 5-9, distinguishes this social group from an "aristocracy" as well as from a "plutocracy."

18Ibid., pp. 386-427.

19Persons, "The Origins of the Gentry," pp. 103-6. One of the
most impressive statements of this blending of democratic social
theory with the ideal of the gentleman is Jefferson's plan for
identifying and nurturing, through a sequence of publicly sup-

ported schools, the natural *aristoi*, whose function was to govern but who might appear in any social strata. See Cady, *The Gentleman in America*, pp. 85-102.

[20]"Accomplished Gentlemen: Points as to California Education," *Overland Monthly*, n.s. 6 (1885): 206-9.

[21]George Henry Calvert, *The Gentleman* (Boston: Ticknor and Fields, 1863). Cf. Emerson's essay "Manners" in *Works*, III: 115-50.

[22]Cady, *The Gentleman in America*, p. 158.

[23]Calvert, *The Gentleman*, pp. 133, 152, 156.

[24]George Frisbie Hoar, *Autobiography of Seventy Years* (London: Bickers and Son, 1904), I: 90-91.

[25]E. L. Godkin, "Chromo Civilization," in *Reflections and Comments, 1865-1895* (New York: Scribner's, 1895), pp. 202-3.

[26]Ibid., pp. 203-4.

[27]Edward Everett Hale, "An American Publisher," *Lend A Hand* 9 (1892): 263.

[28]The problems of competition, noted in the text, are discussed in the essay "Accomplished Gentlemen," *passim*.

[29]E. A. Ross, *Social Control* (New York: Macmillan, 1901), p. 228. More recently, Kenneth Boulding has suggested that the images organizing subcultures are frequently summarized in the form of ideal types of personality. *The Image* (Ann Arbor: University of Michigan Press, 1956), pp. 143-44. Cf. Keller, *Beyond the Ruling Class*, pp. 153-57.

[30]John Townsend Trowbridge, *My Own Story* (Boston: Houghton Mifflin, 1903), p. 388.

[31]Ross, *Social Control*, pp. 358-63.

[32]Roswell-Smith, "The Boy Who Worked," *SN* 1 (1874): 149.

[33]Calvert, *The Gentleman*, pp. 151-53.

[34]Lucy Larcom, *A New England Girlhood*, ed. Charles T. Davis (1889; reprint ed., New York: Corinth, 1961), p. 225.

[35]Ibid., p. 201.

[36]Calvert, *The Gentleman*, pp. 129-30. See also Josiah Gilbert Holland's lecture "Fashion" in *Works*, VIII: 138-67. Emerson's essay "Manners" hinges on the distinction between fashion and the qualities of the true gentleman.

[37]"The Best of a Bad Bargain," *YC* 46 (January 2, 1873): 2.

[38]"The Flirt," *YC* 49 (July 6, 1876): 215.

[39]See, for example, "Sharp Work," *YC* 46 (January 9, 1873): 11.

[40]For an analysis of the competing styles of manners, see Arthur M. Schlesinger, *Learning How to Behave* (New York: Macmillan, 1946).

[41]John Trowbridge, "His Own Master," *SN* 4 (1876): 594.

[42]Ibid., p. 336.

[43]P. Tucker, "Jim," *YC* 52 (August 7, 1879): 261-62.

[44]Trowbridge used the character again in a series for *Our Young Folks*: "Half-hours with Father Brighthopes," *OYF* 1 (1865): 534-39.

[45]See, for example, Martha M. Thomas, "A Night's Adventure on the Ohio River," *OYF* 7 (1871): 523-28.

[46]It is worth noting that, of the twenty-six titles in the *Youth's Companion Library* series available in 1899, seven are collections of stories emphasizing desirable character traits. Of these, five are concerned primarily with courage, one with kindness, and one with student life. Other titles in the series are devoted to travel and to natural history exclusively.

[47]Irvin Wyllie, *The Self-made Man in America* (1954; reprint ed., New York: Free Press, 1966), p. 54.

[48]M. R. Housekeeper, "An Inconsiderate Act," *YC* 61 (September 6, 1888): 421-22.

[49]For this aspect of Alger, see John Cawelti, *Apostles of the Self-made Man* (Chicago: University of Chicago Press, 1965), pp. 101-24.

[50]Louise Chandler Moulton, "Coals of Fire," *OYF* 4 (1868): 551-56.

[51]W. Lloyd Warner, *American Life: Dream and Reality*, rev. ed. (Chicago: University of Chicago Press, 1962), p. 108.

[52]Calvert, *The Gentleman*, p. 157.

[53]Louisa May Alcott, "Jack and Jill," *SN* 7 (1879): 387.

[54]Abby Morton Diaz, "Little Dilly; or the Uses of Tears," *OYF* 4 (1868): 600-608.

[55]Rev. J. Lambdin Harris, "Charley and His Master," *WA* 6 (1878): 172-73.

[56]Rose Terry Cooke, "The Wrong Coat," *SN* 10 (1883): 324-27.

[57]Edgar Fawcett, "Belle Langley's Punishment," *WA* 2 (1876): 280-85.

[58]Julia A. Eastman, "Her Little Life," *WA* 7 (1878): 179.

[59]Ibid., p. 180.

[60]Calvert, *The Gentleman*, p. 151.

[61]J. D. C., "What Came of Making Pickles," *YC* 46 (November 6, 1873): 361; Ella Farman, "The Doll Mission," *WA* 2 (1876): 323-26; Ella Farman, "Kitty's Happy Thought," *WA* 6 (1878): 55-59; Marie B. Williams, "A Golden Rose," *YC* 58 (September 3, 1885): 345-46; Ruth Chesterfield, "Buttons," *YC* 49 (December 7, 1876): 414.

[62]Mary Hartwell Catherwood, "The Assistant," *WA* 15 (1882): 12-18.

[63]Ibid., p. 15.

[64]Charles Barnard, "A Fable for Boys," *SN* 10 (1883): 486-88.

[65]Frank Stockton, "What Might Have Been Expected," *SN* 1 (1873): 24-28.

[66]Lily F. Wesselhoeft, "Milly Brewster's Pride," *YC* 61 (March 22, 1888): 151. Cf. Samuel Osgood, "Books for Our Children," p. 731.

[67]Louisa May Alcott, "Bonfires," *YC* 46 (January 9, 1873): 10.

[68]Louise Chandler Moulton, "Against Wind and Tide," *YC* 46 (September 4, 1873): 282-83.

[69]Ibid., p. 283.

[70]Smith, "The Boy Who Worked," p. 148.

[71]*OYF* 7 (1871): 61.

[72]Ibid., p. 316-17.

[73]John H. Young, *Our Deportment* (Chicago: Union Publishing, 1881), p. 18.

Chapter 4

[1]Philippe Ariès, *Centuries of Childhood*, trans. Robert Baldick (New York: Vintage Books, 1962), pp. 128-32.

[2]Ibid., pp. 329, 411-13.

[3]Monica Kiefer, *American Children Through Their Books, 1700-1835* (Philadelphia: University of Pennsylvania Press, 1948). See also Alice M. Earle, *Child-Life in Colonial Days* (New York: Macmillan, 1899). The anti-Puritanism characteristic of histories of children's literature is discussed in my review essay "American Children's Literature: An Historiographical Review," *American Literary Realism, 1870-1910* 6 (1973): 89-108.

[4]Edmund Morgan, *The Puritan Family*, rev. ed. (New York: Harper and Row, 1966), p. 108.

⁵Ibid., pp. 92-94, 104-5.

⁶Conrad Wright, *The Beginnings of Unitarianism in America* (1955; reprint ed., Boston: Beacon Press, 1966), pp. 85-87.

⁷Bernard Wishy, *The Child and the Republic* (Philadelphia: University of Pennsylvania Press, 1968), p. 22.

⁸Ibid., pp. 1-5.

⁹Max Lerner, *America as a Civilization* (New York: Simon, 1957), p. 562.

¹⁰Wishy, *The Child and the Republic* pp. 27-28. See also Anne L. Kuhn, *The Mother's Role in Childhood Education* (New Haven: Yale University Press, 1947) and William E. Bridges, "Warm Heart, Cold World: Social Perspectives on the Household Poets," *American Quarterly* 21 (1969): 764-79.

¹¹The remark is Stephen H. Taft's, quoted in Fred A. Taft, *An Empire Builder of the Middle West* (Los Angeles: Parker, Stone and Baird, 1929), p. 19.

¹²Susan Archer Weiss, "Nellie in the Light-house," *SN* 4 (1877): 577-80. Bridges, "Warm Heart, Cold World," discusses the pervasive imagery in popular poetry of the memory of the mother as a guide to behavior.

¹³Sunley, "Early Nineteenth Century American Literature on Child Rearing," pp. 156-57, 159-61.

¹⁴Wishy, *The Child and the Republic,* pp. 42-49.

¹⁵Ibid., pp. 35-38.

¹⁶Ibid., pp. 24-25.

¹⁷Alexis de Tocqueville, *Democracy in America,* the Henry Reeve text, revised by Francis Bowen and further corrected and edited by Phillips Bradley (New York: Vintage Books, 1945), II: 62.

¹⁸Ibid., pp. 62-63.

¹⁹Wishy, *The Child and the Republic,* pp. 54-57.

²⁰Lucy Larcom, *A New England Girlhood,* ed. Charles T. Davis (1889; reprint ed., New York: Corinth, 1961), p. 78.

²¹Ibid., pp. 105-6.

²²Margaret Sangster, *From My Youth Up* (New York: Fleming H. Revell, 1909), p. 82.

²³James T. Fields, *Biographical Notes and Personal Sketches* (London: Samson Low, 1881), pp. 223-25.

²⁴William Graham Sumner, "What Our Boys Are Reading," *Scribner's Monthly* 15 (1878): 681-85.

²⁵Ibid., p. 685. See also W. H. Bishop, "Story-Paper Litera-

ture," *Atlantic Monthly* 44 (1879): 383-93; "Literature for Boys," *Scribner's Monthly* 7 (1874): 370-71; Amanda B. Harris, "The Kind of Books That Children Should Not Read," *The Christian Union* 36 (October 6, 1887): 325.

[26]Anthony Comstock, *Traps for the Young,* ed. Robert Bremner (1883; reprint ed., Cambridge, Mass.: Belknap Press, 1967), p. 25.

[27]Ibid., p. 34.

[28]"Books for Children of All Ages," *Nation* 5 (December 26, 1867), 524.

[29]Raymond L. Kilgour, *Lee and Shepard: Publishers for the People* (Hamden, Conn.: Shoe String Press, 1965), pp. 155, 164. Miss Alcott's aversion to "optical delusions" may be examined in "Eight Cousins," *SN* 2 (1875): 616-17. For Optic's reply, see *Oliver Optic's Magazine* 18 (1875): 717-18.

[30]George B. Bacon, "The Literature of Our Sunday-Schools," *Hours at Home* 10 (1870): 455.

[31]Ibid., p. 457.

[32]Ibid., p. 458.

[33]John Townsend Trowbridge, *My Own Story* (Boston: Houghton Mifflin, 1903), p. 330.

[34]"The Ladies' Commission," *Old and New* 4 (1871): 626-29; "The Ladies' Commission on Sunday School Books," *Old and New* 1 (1870): 709-12; "Literature for the Young," *Unitarian Review* 1 (1874): 354-59.

[35]Caroline Hewins, *Books for the Young* (New York: Leypoldt, 1882), pp. 3-4.

[36]Martha E. Brooks, "Sunday School Libraries," *Library Journal* 4 (1879): 341.

[37]The collected papers at this meeting were published in *Library Journal* 4 (1879). See also: Esther Carrier, *Fiction in Public Libraries, 1876-1900* (New York: Scarecrow, 1965).

[38]James Freeman Clarke, "Address," *Library Journal* 4 (1879): 356. See also "Address by Mellen Chamberlain," 4 (1879): 362.

[39]Chamberlain, "Address," p. 363.

[40]Ibid., p. 364.

[41]S. S. Green, "Sensational Fiction in Public Libraries," *Library Journal* 4 (1879): 351.

[42]Ibid., pp. 348-49.

[43]Kate Gannett Wells, "Responsibility of Parents in the Selec-

tion of Reading for the Young," *Library Journal* 4 (1879): 329.

[44]Thomas Wentworth Higginson, "Address," *Library Journal* 4 (1879): 357.

[45]Ibid., p. 358.

[46][Mary Mapes Dodge], "Children's Magazines," *Scribner's Monthly* 6 (1873): 352-54.

[47]Higginson, "Address," p. 359.

[48][Dodge], "Children's Magazines," p. 353.

[49]Ibid., p. 354. In a similar vein, Edward Everett Hale wrote: "Let your moral come in by the way. Virtue is one of the things which is caught by contagion. Never fear for your boy and girl if the people they read about show the glory of a true life, and show the failure of a false one. You need not explain to them why this is so." "On Writing for Children," *The Critic* 5 (December 6, 1884): 266. Didacticism did not disappear, of course; it only seems less obtrusive because it is framed in contemporaneously acceptable forms and values. It was impossible for American writers and others with a concern for socialization to ignore the moral assumptions implicit in books for children. For an analysis of the perennially fresh didactic spirit in American children's literature, see John Rowe Townsend, "Didacticism in Modern Dress," in Sheila Egoff, L. F. Ashley, and G. T. Stubbs, eds., *Only Connect* (Toronto: Oxford University Press, 1969), pp. 33-40.

[50]Louisa May Alcott, "Jack and Jill," *SN* 7 (1879): 775.

[51]Harriet Beecher Stowe, "Pussy and Emily Mature," *OYF* 4 (1868): 464.

[52]Samuel Osgood, "Books for Our Children," *Atlantic Monthly* 16 (1865): 720-35. George Orwell, "Boys' Weeklies," in *Dickens, Dali and Others* (New York: Reynal and Hitchcock, 1946), pp. 76-114.

[53]Howard Mumford Jones, *The Theory of American Literature*, rev. ed. (Ithaca, N.Y.: Cornell University Press, 1965), p. ix.

[54]Edmund Kirke, "The Little Prisoner," *OYF* 1(1865): 32-37.

[55]Ibid., pp. 464-65.

[56]John Townsend Trowbridge, "His Own Master," *SN* 4, p. 594.

[57]"Ran Away," *YC* 46 (October 2, 1873): 314-15. See also Frank Converse, "Going to Sea—A Talk with Boys," *SN* 9 (1882): 292-95.

[58]Rufus Sargent, "Dandy Lyon's Visit to New York," *YC* 46 (June 5, 1873): 178.

[59]Bacon, "The Literature of Our Sunday-Schools, p. 458.

[60]Hewins, *Books for the Young,* pp. 3-4

[61]Rufus Seward, "Number Fifteen," *YC* 46 (March 6, 1873): 73-74; Louise Chandler Moulton, "My Little Gentleman," *YC* 46 (January 2, 1873): 1-2; Martha M. Thomas, "Snowed In," *SN* 1 (1874): 257-61.

[62]"Jack's Treadle," *YC* 46 (April 3, 1873): 104, 112-13.

[63]Horace Scudder, *Childhood in Literature and Art* (Boston: Houghton Mifflin, 1900), 234-40.

[64][Dodge], "Children's Magazines," p. 354.

[65]Green, "Sensational Fiction in Public Libraries," p. 346.

[66]Mary A. Denison, "A Plea for Purity in Literature," *The Writer* 9 (1896): 47.

[67]Wells, "Responsibility of Parents," p. 327.

[68]Harris, "The Kind of Books That Children Should Not Read," p. 325.

[69]Hewins, *Books for the Young,* p. 4.

[70]Kate Douglas Wiggin, "What Shall Children Read?" *Cosmopolitan* 7 (1889): 357. "It is in remembering what books greatly moved us in earlier days; what books wakened strong and healthy desires, enlarged the horizon of our understanding, and inspired us to generous action, that we get some clew to the books with which to surround our children; and a reminiscence of this kind becomes a sort of psychological observation."

[71]Caroline Hewins, *A Mid-century Child and Her Books* (New York: Macmillan, 1926).

[72]Osgood, "Books for Our Children," p. 726.

[73]Ibid., p. 728.

[74]Ibid., p. 730.

[75]Ibid.

[76]Ibid., p. 732.

[77]"Children's Books of the Year," *North American Review* 102 (1866): 236-49.

[78]"Editorial Talks with Contributors," *The Writer* 9 (1896): 144.

[79]Ibid.

[80]P. Tucker, "Jim," *YC* 52 (August 7, 1879): 261-62.

[81]John Townsend Trowbridge, "Half-hours with Father Brighthopes," *OYF* 1 (1865): 586-91.

82Harriet Beecher Stowe, "Pussy and Emily Mature," p. 462.
83Clara F. Guernsey, "Fayette's Ride," *WA* 1 (1875): 150.
84Louisa May Alcott, "Jack and Jill," p. 934.
85Ibid., p. 700.
86Jean Ingelow, "Vale of Childhood," *WA* 1 (1875): 165.

Chapter 5

1"Editorial Talks with Contributors," *The Writer* 9 (1896): 144.
2Ibid.
3Ibid.
4Ibid., p. 145.
5"Urbanism as a Way of Life," in Albert J. Reiss, Jr., ed., *Louis Wirth on Cities and Social Life* (Chicago: University of Chicago Press, 1964), p. 66.
6Hostility toward the city, of course, has a long history in American thought. See Morton and Lucia White, *The Intellectual Versus the City* (Cambridge: Harvard University Press, 1962). Aversion to the city was neither unusual nor peculiarly American in the late nineteenth century; see Robert Nisbet, *The Sociological Tradition* (New York: Basic Books, 1966), 47-106.
7Rufus Sargent, "Dandy Lyon's Visit to New York," *YC* 46 (June 5, 1873): 177-78.
8Loren Eiseley, *The Unexpected Universe* (New York: Harcourt, Brace & World, 1969), p. 73.
9René Dubos, *So Human an Animal* (New York: Scribner's, 1968), p. 79.
10Ibid., p. 98.
11Ibid., p. 105.
12Ibid., p. 159.
13Ibid., p. 141.
14Carl N. Degler, *Out of Our Past* (New York: Harper, 1962), pp. 314-19. Paul Johnstone, "Old Ideals versus New Ideas in Farm Life," *The Yearbook of Agriculture: 1940* (Washington, D.C.: Government Printing Office), pp. 139-64.
15Degler, *Out of Our Past*, pp. 314-19.
16Johnstone, "Old Ideals," p. 139.
17John Hay, *In Defense of Nature* (Boston: Atlântic-Little, Brown, 1969), p. 27.

[18]Celia Thaxter, "Child-life at the Isle of Shoals," *Atlantic Monthly* 31 (1873): 532-39; Rebecca Harding Davis, *Bits of Gossip* (Boston: Houghton Mifflin, 1904); Margaret E. Sangster, *From My Youth Up* (New York: Fleming H. Revell, 1909). Miss Sangster's idea of "childhood in ideal conditions" may be glimpsed in the diary of Caroline Cowles Richards, *Village Life in America, 1852-1872* (New York: Holt, 1912), to which she contributed an introduction.

[19]Davis, *Bits of Gossip,* p. 102.

[20]Sangster, *From My Youth Up,* p. 71.

[21]John Albee, *Confessions of Boyhood* (Boston: Richard G. Badger, 1910), p. 26.

[22]Edward Everett Hale, "Social Forces in the United States," *North American Review* 137 (1883): 407.

[23]Walter B. Platt, "Injurious Influences of City Life," *Popular Science Monthly* 33 (1888): 484-89.

[24]Quoted in Stow Persons, "The Origins of the Gentry," in Robert Bremner, ed., *Esssays in History and Literature* (Columbus: Ohio State University Press, 1966), pp. 107-8.

[25]Davis, *Bits of Gossip,* p. 49.

[26]G. Stanley Hall, "The Contents of Children's Minds," *Princeton Review,* 3d ser., II (1883): 255.

[27]Mary E. Bradley, "Mrs. Pomeroy's Page," *SN* 1 (1874): 341-43.

[28]Charles Kellogg, "Child Life in City and Country," *Journal of Social Science* 21 (1886): 209-14.

[29]Charles L. Brace, "Wolf-reared Children," *SN* 9 (1882): 543-44.

[30]Samuel Dike, "Problems of the Family," *The Century Magazine* 39 (1890), 385-95. See also Washington Gladden, "Three Dangers," *The Century Magazine* 28 (1884): 620-27.

[31]Dike, "Problems of the Family," p. 394.

[32]Charles A. Ellwood, *Sociology and Modern Social Problems,* rev. ed. (New York: American Book, 1924), pp. 147-50.

[33]Ibid., pp. 82-85, 89-90, 160.

[34]Willystine Goodsell, *A History of the Family as a Social and Educational Institution* (New York: Macmillan, 1915), p. 468.

[35]Arthur M. Schlesinger, *The Rise of the City, 1878-1898* (New York: Macmillan, 1933), pp. 128-30, See also Platt, "Injurious Influences of City Life, pp. 484-89."

[36]Davis, *Bits of Gossip,* p. 99.

[37]Rufus Sargent, "Billy's Fifteen Dollars," *YC* 46 (December 4, 1873): 393-94; Edgar Fawcett, "Belle Langley's Punishment," *WA* 2 (1876): 280-85; "Margaret," *YC* 46 (April 3, 1873): 106-7; Caroline A. Howard, "Cash," *OYF* 4 (1868): 45-51; L. G. M., "Pete," *SN* 1 (1874): 117-20.

[38]John Townsend Trowbridge, "Fast Friends," *SN* 1 (1874): 153-60; Lily F. Wesselhoeft, "Milly Brewster's Pride," *YC* 61 (March 22, 1888): 137-38.

[39]Wesselhoeft, "Milly Brewster's Pride," p. 218.

[40]Louisa May Alcott, "Bonfires," *YC* 46 (January 9, 1873): 10; Margaret Brenda, "Little Agnes's Adventure," *OYF* 7 (1871): 425-29; Rose Terry Cooke, "The Wrong Coat," *SN* 10 (1883): 324-27.

[41]Margaret Wright, "Charlie's First Doughnut," *WA* 15 (1882): 295-99, discussed in chapter 2.

[42]"The Pettingills," *YC* 46 (July 3, 1873): 210-11.

[43]Emily H. Miller, "Links in a Chain," *YC* 61 (June 7, 1888): 278. Mrs. Miller edited *The Little Corporal* prior to its merger with *St. Nicholas* in 1873.

[44]Mary Mapes Dodge, "The Family with Whom Everything Went Wrong," *SN* 7 (1879): 32-34.

[45]Edgar Fawcett, "A Country Cousin," *YC* 58 (May 7, 1885): 181-82.

[46]For a story in which a cultivated lady plays a similar role, see Lucy C. Lillie, "Pamela's Fortune," *WA* 23 (1886): 51-54.

[47]Harriet Beecher Stowe, "Little Pussy Willow," *OYF* 2 (1886): 549.

[48]Ibid., p. 674.

[49]Harriet Beecher Stowe, "Emily's New Resolutions," *OYF* 4 (1868): 8.

[50]Harriet Beecher Stowe, "Emily at Home Again," *OYF* 4 (1868): 243.

[51]Ibid., pp. 244-45.

[52]See also Lillie, "Pamela's Fortune."

[53]"City Life in the United States," *The Contemporary Review* 40 (1881): 713.

[54]Lucy G. Morse, "The Ash-girl," *SN* 3 (1876): 386.

[55]Harriet Prescott Spofford, "Little Rosalie," *SN* 15 (1888): 494-501.

[56]"Ran Away," *YC* 46 (October 2, 1873): 314-15; P. Tucker, "Jim," *YC* 52 (August 7, 1879): 261-62; Julia A. Eastman, "Her Little Life," *WA* 7 (1878): 176-80.

[57]Mrs. A. M. Diaz, "The Little Beggar-girl," *OYF* 3 (1867): 556-63.

[58]Caroline A. Howard, "A Modern Cinderella," *OYF* 3 (1867): 280-84.

[59]Caroline A. Howard, "Cash," *OYF* 4 (1868): 47.

[60]Louisa May Alcott, "Little Pyramus and Thisbe," *SN* 10 (1883): 803-7.

[61]"Accomplished Gentlemen," *Overland Monthly* n.s. 6 (1885): 207.

[62]Lucy Larcom, *A New England Girlhood,* ed. Charles T. Davis (1889; reprint ed., New York: Corinth, 1961), p. 188.

Chapter 6

[1]Suzanne Keller, *Beyond the Ruling Class* (New York: Random House, 1963), p. 231.

[2]Louisa May Alcott, "Jack and Jill," *SN* 7 (1879): 387.

[3]Mrs. P. P. Bonney, "Not Reliable," *YC* 40 (January 10, 1867): 1.

[4]M. A. Denison, "A True Story," *YC* 46 (January 9, 1873): 10-11.

[5]Thomas Bailey Aldrich, "Story of a Bad Boy," *OYF* 5 (1869): 1-10.

[6]Jean Ingelow, "Two Ways of Telling a Story," *OYF* 2 (1866): 41-46.

[7]Ibid., p. 46.

[8]Ibid.

[9]S. B. Thresher, "Scraping an Acquaintance," *YC* 61 (January 12, 1888): 14-15.

[10]Ibid.

[11]Arthur M. Schlesinger, *Learning How to Behave* (New York: Macmillan, 1946).

[12]Edgar Fawcett, "A Country Cousin," *YC* 58 (May 7, 1885): 181-82.

[13]Sophie May, "A Family Mystery," *OYF* 7 (1871): 278.

[14]Alcott, "Jack and Jill."

[15]Ibid., p. 775.

[16] George Henry Calvert, *The Gentleman* (Boston: Ticknor and Fields, 1863), p. 153.

[17] Alcott, "Jack and Jill," p. 855, Cf. Lucy Larcom, *A New England Girlhood*, ed. Charles T. Davis (1889; reprint ed., New York: Corinth, 1961), p. 273.

[18] Alcott, "Jack and Jill," p. 942.

[19] See Ednah D. Cheney, *Louisa May Alcott: Her Life, Letters and Journals* (Boston: Little, Brown, 1890), pp. 321-26.

[20] Arabella B. Buckley, "Settling Down in Life," *YC* 61 (May 3, 1888): 220.

[21] G. B. Bartlett, "An Entertainment Under Difficulties," *OYF* 7 (1871): 505.

[22] See J. L. Harbour, "How Ford Hall Came to be Built," in George W. Coleman, ed., *Democracy in the Making: Ford Hall and the Open Forum Movement* (Boston: Little, Brown, 1915); Rebecca Harding Davis, "Naylor o' the Bowl," *SN* 1 (1873): 65-69.

[23] Mrs. S. C. Hallowell, "Nan: The New-Fashioned Girl," *WA* 3 (1876): 21-27

[24] Ibid., p. 393.

[25] Nora Perry, "Kate Oxford's One Talent," *WA* 21 (1865): 13-17.

[26] Ibid., p. 15.

[27] James Russell Lowell, "Uncle Cobus's Story," *OYF* 3 (1867): 416.

[28] John Townsend Trowbridge, "His Own Master," *SN* 4 (1876): 81-90.

[29] Roswell-Smith, "The Boy Who Worked," *SN* 1 (1874): 147-51; "Jack's Treadle," *YC* 46 (April 3, 1873): 104, 112-13.

[30] "Jack's Treadle," p. 113.

[31] "Losing Caste," *YC* 46 (May 1, 1873): 138.

[32] J. D. C., "What Came of Making Pickles," *YC* 46 (November 6, 1873), 361.

[33] Ella Farman, "How Miss Chatty Earned a Living," *WA* 2 (1876): 151-56.

[34] Ella Farman, "Kitty's Happy Thought," *WA* 6 (1878): 55-59.

[35] Emily H. Miller, "Links in a Chain," *YC* 61 (June 7, 1888): 277-78.

[36] Ibid., p. 278.

[37] Rose Terry Cooke, "The Wrong Coat," *SN* 10 (1883): 324-27.

[38]E. Vinton Blake, "Quaker Esther's Ride," *SN* 13 (1886): 380-86.

[39]Ruth Chesterfield, "Miss Baxter's Adventure," *YC* 46 (January 2, 1873): 2-3.

[40]"The Drunkard's Vow," *YC* 49 (December 7, 1876): 413.

[41]C. S. Sleight, "A Brave Boy," *YC* 52 (July 3, 1879): 219.

[42]John Brownjohn, "Pentateuch," *YC* 52 (October 16, 1879): 342.

[43]Geoffrey H. Steere, "Changing Values in Child Socialization: A Study of United States Child Rearing Literature, 1865-1929" (Ph.D. diss., University of Pennsylvania, 1964), p. 22.

[44]See, for example, Annie T. Howells, "Frightened Eyes," *OYF* 4 (1868): 309-11, and the passage on the changing social effects of rum in Elijah Kellogg, "Good Old Times," *OYF* 3 (1867): 294.

[45]M. B. Williams, "The Drunkard's Daughter," *YC* 49 (June 1, 1876): 173-74.

[46]"The Best of a Bad Bargain," *YC* 46 (January 2, 1873): 2.

[47]Ruth Chesterfield, "What Came of It," *YC* 46 (July 3, 1873): 209-10.

Chapter 7

[1]Rowland Berthoff, "The American Social Order: A Conservative Hypothesis," *American Historical Review* 65 (1960): 507.

[2]John Morton Blum, *Yesterday's Children* (Boston: Houghton Mifflin, 1959), pp. xiii-xxiii; Berthoff, "The American Social Order," p. 510.

[3]Jane Addams, "A Modern Lear," in *The Social Thought of Jane Addams,* ed. Christopher Lasch (Indianapolis: Bobbs-Merrill, 1965), 107-23.

[4]Berthoff, "The American Social Order," pp. 510-11.

[5]George Henry Calvert, *The Gentleman* (Boston: Ticknor and Fields, 1863), p. 147.

[6]Ibid., p. 159.

[7]Louisa May Alcott, "Jack and Jill," *SN* 7 (1879): 775.

[8][Mrs. A. D. T. Whitney], "A Summer in Leslie Goldthwaite's Life," *OYF* 2 (1866): 110.

[9]John Townsend Trowbridge, "Half-hours with Father Brighthopes," *OYF* 1 (1865): 586-91.

[10]Thomas C. Cochran, *The Inner Revolution* (New York: Harper and Row, 1964).

[11][Whitney], "A Summer in Leslie Goldthwaite's Life," p. 102.

[12]Ibid., p. 658.

[13]Ibid.

[14]Peter Berger, Brigitte Berger, and Hansfried Kellner, *The Homeless Mind: Modernization and Consciousness* (New York: Random House, 1973).

[15]*Little Lord Fauntleroy* apppeared in *St. Nicholas* (1886) with illustrations by Reginald Burch. Compare the blend of New World and Old World motifs in the rewards hinted at by Mrs. Whitney at the conclusion of "A Summer in Leslie Goldthwaite's Life."

[16]Rebecca Harding Davis, *Bits of Gossip* (Boston: Houghton Mifflin, 1904), pp. 102-6.

[17]Rebecca Harding Davis, "The Enchanted Prince," *SN* 1 (1873): 18-20.

[18]Cf. Mrs. Davis's "Life in the Iron-Mills," *Atlantic Monthly* 7 (1861): 430-51.

[19]William James, "On a Certain Blindness in Human Beings," in *On Some of Life's Ideals* (New York: Holt, 1913), pp. 45-46.

[20]Donald Sheehan, *This Was Publishing: A Chronicle of the Book Trade in the Gilded Age* (Bloomington: Indiana University Press, 1952), pp. 104-21.

[21]E. A. Ross, *Social Control* (New York: Macmillan, 1901), p. 228. For an explanation of the disappearance of the gentry elite, see Stow Persons, *The Decline of American Gentility* (New York: Columbia University Press, 1973), especially Chapter VIII.

[22]Howard Mumford Jones, "The Genteel Tradition," *Harvard Library Bulletin* 18 (1970): 5.

[23]John Tomsich, *A Genteel Endeavor: American Culture and Politics in the Gilded Age* (Stanford, Calif.: Stanford University Press, 1971). The eight are: Richard Henry Stoddard, Thomas Bailey Aldrich, George Henry Boker, Bayard Taylor, George William Curtis, Charles Eliot Norton, Richard Watson Gilder, and Edmund Clarence Stedman.

[24]Henry Dwight Sedgwick, *In Praise of Gentlemen* (Boston: Little, Brown, 1935).

[25]Fred Erisman, "The Strenuous Life in Practice: The School and Sports Stories of Ralph Henry Barbour," *Rocky Mountain Social Science Journal* 7 (1970): 29-37.

[26]Cf. Montrose J. Moses, *Children's Books and Reading* (New York: Kennerly, 1907), and the historical sketch in May Hill Arbuthnot, *Children and Books* (Chicago: Scott, Foresman, 1947), which has been virtually unchanged in two subsequent major revisions of the most influential textbook in the field.

[27]Jennie D. Lindquist, "Caroline M. Hewins and Books for Children," in Siri Andrews, ed. *The Hewins Lectures, 1947-1962* (Boston: Horn Book, 1963).

[28]R. Gordon Kelly, "American Biographies for Children, 1870-1900," *American Literary Realism, 1870-1910* 6 (1973): 123-34. Towle was an editorial assistant for a time on the *Youth's Companion,* as was James Parton, one of the most prolific late nineteenth-century biographers. Brooks wrote for Daniel Lothrop. Perhaps the best biography written for children in the generation following the Civil War was Horace Scudder's life of George Washington.

Selected Bibliography

A number of sources have been useful in establishing a theoretical basis for this study, particularly a recent book in the sociology of knowledge: Peter Berger and Thomas Luckmann, *The Social Construction of Reality* (Garden City, N.Y.: Doubleday, 1966). Lewis Coser's essay "Sociology of Knowledge" in the *Encyclopedia of the Social Sciences,* ed. David L. Sills (New York: Macmillan and The Free Press, 1968) is a good historical introduction. A useful analysis of Mannheim, Scheler, and others is found in Robert K. Merton's chapter, "The Sociology of Knowledge" in *Social Theory and Social Structure* (New York: Free Press, 1968). Alexander C. Kern's "The Sociology of Knowledge in the Study of Literature," *Sewanee Review* 50 (1942): 505–514, adapts elements of Karl Mannheim's *Ideology and Utopia* (New York: Harcourt, Brace, 1936) for purposes of literary analysis. Kenneth Boulding, *The Image* (Ann Arbor: University of Michigan Press, 1956) treats knowledge from an organizational and developmental perspective.

For cultural theory, I have drawn on the following: Ward Goodenough, *Culture, Language, and Society* (Reading, Mass.: Addison-Wesley, 1972): A. I. Hallowell, *Culture and Experience* (Philadelphia: University of Pennsylvania Press, 1955); James Spradley, ed., *Culture and Cognition: Rules, Maps and Plans* (San Francisco: Chandler, 1972); Yehudi Cohen, ed. *Man in Adaptation: The Cultural Present* (Chicago: Aldine, 1968); and Anthony F. C. Wallace, *Culture and Personality,* 2d ed. (New York: Random House, 1970).

For the theoretical and methodological literature of American studies, the best collection of essays is Robert Merideth, *American Studies: Essays in Theory and Method* (Columbus, Ohio: Merrill,

211

1968). Important recent contributions to this literature include: Seymour Katz, " 'Culture' and Literature in American Studies," *American Quarterly* 20 (1968): 318-329; Leo Marx, "American Studies: Defense of an Unscientific Method," *New Literary History* 1 (1969): 75-90; and Bruce Kuklick, "Myth and Symbol in American Studies," *American Quarterly* 24 (1972): 435-450.

An excellent introduction to the sociological study of literature is Levin Schucking's neglected *The Sociology of Literary Taste,* 3d rev. ed., trans. Brian Battershaw (Chicago: University of Chicago Press, 1966). Two recent books in the field are Diana T. Laurenson and Alan Swingewood, *The Sociology of Literature* (New York: Schocken, 1972) and Tom and Elizabeth Burns, eds., *The Sociology of Literature and Drama* (Harmondsworth, Eng.: Penguin, 1973). Among American scholars, William Charvat has most successfully integrated social and economic factors with textual interpretation: *The Profession of Authorship in America, 1800-1870,* ed. Matthew Bruccoli (Columbus: Ohio State University Press, 1968).

The analysis of symbols as means of social integration is extensively developed by Hugh Duncan in *Communication and Social Order* (New York: Oxford University Press, 1962) and *Symbols in Society* (New York: Oxford University Press, 1968). Several papers of the Fourteenth Symposium of the Conference on Science, Philosophy and Religion, collected as *Symbols and Society,* ed. Lyman Bryson (New York: Harper, 1955), discuss the social functions of symbols; see, for example, Karl W. Deutsch, "Symbols of Political Community," pp. 23-54, and Alfred Schutz, "Symbol, Reality and Society," pp. 135-203. Another useful essay is Warren Breed, "Mass Communication and Sociocultural Integration," in Lewis Dexter and David Manning White, eds., *People, Society and Mass Communications* (Glencoe, Illinois: Free Press, 1964), pp. 183-200. Two impressive analyses of symbolic mediation from an anthropological perspective are James Peacock, *Rites of Modernization* (Chicago: University of Chicago Press, 1968), and Clifford Geertz, "Deep Play: Notes on the Balinese Cockfight," *Daedalus* 101 (1972): 1-38. The social symbolism of heroes, villains, and fools is analyzed by Orin E. Klapp in several books and articles; see, for example, "Heroes, Villains and Fools as Agents of Social Control," *American Sociological Review* 19 (February 1954): 56-62. John Cawelti's essay "The

Concept of Formula in the Study of Popular Literature," *Journal of Popular Culture* 3 (1969): 381-90, outlines a method appropriate to popular materials.

For general historical background, the following studies are particularly good: Robert Wiebe, *The Search for Order, 1877-1920* (New York: Hill and Wang, 1967): Samuel Hays, *The Response to Industrialism, 1885-1914* (Chicago: University of Chicago Press, 1957); Eric F. Goldman, *Rendezvous with Destiny* (New York: Knopf, 1952); Carl N. Degler, *Out of Our Past* (New York: Harper and Row, 1959); Louis Hartz, *The Liberal Tradition in America* (New York: Harcourt, Brace and World, 1955); Irvin Wyllie, *The Self-made Man in America* (New Brunswick, N.J.: Rutgers University Press, 1954); Dixon Wecter, *The Saga of American Society* (New York: Scribner's, 1937); Cleveland Amory, *The Proper Bostonians* (New York: Dutton, 1947); E. Digby Baltzell, *Philadelphia Gentlemen* (Glencoe, Ill.: Free Press, 1958); Jay Martin, *Harvests of Change* (Englewood Cliffs, N.J.: Prentice-Hall, 1967); John G. Sproat, *"The Best Men": Liberal Reformers in the Gilded Age* (New York: Oxford University Press, 1968); H. Wayne Morgan, ed. *The Gilded Age*, rev. ed. (Syracuse, N.Y.: Syracuse University Press, 1970); Howard Mumford Jones, "The Genteel Tradition," *Harvard Library Bulletin* 18 (1970): 5-20.

For a sense of the importance of the gentleman as a social type in the nineteenth century, see Stow Persons' work on this subject: "The Origins of the Gentry" in Robert Bremner, ed., *Essays on History and Literature* (Columbus: Ohio State University Press, 1966), pp. 83-119; and *The Decline of American Gentility* (New York: Columbia University Press, 1973). Although primarily a literary analysis, Edwin Cady, *The Gentleman in America* (Syracuse, N.Y.: Syracuse University Press, 1949), provides a useful study of the ideal of the gentleman in the nineteenth century. The colonial Virginia gentry are discussed by Louis B. Wright, *The First Gentlemen of Virginia* (San Marino, Calif.: Henry E. Huntington Library, 1940). The function of the gentleman as an integrative ideal is examined briefly by E. A. Ross in *Social Control* (New York: Macmillan, 1901). A representative view of the nature and social role of the gentleman is George H. Calvert, *The Gentleman* (Boston: Ticknor and Fields, 1863). The following essays by E. L. Godkin, editor of *The Nation*, also discuss the social function of the American gentleman: " 'Short-Hairs' and 'Swallow-Tails' " and

"Chromo Civilization" in *Reflections and Comments, 1865-1895* (New York: Scribner's, 1895); "The Political Decline of the 'Perfect Gentleman,' "*The Nation* 5 (August 22, 1867): 153-54; "Social Classes in the Republic," *Atlantic Monthly* 78 (1896): 721-28. The ideal of the gentleman as the basis for democratic education is examined in the anonymous essay "Accomplished Gentlemen: Points as to California Education," *Overland Monthly* n.s. 6 (1885): 206-209.

For American periodicals, the standard reference remains Frank Luther Mott, *A History of American Magazines* (Cambridge: Harvard University Press, 1938-1968), 5 vols. In addition, two unpublished doctoral dissertations contain detailed information on children's periodicals. Betty L. Lyon's "A History of Children's Secular Magazines Published in the United States from 1789-1899" (Ph.D. diss., Johns Hopkins University, 1942), contains the most complete list of periodicals and publishing data currently available. A study that emphasizes changing educational attitudes is Goldie P. Merrill, "The Development of American Secular Juvenile Magazines, A Study of the Educational Significance of Their Content" (Ph.D. diss., University of Washington, 1938).

There is a need for more work in the area of publishing history, but the following studies are informative. Printing technology is surveyed in Hellmut Lehmann-Haupt, *The Book in America*, 2d ed. (New York: Bowker, 1951). A more limited study stressing the cultural contribution of four publishing houses during the Gilded Age is Donald Sheehan, *This Was Publishing: A Chronicle of the Book Trade in the Gilded Age* (Bloomington: Indiana University Press, 1952). Raymond Kilgour, *Lee and Shepard: Publishers for the People* (Hamden, Connecticut: Shoe String Press, 1965), contains a great deal of factual information on one of the period's most important juvenile publishers. Two other studies by Kilgour also contain information on juvenile books and authors: *Messrs. Roberts Brothers: Publishers* (Ann Arbor: University of Michigan Press, 1952) and *Estes and Lauriat* (Ann Arbor: University of Michigan Press, 1957). Three other useful works are: James D. Hart, *The Popular Book* (New York: Oxford University Press, 1950); Raymond Shove, *Cheap Book Production* (Urbana: University of Illinois Library, 1938); and Frank Luther Mott, *Golden Multitudes* (New York: Macmillan, 1947). The operation and the success of the Stratemeyer syndicate, which mass-produced a number of popular juvenile series, is discussed in " 'For It Was Indeed He,' " which appeared in *Fortune* magazine in 1934 and is reproduced in Sheila Egoff, L. F. Ashley, and G. T. Stubbs, eds., *Only Connect* (Toronto: Oxord University Press, 1969).

Aside from the material in the two dissertations previously mentioned, information on the children's periodicals included in this study is scattered and fragmentary. The best introduction to *Our Young Folks* is the anthology edited by John Morton Blum, *Yesterday's Children* (Boston: Houghton Mifflin, 1959). A short essay by Alice M. Jordan, *"Our Young Folks*: Its Editors and Authors," collected in *From Rollo to Tom Sawyer* (Boston: Horn Book, 1948), has the virtue of enthusiasm if not of penetrating analysis. Considerable insight into the personalities of the magazine's two principal editors, Lucy Larcom and John Townsend Trowbridge, may be gained from the following: Daniel D. Addison, *Lucy Larcom: Life, Letters and Diary* (Boston: Houghton Mifflin, 1894); Lucy Larcom, *A New England Girlhood* (Boston: Houghton Mifflin, 1889); and John Townsend Trowbridge, *My Own Story* (Boston: Houghton Mifflin, 1903).

Horace E. Scudder is discussed by Alice M. Jordan in *From Rollo to Tom Sawyer*, noted above. A sympathetic tribute to Scudder is Alexander V. G. Allen, "Horace E. Scudder: An Appreciation," *Atlantic Monthly* 91 (1903): 549-560. Scudder's own account of the founding of the *Riverside Magazine* is contained in his memoir *Henry Oscar Houghton* (Cambridge, Mass.: Riverside Press, 1897).

St. Nicholas has attracted more attention than any other American children's magazine. Its founding is discussed in Samuel C. Chew, ed., *Fruit Among the Leaves* (New York: Appleton, 1950); by Alice M. Jordan, *From Rollo to Tom Sawyer* (Boston: Horn Book, 1948); and by William Webster Ellsworth, *A Golden Age of Authors* (Boston: Houghton Mifflin, 1919). Mrs. Dodge's editorial policies are discussed uncritically by Florence Sturges in "The *St. Nicholas* Years," in Siri Andrews, ed., *The Hewins Lectures: 1947-1962* (Boston: Horn Book, 1963), pp. 267-95. *St. Nicholas* during the era of Progressivism is examined in a recent dissertation by Fred Erisman, " 'There Was a Child Went Forth': A Study of *St. Nicholas* Magazine and Selected Children's Authors, 1890-1915" (Ph.D. diss., University of Minnesota, 1966). See his essays, "L. Frank Baum and the Progressive Dilemma," *American Quarterly* 20

(1968): 616-23, and "The Strenuous Life in Practice: The School and Sports Stories of Ralph Henry Barbour," *The Rocky Mountain Social Science Journal* 7 (1970): 29-37. Henry Steele Commager writes engagingly of *St. Nicholas* in "Super. This Must Go In! Editing the *St. Nicholas* Anthology," *Publishers' Weekly* 154 (October 30, 1948): 1874-77.

There is no adequate biography of Mary Mapes Dodge; Alice B. Howard's *Mary Mapes Dodge of "St. Nicholas"* (New York: Messner, 1943) is intended primarily for a juvenile audience although the author had access to some of Mrs. Dodge's papers. Tributes to Mrs. Dodge's work in the field of juvenile literature include: William Fayal Clarke, "In Memory of Mary Mapes Dodge," *SN* 32 (1905): 1059-71; "Mary Mapes Dodge," *The Critic* 47 (1905): 291; Sarah McEnery, "Mary Mapes Dodge—An Intimate Tribute," *The Critic* 47 (1905): 310-12; and "A Unique Figure in Juvenile Literature," *Current Literature* 39 (1905): 395.

Wide Awake is discussed briefly by Mott, *History of American Magazines,* III: 508-9. Some biographical information on its publisher is presented by Edward Everett Hale in his tribute to Daniel Lothrop: "An American Publisher," *Lend a Hand* 9 (1892): 253-68.

Somewhat more material is available on the *Youth's Companion*. Mott's sketch of the magazine in volume II of his *History of American Magazines* is useful. An anthology of materials from the periodical, including the original prospectus, has been edited by Lovell Thompson: *Youth's Companion* (Boston: Houghton Mifflin, 1954). An excessively laudatory and uncritical estimate of the *Companion* and of Daniel Sharp Ford is Louise Harris's *"None But the Best"* (Providence, R.I.: Brown University Press, 1966). Ray Stannard Baker discusses the formula for the *Companion*'s short stories in his autobiography, *American Chronicle* (New York: Scribner's, 1945). Daniel Ford's philanthropy is discussed by J. L. Harbour, "How Ford Hall Came to be Built," in George W. Coleman, ed., *Democracy in the Making: Ford Hall and the Open Forum Movement* (Boston: Little, Brown, 1915). M. A. DeWolfe Howe recalls his experiences on the *Companion* in *A Venture in Remembrance* (Boston: Little, Brown, 1941).

The lives of the editors and of those authors who wrote consistently for these magazines remain obscure, owing to the lack of biographical material already noted. A few writers left some

autobiographical material: Louisa May Alcott, "Recollections of
My Childhood," *YC* 61 (May 21, 1888): Rebecca Harding Davis,
Bits of Gossip (Boston: Houghton Mifflin, 1904); Margaret E.
Sangster, *From My Youth Up* (New York: Fleming H. Revell,
1909); Celia Thaxter, "Child-life at the Isle of Shoals," *Atlantic
Monthly* 31 (1873): 532-9. Louise Chandler Moulton has been
memorialized by Lillian Whiting in *Louise Chandler Moulton: Poet
and Friend* (Boston: Little, Brown, 1910).

The literature on children's books is enormous, but the following materials have proved informative. An indispensable, though
not exhaustive, guide is Virginia Haviland, *Children's Literature: A
Guide to Reference Sources* (Washington, D.C.: Library of Congress,
1966), an annotated bibliography. A recent supplement collects
articles published through 1969. R. Gordon Kelly's "American
Children's Literature: An Historiographical Review," *American
Literary Realism, 1870-1910* 6 (1973): 89-108, reviews the development of the history of children's literature and cites scholarly articles not listed in Haviland's bibliography. The standard
history of children's literature is Cornelia Meigs, et al., *A Critical
History of Children's Literature* (New York: Macmillan, 1953). A
recent collection of essays on various aspects of children's literature, limited primarily to articles published during the 1960s, is
Sheila Egoff, L. F. Ashley, and G. T. Stubbs, eds., *Only Connect*
(Toronto: Oxford University Press, 1969). The essays as a whole
suggest that the basic problems of writing for children in America
that were articulated in the nineteenth century are still vigorously
debated.

Several essays that appeared in the decade after the Civil War
are essential for understanding the issues facing children's authors during the period: "The Ladies' Commission on Sunday
School Books," *Old and New* 1 (1870): 709-12; "The Ladies'
Commission," *Old and New* 4 (1871): 626-9, the annual report for
that year; George Bacon, "The Literature of Our Sunday-
Schools," *Hours at Home* 10 (1870): 293-300, 450-59, 558-67. The
papers delivered at the 1879 Boston conference on fiction and
the reading of school children are collected in the *Library Journal* 4
(1879). Samuel Osgood's early essay, "Books for Our Children,"
Atlantic Monthly 16 (1865): 724-35, is an exploration of the needs
to be met by a truly democratic children's literature.

The reaction against sensational literature may be studied in

the following, of which the first two essays are particularly impor-
tant: W. H. Bishop, "Story-Paper Literature," *Atlantic Monthly* 44
(1879): 383-93; William Graham Sumner, "What Our Boys Are
Reading," *Scribner's Monthly* 15 (1878): 681-85; Amanda B. Har-
ris, "The Kind of Books That Children Should Not Read," *The
Christian Union* 36 (October 6, 1887): 325; Anthony Comstock,
"Half-dime Novels and Story Papers," in *Traps for the Young* (New
York: Funk and Wagnalls, 1883); Mary A. Bean, "The Evil of
Unlimited Freedom in the Use of Juvenile Fiction," *Library
Journal* 4 (1879): 341-3; Mary A. Denison, "A Plea for Purity in
Literature," *The Writer* 9 (1896): 46-47; Kate Douglas Wiggin,
"What Shall Children Read?" *Cosmopolitan* 7 (1889): 355-60; Sara
E. Wiltse, *The Place of the Story in Early Education* (Boston: Ginn,
1892).

   The principles of criticism used to evaluate children's literature
following the Civil War are explored in a first-rate monograph by
Richard L. Darling, *The Rise of Children's Book Reviewing in
America, 1865-1881* (New York: Bowker, 1968). Story-paper literature is placed in the context of the period's literary conventions by Mary Noel, *Villains Galore* (New York: Macmillan, 1954).
An analysis of the rise of popular literature written by and for
women during the nineteenth century is Helen Waite Papashvily,
All the Happy Endings (New York: Harper, 1956). Ms. Papashvily
has some provocative comments on the popular domestic novel as
a fictional response to male dominance.

   During the Gilded Age, several authors, editors, and librarians
recorded their own standards of what was desirable in children's
literature. The classic statement of the aims of a children's
magazine is [Mary Mapes Dodge], "Children's Magazines,"
Scribner's Monthly 6 (1873): 352-54. Caroline Hewins stated her
principles in her introduction to *Books for the Young* (New York:
Leypoldt, 1882). See also her "Literature for the Young," *Library
Journal* 7 (1882): 182-90. Miss Hewins' influence is discussed by
Jennie D. Lindquist, "Caroline M. Hewins and Books for Children," in Siri Andrews, ed., *The Hewins Lectures, 1947-1962* (Boston: Horn Book, 1963).

   Others who expressed their critical philosophies include: Edward Everett Hale, "On Writing for Children," *The Critic* 5 (December 6, 1884): 266-67; Horatio Alger, Jr. "Writing Stories for
Boys," *The Writer* 9 (1896): 4-5. The editors of the *Youth's*

Companion stated their principles in "Editorial Talks with Contributors," *The Writer* 9 (1896): 143-5.

Children's literature has been effectively used by several historians in the analysis of popular values. Two of the best essays are John Cawelti's chapter on Alger in his *Apostles of the Self-made Man* (Chicago: University of Chicago Press, 1965), and Russell B. Nye, "The Juvenile Approach to American Culture, 1870-1930," in Ray B. Brown, ed., *New Voices in American Studies* (Lafayette, Ind.: Purdue University Press, 1966). Another excellent essay is George Orwell, "Boys' Weeklies" in *Dickens, Dali and Others* (New York: Reynal and Hitchcock, 1946). Henry Steele Commager makes a useful point about the increasing separation, in this century, of authors who write for children from those who write for adults: "When Majors Wrote for Minors," *Saturday Review* 35 (May 10, 1952): 10-11. Edmund Leach discusses Jean de Brunhoff's popular Babar series from an anthropological perspective in "Babar's Civilization Analyzed" in Sheila Egoff, L. F. Ashley, and G. T. Stubbs, eds., *Only Connect.* David Riesman's analysis of a popular children's story, "Tootle: A Modern Cautionary Tale," is well worth reading in *The Lonely Crowd* (New Haven: Yale University Press, 1950). Colonial children's literature is analyzed by Monica Kiefer in *American Children Through Their Books, 1700-1835* (Philadelphia: University of Pennsylvania Press, 1948), but the study suffers from the author's assumption that literature directly mirrors social practices. An informative essay on the image of family life in German literature for children is Rhoda Metraux, "A Portrait of the Family in German Juvenile Fiction," in Margaret Mead and Martha Wolfenstein, eds., *Childhood in Contemporary Cultures* (Chicago: University of Chicago Press, 1955).

The image of the family in popular nineteenth-century verse has been examined by William E. Bridges, "The Family Circle in American Verse: The Rise and Fall of an Image" (Ph.D. diss., Brown University, 1963); see his "Warm Hearth, Cold World: Social Perspectives on the Household Poets," *American Quarterly* 21 (1969): 764-79. Children's literature as a vehicle for social reform thought is discussed by John C. Crandall, "Patriotism and Humanitarian Reform in Children's Literature, 1825-1860," *American Quarterly* 21 (1969): 3-11.

A number of recent statements about children's reading suggest that the issue of moral and cultural responsibility central to the late nineteenth-century debate over children's literature are still of concern. John Rowe Townsend traces the still-vigorous tradition of moralism in literature for children in "Didacticism in Modern Dress" in Sheila Egoff, L. F. Ashley and G. T. Stubbs, eds., *Only Connect*. One of the most influential statements of the moral function of literature for children is Paul Hazard, *Books, Children and Men*, 4th ed., trans. Marguerite Mitchell (Boston: Horn Book, 1960). The contribution made by children's literature to the process of socialization is discussed by May Arbuthnot, *Children and Books*, 3d ed., (Chicago: Scott, Foresman, 1964). An effort at clarifying critical principles appropriate to children's literature is James Steel Smith, *A Critical Approach to Children's Literature* (New York: McGraw-Hill, 1967). Some dangerous tendencies in contemporary book production for children are the subject of Jason Epstein's essay, " 'Good Bunnies Always Obey': Books for American Children," *Commentary* 35 (1963): 112-22. Other useful discussions of the relationship between children's literature and social needs include: Leland B. Jacobs, "Culture Patterns in Children's Fiction," *Childhood Education* 23 (1947): 431-4; Edward W. Rosenheim, Jr., "Children's Reading and Adults' Values," in Sara I. Fenwick, ed., *A Critical Approach to Children's Literature* (Chicago: University of Chicago Press, 1967); Jacquelyn Landers, "Psychological Significance of Children's Literature," in Fenwick, ed., *A Critical Approach to Children's Literature*; Helen R. Sattley, "Children's Books for Democratic Survival," *Elementary English* 22 (1945): 77-80, 93; Evelyn Wenzel, "Children's Literature and Personality Development," *Elementary English* 25 (1948): 12-31. One of the most engaging essays on writing for children is C. S. Lewis, "On Three Ways of Writing for Children," in Sheila Egoff, L. F. Ashley, and G. T. Stubbs, eds., *Only Connect*.

The study of childhood is inseparable from the study of family life, and I am indebted to a number of studies that bear on the problem of the American family in the late nineteenth century. A useful review of the historiography of the American family is Edward N. Saveth, "The Problem of American Family History," *American Quarterly* 21 (1969): 311-29. Two recent articles challenge the long-accepted view that industrialization destroyed traditional family structures: Frank F. Furstenberg, Jr., "Industrialization and the American Family: A Look Backward," *American Sociological Review* 31 (1966): 326-37 and Sidney M. Greenfield, "Industrialization and the Family in Sociological Theory," *American Journal of Sociology* 67 (1961): 312-22.

The standard history of the American family is still Arthur W. Calhoun, *A Social History of the American Family* (Cleveland: Arthur H. Clark, 1919), 3 vols. A shorter study is Willystine Goodsell, *A History of the Family as a Social and Educational Institution* (New York: Macmillan, 1915). Charles Franklin Thwing, *The Family* (Boston: Lee and Shepard, 1887), presents a late nineteenth-century view of the family as a divinely authorized social institution. The centrality of the family in social progress is urged by Sarah J. Hale, the influential editor of *Godey's Ladies' Book,* in *Manners: Happy Homes and Good Society All the Year Round* (Boston: Lee and Shepard, 1889).

Edmund S. Morgan's *The Puritan Family,* rev. ed. (New York: Harper and Row, 1966) is an admirable study of the early New England family and Puritan child-rearing practices; see also Sandford Fleming, *Children and Puritanism* (New Haven: Yale University Press, 1933), and Lewis B. Schenck, *The Presbyterian Doctrine of Children in the Covenant* (New Haven: Yale University Press, 1940). The function of the family in transmitting culture is examined by Paul Schrecker in "The Family: Conveyance of Tradition," in Ruth Nanda Anshen, ed., *The Family: Its Function and Destiny* (New York: Harper, 1959). See also William E. Bridges, "Family Patterns and Social Values in America, 1825-1875," *American Quarterly* 17 (1965): 3-11.

A good introduction to the process of socialization from the perspective of social role theory is Frederick Elkin, *The Child and Society* (New York: Random House, 1960). Nineteenth-century child nurture literature is also examined by Bernard Wishy, *The Child and the Republic* (Philadelphia: University of Pennsylvania Press, 1968). Changes in child-rearing practices during the last century and a half are described and assessed by Daniel R. Miller and Guy E. Swanson, *The Changing American Parent* (New York: Wiley, 1958). The increased emphasis placed upon the mother's responsibilities in child nurture during the generation before the Civil War is surveyed by Anne C. Kuhn, *The Mother's Role in Childhood Education: New England Concepts, 1830-1860* (New Haven: Yale University Press, 1947). A good, brief analysis of pre-Civil War nurture literature is Robert Sunley, "Early Nineteenth Century American Literature on Child Rearing," in Margaret Mead and Martha Wolfenstein, eds., *Childhood in Contemporary Culture* (Chicago: University of Chicago Press, 1955). The Reisman thesis is critically examined by Forrest J. Berghorn and Geoffrey Steere, "Are American Values Changing? The Problem of Inner- or Other-Direction," *American Quarterly* 18 (1966): 52-62, and by Fred I. Greenstein, "New Light on Changing American Values: A Forgotten Body of Survey Data," in Seymour Lipset and Richard Hofstadter, eds., *Sociology and History: Methods* (New York: Basic Books, 1968). See also Geoffrey Steere's "Changing Values in Child-Rearing Literature, 1865-1929" (Ph.D. diss., University of Pennsylvania, 1964).

For changing attitudes toward the child, I have found the following informative. Reactions of foreign travelers to American children are described and analyzed by Richard Rapson, "The American Child as Seen by British Travelers, 1845-1935," *American Quarterly* 17 (1965): 520-35. A readable and perceptive look at the American family is provided by the English traveler James F. Muirhead, *America: The Land of Contrasts,* 3d ed. (London: John Lane, 1902). Other late nineteenth-century statements on the child include: Alexander Francis Chamberlain, *The Child: A Study in the Evolution of Man* (London: Walter Scott, 1900); G. Stanley Hall, "The Contents of Children's Minds," *Princeton Review,* ser. 3, 11 (1883): 249-72, and "The Moral and Religious Training of Children," *Princeton Review,* ser. 3, 9 (1882): 26-48; John Johnson, Jr., "The Savagery of Boyhood," *Popular Science Monthly* 31 (1887): 796-800; Rev. Anna Garland Spencer, "Social Responsibility toward Child-life," *Lend a Hand* 11 (1893): 105-21; and Ednah D. Cheney, "The Relation of the Child to the Home," *Unitarian Review* 1 (1874): 336-46.

For material on the city, see Dwight W. Hoover, "The Diverging Paths of American Urban History," *American Quarterly* 20 (1968): 298-317. Arthur M. Schlesinger, *The Rise of the City, 1878-1898* (New York: Macmillan, 1933) is still provocative. More recent is Blake McKelvey, *The Urbanization of America, 1860-1915* (New Brunswick, N.J.: Rutgers University Press, 1963). The image of the city can be fruitfully explored using Anselm Strauss, *The American City: A Sourcebook of Urban Imagery* (Chicago: Aldine, 1968). Also instructive is Louis Wirth's pioneer essay "Urbanism as a Way of Life," *American Journal of Sociology* 44 (1938): 1-24.

The following materials bear on the city perceived as a threat, especially to the family: George M. Beard, "Physical Future of the American People," *Atlantic Monthly* 43 (1879): 718-28; Charles A. Ellwood, *Sociology and Modern Social Problems* (New York: American Book, 1910); Washington Gladden, "Three Dangers," *The Century Magazine* 28 (1884): 620-27; Edward Everett Hale, "The Congestion of Cities," *The Forum* 4 (1888): 527-35; Charles D. Kellogg, "Child Life in City and Country," *Journal of Social Science* 21 (1886): 207-23; Grace Peckham, "Infancy in the City," *Popular Science Monthly* 28 (1886): 683-89; Walter B. Platt, "Injurious Influences of City Life," *Popular Science Monthly* 33 (1888): 484-89; Morrison I. Swift, "Building Cities for Health," *Unitarian Review* 34 (1890): 270-76; Robert Archey Woods, *The City Wilderness* (Boston: Houghton Mifflin, 1899); Charles Loring Brace, "Wolf-Reared Children," *SN* 9 (1882): 542-54; and Samuel Dike, "Problems of the Family," *The Century Magazine,* 39 (1890): 385-95. The general degeneration of the family allegedly taking place under democratic conditions is questioned early in the period in "Democratic Homes," *The Nation* 6 (February 13, 1868): 128-29.

Index